BLOWBACK

An alumnus of La Martiniere College, Lucknow, the National Defence Academy, Pune, and the Indian Military Academy, Dehradun, Mukul Deva was commissioned in December 1981 into the Sikh Light Infantry of the Indian Army. He took early retirement after fifteen-plus years of service, including a decade of active combat duty in India and overseas. Mukul is now an entrepreneur, consultant, Writing, Leadership and Business Coach. He is the author of *Time After Time…It All Happened*, *S.T.R.I.P.T.E.A.S.E: The Art of Corporate Warfare*, *M.O.D.E.L.: The Return of the Employee*, *Lashkar* and *Salim Must Die.*

Praise for Mukul Deva

'Deva has a Nostradamus touch.'

– *The Statesman*

'India's literary storm trooper.'

– *Business Standard*

'Deva comes as a pleasant surprise... it is rare to find a successful, celebrated man who has enough vulnerability.'

– *New Indian Express*

'You can smell the gunpowder. Such is the power of the words of Mukul Deva... India's first military action thriller writer.'

– *The Hindu*

'India's only military thriller writer.'

– *The Week*

'Deva needs to be congratulated for being part of the pioneering group in the genre of the Indian thriller novel.'

– *The Deccan Herald*

'Mukul Deva wears the crown of India's premier military thriller writer with great skill and panache.'

– *www.indepepal.com*

Praise for *Lashkar*

'An edge-of-the-seat-thriller.'

– *The Hindustan Times*

'Exciting... with some action, some introspection, some retrospection... A racy read.'

– *The Times of India*

'For the first time, an Indian thriller set in contemporary times… a gripping tale.'

– *Pioneer*

'*Lashkar* tries to make sense of the terror that surrounds our lives.'

– *The Hindu*

'Ludlumesque.'

– *Tribune*

'A glance is enough to discover... this is a Tom Clancy on the LOC.'

– *Time Out*

'A real page-turner… a riveting read.'

– *Business Standard*

'Written with style and panache.'

– *Sahara Time*

'A real-life take on how the so-called jehadis are picked up from anonymous Indian streets… *Lashkar* tells many tales with great ease.'

– *MetroPlus*

'*Lashkar* is gripping... racy and visually captivating.'

– *Indo Asian News Service*

'A compelling read.'

– Govind Nihalani, film-maker

Praise for *Salim Must Die*

'Deva is back and how! Uncannily prescient. Unputdownable. *Salim Must Die* enthrones Deva as the undisputed Master of Thrills.'

– Sarthak Dasgupta, film-maker

'Taut and gripping... technical knowledge and research are remarkable, as is the plotting and the premise. Great read for the fans of Tom Clancy.'

– *Delhi Times*

'A ripping, edge-of-your-seat, burn-the-midnight-oil, good read. Deva sets a frenetic pace. The author's attention to detail and prodigious research skills are evident.'

– *www.indepepal.com*

'After his much acclaimed *Lashkar... Salim Must Die* continues its Tom Clancy-eqsue (run). Deva scores... you can sense the passion.'

– *Mail Today*

'Finally, an Indian thriller of quality... where neither the tautness nor the pace collapses. Here comes India's Clancy or Ludlum or Forsyth.'

– *Outlook*

'Deva is an equal with the likes of Robert Ludlum and Sidney Sheldon… a tight plot bound together by intricate but brilliant narration leaves the reader in awe.'

– *Deccan Herald*

'A prescient tale… racy, keeps you hooked… definitely written for the movies.'

– *The Hindu*

'India's answer to Tom Clancy… *Salim Must Die* is as real as it gets… gut wrenching action and a deeper look into the terrorist's psyche.'

– *Khabar Dilli Se*

What Readers Have to Say

'Both *Lashkar* and *Salim Must Die* are serious page-turners. He is one of the best authors that I have ever come across.'

– Sayan Acharya, acharya.sayan@gmail.com

'The sharp zigzags of the plot kept me on edge and made for a very racy pace.'

– Amit Kumar Bose, bose.amitkumar@gmail.com

'*Lashkar* and *Salim Must Die* will find an answering chord with many and both are bound to be made into films and have multiplexes filled with patriotic cheers.'

– Anjana Basu, anjanaorama@gmail.com

'Every scenario described here is realistic and scary. I truly enjoyed it... I feel that *Salim Must Die* should not only be read by every Indian but also be read the world over.'

– Shailesh Karkhanis, shaileshkar@gmail.com

'Reality, Thriller, Action – *Lashkar* and *Salim Must Die* present an amazing vision to see the reality, on such sensitive issues.'

– Sadiya Khan, sadiyakhan@hotmail.com

'Finally, an Indian writer who keeps you on the edge and wanting more. Go, Mukul, go; let your pen flow!'

– Hari Kumar, harismind@gmail.com

'I still remember my first thriller, an Alistair Maclean, which I read twenty-nine years ago. Reading *Salim Must Die* gave me a similar high.'

– Ashish Kumar, ashish.kulshreshtha@gmail.com

'Gripping storylines with excellent coverage and explanations of the global geo-political scenario. Mukul Deva is probably amongst the best authors globally.'

– Monish Navlani, monishn@live.com

'*Laskhar* was pacy, tight, well-knit and pleasantly vindicating. Mukul deftly blends his knowledge of military operations with his knack for thriller writing.'

– Gul Panag, gulpanag@gmail.com

'I put off everything once I started reading Mukul Deva's series and then I told all my friends. Clancy, sure, but I'm thinking the next Ken Follett.'

– Fran Lebowitz Rittman, flebowitz@yahoo.com

'Had the pleasure of reading *Lashkar* and *Salim Must Die* and am thrilled to see this kind of a writing from a fellow Indian. I read that people are comparing your writing to Ludlum and Clancy but in my eyes you are way beyond them... somewhere close to Mathew Riley and Allen Folsom... Cheers and keep 'em coming!'

– Anunay Shrivastava, anunay.shrivastava@gmail.com

'While *Lashkar* is unputdownable, *Salim Must Die* takes the thrills to the next level! Current themes about proliferation and "non-state" actors make the story very relatable to anyone who reads the newspapers regularly.'

– Deepak Subramanian, Deepaksub@yahoo.in

'Mukul has a very definitive style of writing and it makes the reader literally feel like he is part of the entire plot, witnessing each and every thrill in real time.'

– Arijit Sen, arijit.sen@kotak.com

'Mukul Deva's writings are a sure recipe to entertain. *Salim Must Die* catapulted me into a virtual world of action where I smelt gunpowder, felt the shocks of mortar and grenade explosions, and survived the labyrinthine espionage of the next-door enemy all of us love to hate.'

– Kulpreet Yadav, kulpreetyadav@gmail.com

BLOWBACK

MUKUL DEVA

HarperCollins *Publishers* India

First published in India by
HarperCollins *Publishers* in 2010

Building 10, Tower A, 4th Floor, DLF Cyber City, Phase II,
Gurugram Haryana – 122002, India
www.harpercollins.co.in
2 4 6 8 10 9 7 5 3

P-ISBN: 978-81-7223-921-3
E-ISBN: 978-93-5029-593-9

This is a work of fiction and all characters and incidents described in this book are the product of the author's imagination. Any resemblance to actual persons, living or dead, is entirely coincidental.

Typeset in ClassGaramond BT 10/13
Jojy Philip, New Delhi 110 015

Printed and bound at
MicroPrints India, New Delhi

For Aryan, my favourite younger son –
we are really proud of you, kid.

Sandman the handsome (Rest in Peace).

Sasha of the soulful eyes
and
Tipsy, my dowry.
Have a great life!

AUTHOR'S NOTE

This book is a work of fiction although some of the events mentioned here have actually taken place.

All the characters, countries, places and organizations described or mentioned in this book are fictitious or have been fictitiously used and any resemblance to any person, living or dead, is unintentional.

The technical details of the various weapon systems, the specifications and methodologies of bomb making and weaponry, as well as the tactics and security procedures employed by any police, military, intelligence organization, airline, airport security and/or militant organization, as also all criminal, forensic and investigative procedures, have been deliberately kept vague, inaccurate and/or incomplete to prevent any misuse, accidental or otherwise.

There is no slur or malice intended against any religion, race, caste, creed, nation, organization or people.

PREFACE

The responses (from readers, critics and the media) that came in when *Lashkar* and *Salim Must Die* were released were overwhelming, to say the least. I was totally surprised at the heat and debate the two books generated. In the past two years not a week has gone by without at least one mail coming in; either pointing out or commenting on something in these books or asking me when the third book of the Force 22/Iqbal saga would be out.

I must also confess that I have really been hard pressed (while working on this book and the fourth one of the series, which is due to be out next year) not to be swayed or affected by the comments and feedback that have poured in. Even though I felt that there was substantial merit in some of the comments and I was often tempted to stray down the avenues that they opened up, in the end I have stuck rather rigidly to the storyline that had been originally charted by me for all four books.

I have tried very hard to present each book in a different visual format and to ensure that they all work as standalone books, but I must also admit I am extremely aware of the fact that with every successive book reader expectations have been climbing. In many ways I welcome this pressure since it has made me work doubly hard on this book and the one coming up next. Whether I have succeeded or not, I leave to you to decide.

Mukul Deva

'Terrorism is the tactic of demanding the impossible, and demanding it at gunpoint.'

Christopher Hitchens

ONE

The man was unusually tall and built like a tank. The harsh, messianic glint in his eyes and the long, angular scar running across his right cheek left an indelible impact on all who set eyes on him. Though it was nowhere as horrendous as the scars he sported elsewhere on his body, it was the only one that was visible, and he carried it with the pride of a soldier sporting a medal. For him it was infallible proof that Allah wanted him around on earth for some more time, at least until his task was complete.

He stood in one corner of the dimly lit room, dressed in his trademark black Pathani suit, surveying the men seated in an uneasy U along the three walls. The house lay in the middle of a nondescript village in the Angoor Adda area of South Waziristan, almost in touching distance of the Afghanistan-Pakistan border. The venue had been chosen at the insistence of those coming in from Afghanistan, despite the dangerous proximity of the American Joint Special Operations Command (SOC) forces; most of them were uncomfortable with the idea of placing themselves at the uncertain mercy of the man who had called the meeting. Given a choice, they would have preferred someplace in the Swat Valley which lay safely out of range of the American missiles. But that was out, given the equation between the two men who led the jihadi forces in those two areas. Eventually, the will of the man occupying centrestage this night had prevailed. And, of course, the fact that Omar the One-eyed, presently ensconced in the shadows of Quetta, had given his personal assurance of safety to every man present and stressed the importance of the meeting.

It was a large room but the eighteen black-clad, heavily armed men crammed into it and the depressing yellow trickle of light from the solitary bulb hanging nakedly in the centre made it seem much smaller. Together, these men represented Al Qaeda and every other credible group of the Afghan and Pakistani Taliban. It was they who dictated the ebb and flow of violence on both sides of the Durand Line; they who controlled every ounce of opium that was grown in or moved out of the area, and every possible illicit activity that took place in that rugged terrain which had been controlled for hundreds of years by warlords such as them. More than half a billion dollars from these nefarious activities passed through their hands every year. They were the ones that decided who would live and who would die and which city or marketplace would encounter the next suicide bomber.

Barring the low, divan-like seating along three walls and a large full-length mirror at the far end, the room was devoid of furniture. Every door and window of the house was covered with heavy drapes and the smell of sweaty, unwashed bodies and gun oil was all-pervasive.

The meeting had been called at short notice and was being conducted under tight security. To ensure that Electronic Intelligence (ELINT) did not detect any trace of the meeting, only trusted human couriers carrying verbal messages had been employed to set it up. Over a hundred hardened, heavily armed fighters, strung out a dozen miles in each direction, guarded every possible route in and out of the village. On this night, anyone who tried to fight their way in would meet with brute force every inch of the way.

The man spoke as soon as the last of them had settled down. 'You all know why we have gathered here today.' His voice shook slightly with the force of his emotions. 'The movement is losing focus and direction.'

'Things have changed ever since Sheikh Sahib was martyred and the others went underground,' one of them offered plaintively. 'We have been rendered leaderless.'

'We are running low on arms, ammunition and medical supplies,' said another. 'Even sustenance money is hard to come by now that the Pakistan government's support is treacherous and uncertain.'

'Stop whining! The jihad does not depend on any one man... no matter who or how important he is.' His voice was a whiplash, daring them to contradict him. Combat hardened and ruthless though they all were, most of them avoided meeting his gaze. 'So what if the Sheikh is dead and the others underground? So what? None of us is indispensable. None!'

'What would you have us do?' someone asked hesitantly.

'To begin with, we must all understand that our cause is the same. We may belong to different groups, different tribes, different regions, but the god we worship is the same, and before everything else we are Allah's soldiers. We have to bury our differences and get ready for the surge of fresh troops that the American president is sending into Afghanistan soon. We must greet them with such fury that they will never dare return. Their new president must realize that it is we who call the shots in this part of the world. Perhaps he has forgotten that Afghanistan is called the Graveyard of Empires. It is our duty to remind him.'

His listeners murmured in agreement.

'Also understand that victory can only be ours if we fight together under one banner, just like our enemy. See how effectively they have forged together the coalition of Crusaders, Zionists and Hindus. Now the kafirs have even started chipping away at the loyalty of our Muslim brothers.'

'True! They have managed to wean away staunch

loyalists like Abdul Salaam – he is now a district administrator in Afghanistan.'

'I know, but I wouldn't worry too much about such treacherous weaklings,' he said coldly. 'We will take care of them when the time comes. We will make such an example of them and their families that no one else will even dream of selling out to the kafir.'

'But the kafir alliance is so big and powerful, what can a handful of us do?'

'Don't worry, all that will soon change.'

'How?' The solitary word came from Saifullah, the frail looking mullah seated in the far corner of the room. With his strong links with Mullah Omar's Quetta-shura and his undisputed overlordship of the Swat Valley, Saifullah was a formidable opponent to the man who had called this meeting. So large was his following that even the Pakistan Army hesitated to jam the radio station he used to ensure his writ ran unchecked over the once beautiful, now devastated Swat Valley.

'Trust me. Can't you see the gains we have already made in Pakistan?'

'We?' Saifullah bared unexpectedly large, stained teeth derisively. 'That is what I was doing while the rest of you were busy fingering each other.'

The others shifted restlessly in their seats. Their honour was being called into question and this was not something they took lightly.

The man chairing the meeting quickly intervened.

'Who do you think got rid of that conniving politician bitch the Americans were trying to thrust on us yet again?'

'Any fool could have done that,' Saifullah scoffed.

'But no one did. *I* had to do it. Anyway, just give me some time to put it all together and then see what we can achieve,' he said, his eyes glinting wildly. 'It will not be long before the kafir is on the run and the One God rules the world.'

'That's easier said than done,' the mullah retorted. 'How do you...'

'Do you forget how it all began in Afghanistan?' the man replied smoothly. 'They were just a handful but it didn't take them long to take over Afghanistan.'

'And then?' Saifullah sneered. 'We all know our history. Don't you remember what happened to them?'

'I do,' he conceded without a pause. 'Mistakes were made, but we have learnt from them and they will not be repeated. *That* is what makes our victory inevitable.'

'That may be so, but what can you do that is different from what the Tehrik-e-Taliban Pakistan was set up to do in the first place?'

'The TTP is too loose a conglomerate and won't be able to match up to the forces that we face in the field. Even as we speak, the Americans are pumping more troops into the area.'

'So? What do you propose?'

'What I propose goes far beyond anything the TTP could have hoped to achieve. It will change the way the battle is fought. I want to expand our base and embroil the kafir in a quagmire of conflict that spans every corner of the globe.'

'If you say so, my friend, but until now we have only heard words. Words don't win wars.' Saifullah laughed. 'We have made far more progress in the Swat Valley than you have in any other area,' he said disdainfully. 'Now tell us what you plan to do and how. Then, maybe then, we will be able to decide which banner to follow.'

Yours or mine?

Though they remained unspoken the words rang clear in the musty, dimly lit room. The mullah did not know it, but he had just signed his death warrant.

'We could just as well follow your banner, my friend,' the giant in black countered, 'as long as you can do what needs to be done... what I promise you that I will do.'

'Which is what?'

By now the tension between the two men had everyone on the edge of their seats.

Aware of the enormity of the task confronting him and the fact that an opportunity like this would never come again, the man began to speak, choosing his words with care and delivering them with practised ease. When he finished, a stunned silence filled the room.

An elderly mullah parked a few seats away stood up slowly and began to clap. Though everyone knew the mullah was the man's mentor, no one could be sure whether this was a premeditated move or spontaneous. In the end it did not matter, because the rest of the room was also applauding wildly. Reluctantly, Saifullah joined in the applause. He could see the way the wind had begun to blow and knew that this was not the time to buck the trend, not if he wanted to leave the room alive. Clearly, he had underestimated his opponent.

After that, one by one, they all departed. And as they went, each one swore allegiance to the man who had called the meeting, the man they now referred to as Ameer ul Momineem, the Commander of the Faithful. The man who had clawed his way up from being a tribal militia leader and kept going until one day, the mantle of Ameer of Waziristan had fallen on him, bestowed by none other than Omar the One-Eyed. Despite Omar's blessings, the Ameer had had to fight off and subdue several contenders. Today, both Al Qaeda and the Taliban accorded him the respect and importance he felt he deserved.

The Ameer waited till the last of them had gone before he spun around towards the large, full-length mirror at the far end of the room. When he gestured, the mirror swung to one side and a man emerged from a tiny cubbyhole behind it. Like the Ameer, the newcomer was dark with saturnine features. Like him, he was unusually tall – but that was where the similarities ended. The newcomer's slender, almost athletic build and demeanour were such that they wouldn't raise a second glance. He could blend effortlessly into any crowd, in any society, in most of Asia.

'What do you think?' The Ameer raised his eyebrows.

'It couldn't have gone better,' the man replied with a smile.

'What about Saifullah?'

'He could be trouble – if he is allowed to live, of course.'

'Take care of him then,' the Ameer said impatiently.

'Consider it done.'

'Good. What's your plan now?'

'The director has placed me at your disposal, Ameer.'

'So you can report to him about everything we do?'

'If you want me to.' The man eyed him levelly, aware that the more he tried to justify his position, the less he would be believed. 'Only if you want me to.'

'Really?' The Ameer stared at him unblinkingly. 'Why should I trust you? Your agency is not exactly the benchmark of trust and truth. And these days, with the American pressure, how can anyone know which way you will turn?'

'You'll have to take my word for it,' the man said. 'My loyalties lie with Allah... only with Allah.'

'Are you sure?'

'Try me.'

'And how does your director feel about this?'

'This area is not even in my beat any more, but he still sent me here, didn't he?'

'That is because I specifically asked for you. He knows I will not deal with anyone else.'

'You can read what you want into it.' The man shrugged.

The Ameer stared at him. Finally, he nodded. 'Fine, I believe you.'

'Then tell me, what is it that you wish to do and...'

'Not wish; this is what I *am* going to do.'

In a low tone, the Ameer repeated some of what he had said earlier, but this time there were subtle yet powerful differences in what he outlined. His one-man audience listened with total attention, his impassive face giving away none of the excitement the words unleashed in his mind.

'Excellent,' he said when the Ameer finally stopped. 'You can bank on us for whatever help you need, but rein in your loose cannons – we need to maintain a low profile for some time.'

'You don't need to check with your director?'

'No. Trust me. I have carte blanche on this one. In fact, I'll personally take care of the India operations.'

'That would be perfect.' The Ameer looked satisfied. 'Will you go there yourself?'

'Of course! I'll brief the director and move immediately.'

'You must tell him not to rush me on this one. It may take a year, maybe more, but I'll make it happen.'

'These things take time, we all understand that.' The man nodded understandingly. 'But if anyone can do it, you can.'

'Thank you for your trust.' The two men embraced.

'Keep in touch the usual way,' the Ameer said in parting. 'And yes, don't forget to resolve my Swat problem before you leave.'

'Consider it done. Allah hafiz!'

As he walked out to the waiting jeep, the man pulled out a Thuraya satellite phone from his pocket. Unlike the Iridium, Inmarsat or the newly launched Globalstar satellite phones, the UAE-based Thuraya phone was the communication weapon of choice for many because it was much harder for anyone to track or monitor conversations on the Thuraya channel.

'Afghan Force Headquarters.' The high-pitched nasal American accent crackled through loud and clear, making the caller wince slightly and move the handset away from his ear.

'Colonel Johnson, please.'

'May I know who is calling?'

'Sher Khan.' The ISI agent provocateur had used and discarded so many names by now that he barely remembered his real one.

'Yes, Sher Khan?' A moment later the colonel was on line. 'How is it going?'

'Chugging along sir, chugging along,' replied the man with many names in fluent, almost unaccented English, his tone light and cordial. 'I've got some news for you.' He lowered his voice as he named Saifullah and mentioned his whereabouts.

'Good job, Sher Khan!' The colonel was unable to mask his satisfaction. 'We've been trying to pin the bastard down for a long time.'

'That's what you pay me for, sir.'

'Subtly put, buddy!' said Colonel Johnson with a laugh. 'Don't worry, the payment will reach your bank the usual way... if the intel is good.'

'It's as good as gold, sir, don't worry about that.'

'We'll find out soon enough.' The colonel chuckled. 'A couple of our birds are already up and about. Let me divert them in the right direction.'

'Happy hunting then! I'll find out on the morning news, sir.'

From memory, the man called another number. Like every experienced operative, especially one working on the dark side, he didn't have any phone numbers stored in the memory of his sat phone – one never knew whose hands it might fall into. This time it took a while for the phone to be answered.

'Yes?' The male voice at the other end was peremptory. Like Sher Khan, the ISI director spoke fluent English, although his accent was more pronounced, an unavoidable hangover of his British education. But his years at home and the nature of the job he held had eliminated all traces of finesse from his speech. 'What did the bugger want?' he asked.

'Exactly what we want, sir,' the agent provocateur replied. 'He's talking about Project Mike, sir.'

'You must be joking!'

Sher Khan could almost visualize the shock on the director's face. 'No, sir. I couldn't believe it either when he told me.'

'He mentioned the... it... by name?'

'No, no, but the game plan he spelled out is aiming for pretty much the same thing.'

'Hmm. He thought of it on his own, or did you help him along?'

'A bit of both, sir... a bit of both,' Sher Khan said triumphantly. 'I tweaked him as we went along, making it amply clear that our support would only be forthcoming if things went according to plan.'

There was a moment's silence at the other end. 'In the circumstances, he is our best bet, isn't he?'

'That he is, sir,' Sher Khan replied without hesitation. 'The others are too erratic and unreliable.' For a moment he wondered whether to mention Saifullah and the fate he had condemned him to. *Sometimes these arseholes warming the chairs at*

Headquarters think they know it all. In any case, what the boss doesn't know can't hurt him. Sher Khan had no illusions about his dispensability. He knew that upsetting the director of the ISI, especially this particular man, was not a career enhancing proposition; it could well turn out to be a life threatening one.

'I agree with you.' There was another short silence. When he finally spoke, there was a sharp, decisive edge in the director's voice. 'Okay, then you go ahead to India and get the operation going again, but be very careful... there should be no fuckups... We can't handle the fallout if you're taken alive. Not after what happened in Mumbai.'

'Don't worry, sir.'

The director rang off and Sher Khan resumed his journey in a much happier frame of mind. Nothing that lay in the future bothered him in the least. *God, country, new challenges every day... and of course, money – lots of it. What more could a man want?* He smiled as he tossed the phone down on the seat beside him, settled himself behind the wheel and roared into the night.

A few weeks later, he would surface in the central Indian town of Aligarh. Here he would go by the name Mujib. Mujib, who bore an uncanny resemblance to the man named Mukesh who showed up occasionally in the northern desert town of Jaipur. And to the man named Michael in the southern coastal town of Kochi.

Sher Khan had barely left the house when the elderly mullah who had started the applause joined the Ameer who was standing just outside the door, gazing sightlessly into the darkness, in the direction in which Sher Khan had vanished.

'Did he buy it?'

'Of course he did.' The Ameer laughed. 'People always hear what they want to hear.'

'They *only* hear what they want to hear.' He joined in the Ameer's laughter. 'You are confident they will do what we want and give us what we need?'

'Do they have a choice? They have hankered after this for so long that the buggers must be salivating right now.'

'So while they drool over their fabulous Project Mike, we go ahead with our plan?'

'Of course we do. This time there will be no half measures. We'll strike only when every cog is firmly in place. By the time they realize what the game is, it will be too late for anyone to do anything about it.'

'True... And have you located the other Ameers?'

'Not yet, but I know I will. They are out there, just waiting to be found.' The Ameer's eyes gazed into some distant horizon. 'It will be the Tanzim of all Tanzims,' he whispered. 'And once they are in place and the nuclear arsenal is in our hands, nothing can stop us.'

Both men stood in the darkness, silently watching

the night deepen around them as they dreamt of the future... a future they hoped would arrive soon.

The director of the ISI was not actually salivating, but he was close to it. He sat for a long time pondering over the conversation he had just had with Sher Khan. Then he picked up his phone and made another call. Considering the late hour, it was not surprising that the man who answered the phone in Dacca, the capital of Bangladesh, sounded groggy.

'Wake up, my friend, this is no time to be sleeping. Project Mike has just been given a new lease of life.'

'What?' The man, who had very recently been appointed the director of the DGFI (Directorate General of Forces Intelligence) in Bangladesh, came awake at once. 'What are you saying?'

'Exactly what you just heard,' the ISI director replied.

'Allah be praised! Tell me about it.'

So he told him. When they finally went back to bed, it was with great satisfaction and a marked sense of achievement. At last things had begun to move in the desired direction. Op TOPAC was finally going to succeed.

At the same time, several hundred miles to the northwest, an MQ-9 Reaper UAV sliced through the cold, dark night, unseen and unheard, and closed in on the unsuspecting target below.

Unlike the lightweight MQ-1B Predator, the Reaper is a weapon system and not just an individual drone. Initially called Predator B, it was finally renamed the MQ-9 Reaper, the 'M' to signify its 'multi-role' designation and the 'Q' to imply an unmanned aircraft system. Each Reaper system consists of four individual Reaper drones operated by different flight teams. Weighing 2223 kilograms and powered by a 900-horsepower turboprop engine, a Reaper can carry 1814 kilograms of fuel and 1701 kilograms of weaponry. Its arsenal is a mix of laser guided bombs and missiles, typically fourteen Hellfire missiles, as against the two Hellfire missiles that a Predator drone can carry. Like most standard fighter jets, the Reaper can also carry two bombs – normally the 226-kilogram GBU-12 laser guided precision bombs – but it can also be fitted with GBU-49s that are equipped to strike any target in any kind of weather without the need of a laser designator. Though still not as visible or notorious in the Af-Pak theatre of war as the more often used Predator drone, with its top speed of 482 kilometres per hour the Reaper is a hunter with the ability to destroy time-sensitive targets with persistence and precision.

Tonight, only one of the four drones would be used, and that was more than enough to deliver the desired destruction. In fact, the massive firepower it had on board could easily have taken out several more such targets without difficulty.

The Reaper took one final circuit of the sleeping village and then there was a sudden flare of light and two pairs of Hellfire II missiles slid off the firing rails and escaped into the night.

Hellfire II is an optimized version of the AGM-114 Hellfire, a laser or radar guided air-to-ground missile system designed to defeat hard targets while minimizing the exposure of the launch vehicle to enemy fire. Designed in the early 1970s and first used as a multi-mission, precision attack weapon in 1985, the Hellfire missile is a miniature aircraft in itself, complete with a guidance computer, steering control and a propulsion system. Depending on the variant used, the Hellfire AGM-114K payload can be a High Explosive Anti-Tank (HEAT) warhead, powerful enough to burn through the heaviest of armour; or the AGM-114M blast fragmentation warhead used to defeat bunkers, other urban targets or light vehicles; or the AGM-114N where a metal augmented charge (MAC) is used against ships and enclosed structures such as caves and bunkers. The first three generations of this missile used a laser seeker that was highly accurate but needed the missile operator or launch platform to deliver it to the target, thereby exposing itself to enemy fire. The fourth generation is an air launched, radar guided, inertially guided missile that utilizes millimetre wave radar technology to seek its target. This guidance is impervious to clouds or obstacles, making it truly 'fire and forget' and capable of engaging multiple targets simultaneously.

With shocking speed, the four 64-inch long, 100-pound Hellfire II missiles lunged forward, and seconds later the three-room, single-storey house that they targeted disappeared in a blinding explosion of sound and light. By the time the dust settled, the mullah from Swat Valley had ceased to exist; parts of his body were scattered amidst the bloody debris.

As were those of sixteen others who happened to be in the vicinity. Only seven had anything to do with the Taliban or Al Qaeda. The nine others were merely bystanders, neighbours, or villagers whose only fault was that they happened to be in the wrong place at the wrong time. But such are the vagaries of war.

TWO

Asif Sharif's distinguishing feature was the glint in his eyes. His eyes glowed with the cold, mesmerizing light of a zealot – or a psychopath. A barely average student with no exceptional skills, barring his extraordinary street-smartness, twenty-one-year-old Asif would have passed through life unnoticed and unremembered had it not been for a chance encounter with Mansoor Ahmed Salafi, one of the founders of Youth for Purity in Society (YPS).

The YPS was set up in Aligarh in April 1997. It began as a students' movement with the stated objective of liberating India from decadent, materialistic Western influences and converting it into an Islamic state where pure Islam would reign supreme, unfettered by the shackles of democracy. Its main architect was a student of journalism called Ishtiyaque Khan. It was a matter of great discomfort for YPS that, a couple of years later, Ishtiyaque Khan succumbed to the same deplorable Western influences that he had earlier attempted to eliminate, and migrated to America where he began to teach the virtues of free speech and journalism to college students.

The nine-year-old organization was still struggling to establish an identity for itself when Salafi picked Asif as one of its office-bearers. Asif had then been trying, and not very successfully, to graduate from the University of Aligarh. For him, this sudden call to potential glory and fame was irresistable.

Salafi was fuming when he left the weekly YPS meeting midway. 'I don't understand why these idiots can't see the writing on the wall!' The short man with his stylish goatee, prominent Adam's apple and horn-rimmed spectacles was walking so fast that Asif had to struggle to keep up. 'All they want to do is sit around and talk all day, or spend hours drafting stupid petitions to be submitted to the government. Bloody morons!'

For want of anything better to say, Asif made the appropriate noises. In any case, he was still too much in awe of Salafi's knowledge, enthusiasm and energy to express an opinion in front of him, especially when Salafi was in such a frenzy. They strode on through the corridor, their leather shoes clicking sharply on the erratic stone tiles.

'While these fools are faffing around, the kafir government is screwing us all over the place.' Salafi hawked loudly and spat out a blob of bile. It hit the corridor wall and trickled thickly down the yellowing walls, which were already streaked with betel juice. 'Can't they see how Muslims are driven into a corner and stepped upon all the time? Ayodhya, Gujarat, Kashmir... are they blind?' Salafi fumed in silence for a while. 'The more I listen to these fools, the more I begin to believe that Mujib is right.'

'Who is Mujib?' Asif asked after he had run through the list of YPS office-bearers in his head and failed to put a face to the name.

'You have not met him – yet!' Salafi threw out the last word theatrically. 'But I think the time has come for us to sit with him and work out a more action-oriented plan that will actually allow us to achieve our goals.' He paused for thought, his goatee tilted upward. 'If we want to achieve something, we must be more aggressive and take action... instead of farting around with our mouths like those morons.' This last was thrown back contemptuously at the others who were still at the YPS meeting.

'If you say so, bhaijaan,' Asif replied. Salafi's words always stirred something deep inside him. 'I am with you.'

'I know you are, Asif!' Salafi bestowed a keen, approving look on him. 'You are the kind of person we need if YPS has to make a mark.'

They met Mujib late that night, when even the confirmed insomniacs of the college had finally gone to sleep. He was waiting for them in a dirty, beaten up SUV outside the campus gates.

'Salaam waleikum, Mujib bhai,' Salafi greeted him in what struck Asif as a strangely deferential tone as they got into the rear seat of the SUV. 'This is Asif... Asif, Mujib bhai.'

The two men shook hands cautiously, each assessing the other in the murky darkness of the car. The cigarette smoke made Asif want to cough. He wound down the window a little.

'Can we talk in front of him?' Mujib asked Salafi, throwing an almost spent cigarette stub out of his window before rolling it up again.

'Of course, bhai!' Salafi was emphatic. 'Would I have brought him along otherwise? He is trustworthy... one of us for sure.'

'Uh huh.' Mujib stared at Asif. 'Where are you from?'

'Azampur.'

'How long have you known him?' Mujib gestured at Salafi.

'For many years now, bhaijaan. We are neighbours... In fact, our parents have known each other a long time.'

'What are you doing here in Aligarh?'

'I'm in the final year. Eco Honours.'

'You understand what loyalty and secrecy mean?'

'Of course.'

'And you understand that we will not take it lightly if you betray us in any way?' There was a sudden edge in his voice as he turned and looked at Asif.

Asif met his gaze and nodded. Mujib finally looked away, seemingly satisfied, at least for the moment. 'Good.' He started the vehicle and they began to crawl through the dark, narrow streets of Aligarh. 'So what have you decided, Salafi?'

'I'm beginning to believe you are right, Mujib bhai. The others are just wasting our time with all their talk, petitions and shit like that.' Salafi thumped the seat with his fist. 'We need to take action! We need to make those bastards sit up and take notice of us... and treat us with respect.'

'How exactly are you are going to do that? And more importantly, who is going to stand by you in this battle?'

'I know who is with me. Asif is, for one. Aren't you?' He looked at Asif.

'Why else am I here, bhaijaan?'

'I am pretty sure that some of the other key members are also with me... Irfan, Zaheer, Nissar and...' He reeled off a few more names before his voice trailed away.

After a moment, Mujib asked softly, 'And who is against us, miyan? Knowing your friends is good, but it's far more important to know your enemies.'

Asif was not sure why, but he intuitively knew that something important was about to go down. Salafi's voice was low when he replied.

'I know for a fact that Omar and Shafique are going to oppose anything we try to do. Those damn do-gooders are definitely going to fight us tooth and nail. As for the others...' He thought for a moment. 'They are fence sitters. Bloody sheep! They'll just flow with the tide. But Omar and Shafique – they certainly are the enemy.'

'So be it!' Mujib's voice was cold and sent a shiver down Asif's spine. 'What are we going to do about them?'

'I don't know,' Salafi replied, almost petulantly.

'What do you think we should do, Salafi?' Mujib continued, his voice still chillingly low. 'What *does* one do with the enemy?'

Silence shrouded the occupants of the car. The game had changed, and each of them was acutely aware of it. They were no longer young students playing at bringing about a change in society or attempting to bring their misguided co-religionists back into the folds of pure Islam. Suddenly there was something else riding with them, something grim and ominous.

'What do you suggest, Mujib?' Salafi's words came out a strangled whisper, as though he was having trouble speaking. The sudden display of weakness in someone he admired so much shocked Asif more than he cared to admit and this unexpected betrayal caused a sudden rush of anger in him.

'What does one do with the enemy?' Mujib repeated softly, his tone neutral.

He needs to know which side of the fence Salafi is on. The thought hit Asif immediately. *And so do I.* He found himself watching Salafi carefully.

Talking the talk and walking the talk are two different things.

Salafi seemed to be struggling with his thoughts, his inner turmoil evident. Both men watched him closely.

'Fight those who believe not in Allah nor the Last Day, nor hold that forbidden which hath been forbidden by Allah and His Messenger, nor acknowledge the religion of Truth (even if they are) of the People of the Book, until they pay the Jizya with willing submission, and feel themselves subdued.' Mujib chanted the sura in a low, flat tone, almost in a whisper. He was among those who had helped design the Al Qaeda recruitment and training manuals; he knew when the time was right to quote from the Scriptures.

'But they are also believers, Mujib,' Salafi protested weakly. 'We must give them the chance to see...'

'Are they? Then they will understand that the jihad takes supremacy. After all, battles are not won without martyrs.' Mujib pulled over to the side of a deserted road; the shadow of a tree smothered what little light there had been inside the vehicle. 'So what *do* we do with the enemy?' he asked again, swivelling around in the driver's seat to face Salafi.

'We kill them.' Salafi swallowed as he whispered the answer, his Adam's apple bobbing comically in his throat. Asif suppressed a sudden, ridiculous urge to laugh.

'And do you have it in you?' Mujib continued in a low voice. Salafi's goatee and his Adam's apple did another rapid bob.

'No!' he finally replied in a strangled whisper. 'I cannot ki...' Even the word eluded him and his voice faded into the night.

Salafi's weak, whining voice was beginning to irritate Asif. He could not believe that this was the same man he had admired for being strong in his beliefs and clear in his call for action.

Mujib did not remove his unwavering gaze from Salafi's face. 'You don't have to dirty your hands, miyan.' His voice was edged with contempt. 'We'll do that for you.'

'Then what do you want me to do?'

'Just get back in there and keep them talking. Keep them busy and use the nice, clean network the YPS is creating to build a strong nationwide network for us; a network that will provide support, finance and when required, media and legal support; a network which we can cull for the right kind of people from time to time.' His tone hardened. 'People who are not so squeamish... people who are ready to kill for Allah.' He leaned forward, pushing his face closer to Salafi's. 'Are you ready to do that at least?'

'Yes!' Salafi's breathing was ragged but he nodded his head vigorously. 'Yes, yes, of course I am... I will... but...'

'Good.' Mujib pulled away from him slightly.

'Always bear in mind that there are others out there who are going to put their lives on the line for the cause. They are the flag bearers of the jihad. Don't ever let them down – *ever.*' The last word hissed out with such shocking vehemence, it made Salafi flinch as though he had been slapped.

'Never!' he croaked back. 'I swear by all that is holy, I will make sure they are never let down.'

'For your sake, I hope so,' Mujib replied, his tone almost conversational. Immediately, the atmosphere in the vehicle eased up. 'Remember this is the best combination in the world.' He saw the question in Asif's eyes and explained, 'While YPS functions over the ground, completely legally, and is thus in a position to provide the propaganda, media support and required legal cover, the Indian Mujahideen shall be free to hit out with a series of terror spectaculars all over the country. The bastards will not even know what hit them.'

'The Indian Mujahideen?' Salafi asked.

'Yes, the Indian Mujahideen.You obviously don't remember our jihadis. Have you forgotten Shah Ismail Shaheed and Sayeed Ahmed Shaheed?' Mujib shook an accusing finger at Salafi. 'Have you forgotten the jihad they waged at Balakot?' He didn't wait for a reply. 'YPS will ensure that every time one of our fighters falls in battle, there will be charges of discrimination and persecution. The ensuing riots must bring life to a standstill.'

'How will that help, bhai?'

'Every time it happens, some friendly politician with his own axe to grind will stand by us and ensure that the government becomes wary of us. The mere threat of a communal riot will give us the edge. The aim is to keep the government on tenterhooks and make sure they shy away from confronting us openly.'

'I see.' Salafi nodded excitedly.

'What about you, my young friend?' Mujib suddenly turned to Asif. 'Do *you* have it in you – or are you also too squeamish to bloody your hands?'

'Try me!' Asif shot back angrily, irritated with Salafi and annoyed that his faith was being questioned.

Mujib held his gaze, a faint smile on his lips. 'I will,' he said softly. His hand came up, over the seatback between them. The silenced pistol in his hand exploded into life. The sound was muted, but in the closed confines of the vehicle, it was like thunder. Asif watched shell-shocked as Salafi's body slammed against the back of the seat. Salafi's expression changed from disbelief to horror as he looked from Mujib to the hole in his chest, from which blood had begun to gush. Then suddenly his body slumped forward with a tired, hissing sigh, like the sound of air escaping from a punctured balloon. In horrifying slow motion he slid sideways until the door of the vehicle arrested his fall.

Mujib reached out and checked the pulse on the

side of Salafi's neck. Satisfied, he looked at the still open-mouthed Asif. 'He was weak. Weak people turn traitor and betray the cause.' He leaned forward slightly, the pistol in his hand not pointing at Asif, but menacingly rocksteady. 'No?'

Abruptly closing his mouth, Asif replied, 'I think so too.' There was a slight tremor in his voice. 'Weakness should never be tolerated.'

'I am glad we agree.' The pistol dropped out of sight. 'Throw him out!' He gestured at the body. Asif reached across and opened the door. Mujib watched closely as he gripped the body, gingerly at first and then with confidence, and began to push it out. As the body shifted, a fresh surge of blood gushed out from Salafi's chest. Asif flinched, pulling back instinctively to avoid being splashed.

'Don't worry, it won't hurt you.'

'It doesn't bother me,' Asif replied, his head pounding with sudden excitement. 'I just don't want to mess up my clothes.' Salafi's body toppled out slowly, almost in slow motion, hitting the black, tarmacked road with a meaty thud. As Asif closed the door, Mujib started the engine and they drove into the night.

'I like you,' Mujib said after a few miles of silence. 'I think we'll work well together. No?'

'Yes, we will.'

'Are you saying that because you truly believe it – or because of the pistol in my hand?'

'What do you think?' Asif countered with a

touch of belligerence, instinctively aware that any display of weakness would not go down well with the other man.

'I like you.' Mujib laughed. 'I knew you had fire in your belly the moment I laid eyes on you. We will certainly work well together.'

'What do you want me to do?'

'Just continue the work they give you at YPS, but while you do that, seek out other suitable people, people like us, who are not afraid to kill... or die. Then we'll strike.'

'How?' Asif asked. 'What can a handful of us do? We need money, arms and...'

'You leave all that to me,' said Mujib, cutting him off.

'You? Who *are* you? Where will you get them from?'

'I'll get them... that's my problem.'

'But who are you?'

'Slowly, miyan.' Mujib laughed. 'All in due course... For now, just keep your eyes and ears open, and learn. You have a long way to go.'

Asif mulled over his words for a while. Then he nodded. 'What about him?' He gestured vaguely over his shoulder, in the direction in which Salafi's body lay. 'How do we explain his death?'

'Why should we explain it at all?' Mujib countered. 'Don't you see...' He broke off in mid-sentence. 'How do you think we can make use of his death?'

Asif did not take long to reply. 'Why don't we just blame the kafir for it? Proclaim Salafi a martyr who was doing great work for Islam and was becoming so popular and powerful that they killed him.'

'Excellent!' Mujib sounded delighted. 'You learn fast!'

'Like you were saying, maybe we can even get the YPS people to hit the streets to protest his murder and inflict some more pain on the government.'

Mujib laughed again. 'You *are* good!'

'Thank you,' Asif murmured, actually blushing at the compliment. He didn't know that Mujib was following a well-choreographed script – *Praise the potential recruit.* Even if Asif had given a foolish answer, Mujib would have guided him towards the right one, made him feel that he had thought it up on his own.

'Fabulous! You must always try to capitalize on every situation. After all, just because he was a coward does not mean he cannot contribute to the jihad with his death.'

'What about Omar and Shafique – and the others at YPS whom Salafi mentioned?'

'Leave the fools alone. Let them talk themselves to death and build up the organization. We'll use them to find the cadres and the support we need to complete our mission. There's no need for them to know about us.'

'But they will eventually find out,' Asif protested.

'It's impossible that they won't. One or the other person we try to recruit is bound to tell them.'

Mujib shrugged. 'When that happens, I guess some more cowards will be murdered by the kafir.' Both men laughed again.

By now they were almost back at the university gates where Mujib had met them.

'Take this.' Asif was getting out when Mujib handed him a mobile phone. It was a snazzy, top-of-the-line model. Asif turned it around in his hand admiringly, unable to keep the gleam out of his eyes. It did not occur to him that the phone had been meant for Salafi. 'I'll call you when I need to talk to you. Use it only, and I mean *only,* to speak with me. Do not make any calls from it or give the number to anyone else. Remember that.'

'But how do I call you if I need to contact you? I don't have your number.'

'Here it is.' Mujib scribbled on a piece of paper he picked out of the glove compartment and handed it to Asif. 'Memorize it and then destroy this paper. And make sure you don't call me unless it's an earthshaking event and even if you have to, call *only* from a public phone,' he stressed. 'Got it? Call only if it's an emergency! And call only from a PCO! That's how we'll always communicate. Okay?'

By now Asif was starting to look a little bewildered.

'Don't fret.' Mujib reached out and patted his

shoulder. 'Just take one thing at a time. To begin with, focus on the task I've given you.'

'Don't worry, bhaijaan. Leave it to me. I'll put together a group that will make us proud.'

'Good! I'll be in touch with you soon!' Mujib engaged gears and drove away.

Asif turned and began the long walk back to the college hostel through the early morning fog. The task given to him was clear in his head.

The Indian Mujahideen. He rolled the name on his tongue, savouring it. *I'll start tomorrow,* he promised himself as he entered the gates. *Tomorrow, I will put together the fiercest band of warriors the jihad has ever seen.*

And so he did. Constantly aided and abetted by Mujib who kept to the shadows, over the next few months Asif slowly swelled the ranks of the Indian Mujahideen.

'Stay away from your relatives, Asif,' Mujib had advised when he started, 'unless there is someone exceptional you really need.'

'Why?'

'It can get very emotional with relatives,' Mujib explained. 'It's better to focus on people who are from your native place. That way you still have the advantage of familiarity and yet no emotional complications to hamper decision making.'

What Mujib did not tell Asif was that this would also ensure his removal from 'the bad environment he lived in' and push him towards 'a good environment to improve his faith' – one of the basic steps outlined in the recruitment manual for terror masters.

The first six men Asif recruited were from his native place, Azampur; none of them was related to him. And through them he found fourteen more, from colleges in Pune, Mumbai, Hyderabad, Delhi and Aligarh.

'Remember,' Mujib had warned, 'security forces today are very well organized, that is why we need people who are educated, smart and mentally mobile.'

'Aren't such men harder to recruit? Aren't they more likely to question everything?'

'They certainly will,' Mujib replied, 'but in the end it will be worth the extra effort. They'll help us to execute missions more efficiently and will be smart enough to hide their tracks well.'

And so the cadre of Indian Mujahideen that Asif finally put in place was comprised almost entirely of graduates, postgraduates and young urban professionals.

'Excellent!' Mujib said as he saw the ranks swell. 'They are a good lot.'

'They're all from good family backgrounds,' the eager-to-please Asif pointed out.

'I can see that,' Mujib replied, 'and it's useful. Should any of them be captured or killed, their families will make a great hue and cry, which is exactly what we need. Just keep going, Asif, you are doing a great job. Trust me.'

Mujib was right. Asif was amazed at the efficiency of the first strike. The bombs were planted with great care. They exploded with meticulous timing. And the people of Jaipur could only stand by as the bodies were counted.

THREE

For Iqbal and Tanaz, barring the escalating pain of the gunshot wound that held Iqbal in its talons, the return journey from Murree to the rendezvous on the Indo-Pak border was so uneventful that it was almost an anti-climax. The pressure of the field dressing that Tanaz had tied on his arm had staunched the bleeding considerably, but the pain intermittently lanced through the fog of painkillers that she had fed him. The shock of Azam Cheema's bullet to his flesh and the tremendous loss of blood had drained him.[1] Whenever he floated out of his state of semi-consciousness, he saw Tanaz watching over him. And in those fleeting moments of lucidity, Tanaz and he spoke, more with their eyes than with words.

Iqbal knew little about the beautiful woman who tended to him as they raced back towards the safety of the Indian border, apart from the fact that both her brothers had been recruited by the Jaish-e-Mohammed and used as cannon fodder in the

[1] Told in *Salim Must Die* (2009).

endless, aimless terrorism that engulfed the Kashmir Valley. He knew that this was what had motivated her to join the Research and Analysis Wing, India's intelligence agency. It was certain that her life on this path had not been easy and had hardened her considerably. But the more Iqbal thought about it, the more convinced he was that he didn't wish to delve any further into her background. Whatever he had seen and heard so far was enough for him.

For Iqbal too had suffered at the hands of the terrorists. Recruited by a maulavi in Delhi and sent for training to the Lashkar-e-Toiba camp in Pakistan, he had returned to India to find that his mother and sister had been killed by bombs that had been planted by the same group.[2]

The sun had begun to recede into the shadows of another night when they finally reached the turning for the border crossing that would take them back to India.

Twenty-five minutes later, Captain Vikram Tiwathia brought the red and white station wagon to a halt near the solitary hut on the edge of the field where they had linked up with Tanaz the previous day. Their guide Rahmat was waiting for them.

'Give us a few minutes to rig up a stretcher for Iqbal,' the young Indian Army captain told Tanaz as he leapt out of the vehicle.

[2] Told in *Lashkar* (2008).

Tiwathia was in his late twenties but had probably seen more action in his tenure with the Special Forces than most regular army officers see in a lifetime. He had been part of both Force 22 operations into Pakistan, the first in retaliation against the Sarojini Nagar terror bombings and the second one to eliminate Salim. He was a die-hard optimist who never failed to see the brighter side of any situation. However, at this moment his dust-streaked face was lined with worry.

'Do you think it's a good idea for you to attempt the border crossing with Iqbal in this state?' Tanaz asked, stepping out of the vehicle. Anxiety marred the radiance of her finely chiselled features. 'What if his condition worsens along the way? He'll slow you two down, and may even inadvertently give you away.'

'We can't leave a buddy behind, Tanaz!' Captain Mohammed Sami, who was seated next to Tiwathia, exclaimed as he climbed out of the vehicle. Sami was the seniormost officer and second-in-command of Force 22. A tall, heavily built man with surprising grace and agility, Sami had also been on both Force 22 missions into Pakistan. 'Don't worry. We'll get Iqbal across. In any case, how will he manage alone?'

'He's not alone,' she answered softly. 'Not unless he wants to be.'

For a long moment there was only the crackling sound of the hot engine as it slowly cooled. Iqbal lay huddled on the rear seat of the station wagon, listening to the conversation. Sami and Tiwathia saw him exchange a glance with Tanaz. She looked away immediately, her face devoid of expression.

'No, I am not alone.' Iqbal finally broke the silence. 'I need to get better and continue the fight. There will be many more Salims and Cheemas to take the place of the ones we have killed.'

'True, but there will also be many more Iqbals,' Sami pointed out. 'This is going to be a long war, long and bloody... and it's not just your problem.'

'It's everybody's problem. All of us have to act, and I, having been through the mill, am relatively better positioned to contribute to the fight. In any case, I have much to atone for...' He looked up abruptly. His breath was running short and he was clearly in pain, but there was a firm resolve in his gaze. 'I will stay here.'

Tanaz turned to the commandos and smiled. *See!* she seemed to be saying. *I told you so.*

'He needs a doctor,' Tiwathia pointed out. 'And he needs one fast.'

'I can get him to one much faster than you can,' Tanaz countered immediately.

'Here? Is that sensible?'

'Someone who won't ask any questions... he is one of us.'

'Where do you plan to go?' Tiwathia asked.

'Eventually?' She raised a quizzical eyebrow. 'To the desert, of course.' Tanaz waved westwards. 'I was born and brought up in the desert. I know it well. The sands will hide us.'

The two commandos exchanged a rapid glance. Sami nodded briefly. 'Okay. Take care then. And Tanaz, I suggest you move fast. You have to get him to a doctor before…' He broke off, then added softly, 'He's losing a lot of blood.'

Sami and Tiwathia helped to move Iqbal to the front seat and made him as comfortable as possible. They were walking away towards their waiting guide when Iqbal called out weakly, 'Please tell the colonel that I'm sorry for...'

'Don't worry about the past, Iqbal.' Sami turned to face the young man. The troubled expression on Iqbal's face reached out to him. 'We all make mistakes but very few of us have the courage to try and redeem ourselves. To my mind, you've already atoned for whatever wrong you may have done. Now it's time for you to put away the past and set yourself free. Go man, your future awaits you… and wherever you go, whatever you do, may Allah watch over you.'

'Thank you… very much.' Iqbal's voice was unsteady as he spoke. 'Tell the colonel that he can always call on me whenever the need arises. I will not fail him.' There was an awkward pause as he looked at the Force 22 commandos. 'In fact, it would be an honour.' He sketched an awkward salute, fighting back the waves of pain, and then turned wordlessly towards Tanaz. Without a moment's delay, she powered the engine and gunned the vehicle.

The two commandos watched the station wagon race away into the gradually gathering darkness, towards the waiting desert sands.

They had been on the road, a narrow, bumpy dirt track, for about two miles when there was a sudden, explosive burst and the station wagon skidded to the right. Tanaz fought the wheel as she struggled to keep the heavy vehicle from ploughing through the muddy embankments on either side of the road.

If it gets into the fields, we've had it. There's no way I can get Iqbal away from here on foot. He'll never make it in this condition.

She fought to bring the vehicle to a shuddering halt just as the front wheels climbed the embankment on the right of the dirt track. Heaving a sigh of relief, she turned to Iqbal. The loud explosion of the tyre had jolted him awake. He was clutching the handrest tightly with both hands, anxiety writ large on his face.

'Damn! What a time to run into a flat!' Tanaz forced a smile. 'Let me get the spare wheel out.' She opened the door and got out.

'I'll help you...' Iqbal struggled to pull himself upright.

'No!' Tanaz said sharply. 'Don't get heroic, Iqbal. The best way for you to help is to stay still and keep that wound from bleeding. I'll manage the tyre change on my own. If you move around and it starts bleeding again, we're in bigger trouble.'

'But...'

'No buts, Iqbal,' she said firmly. 'Just stay put.'

Iqbal watched in silence as Tanaz got the jack and heavy spare wheel out from the rear of the station wagon. Despite her slight build, she was strong and handled the wheel with relative ease. She had just managed to wheel the spare up to the front of the station wagon and was about to insert the jack under the vehicle when the deep-throated roar of an engine burst in on the silence.

Tanaz dropped the jack and moved swiftly to the driver's side of the station wagon. She reached in and grabbed the Uzi. The weapon disappeared between the folds of her burqa with minimal movement. Simultaneously, she dropped the hijab and veiled her face again.

Inside the vehicle, Iqbal struggled to sit up. He grabbed the second Uzi from under his seat and hid it inside the folds of the shawl Tiwathia had draped around him. He quickly checked to ensure the shawl concealed his blood-soaked clothes. The sudden movement sent fresh waves of pain through him and he struggled to force a deadpan expression on his face.

A hundred feet ahead, a Pakistan Army jeep rounded the bend in the track and began to close in on them with tremendous speed.

The army jeep sported the typical sand-green-and-yellow camouflage commonly used by military vehicles. Its canopy cover was rolled forward as it thundered up to them. Four soldiers were perched on the rear seats and two in the front cabin. The four men at the back cradled the standard POF (Pakistan Ordinance Factory) manufactured PK-7 short assault rifles in their hands.

The weapons were placed casually between their legs, their barrels pointing safely skywards, but neither Iqbal nor Tanaz had any doubt about the speed with which they could be brought into action by a trained soldier, or the lethality of the heavy 7.62 mm slugs that they could spew out with blazing rapidity. Each of the standard magazines fitted on the PK-7 rifle cradled twenty rounds and the eighty rounds in those four rifles could be unleashed within seconds.

The jeep came to a noisy, creaking halt next to the stranded station wagon that blocked most of the narrow track. There was a sudden silence as the soldier behind the wheel turned off the engine and the billowing dust in its wake slowly settled around the jeep.

'What's all this?' The thirty-something man who leaned out from the front passenger's side had the bullying arrogance of a typical army NCO (Non Commissioned Officer). He was clearly irritated at being forced to stop.

'Sorry, janab,' Tanaz called out, her tone remarkably calm and even. 'The tyre got punctured. I'll just change it and clear the road in a moment.'

'It would be much faster if you got that idiot sitting inside to help you.' The NCO pointed at Iqbal. 'You! Aren't you ashamed of yourself, warming your butt while you make the woman work?'

'That's my husband, janab,' Tanaz replied before Iqbal could open his mouth. 'He is ill. In fact, I was taking him to the hospital when the tyre got punctured.'

She was still speaking when the NCO threw open the jeep door and jumped out, his metal-jacketed boots hitting the ground with a dull clang. Perhaps it was only force of habit or maybe he had noticed something that made him suspicious, but he was toting a carbine in his hand when he hit the road.

'What's wrong with him?' the NCO asked as he approached the station wagon, heading towards Iqbal's side of the vehicle.

Tanaz exchanged a rapid glance with Iqbal as the NCO approached. She seemed to be asking him what to do. His expression made it clear to her that they could not take a chance. She nodded imperceptibly, her eyes swivelling to the four soldiers in the rear of the jeep, as though letting him know she would take them on, leaving him to sort out the other two. Behind the folds of her burqa, she soundlessly clicked the Uzi to automatic fire mode. The NCO was still a dozen feet away when the Uzi chattered to life. Despite the awkwardness of the loose, flowing fabric, Tanaz's opening burst almost instantly cut down the two men at the back.

Perched high in the open rear of the jeep, they were unmissable targets. Both men died before they even knew the firing had begun. The other two were marginally luckier. Despite the suddenness of the assault, they almost managed to jump clear of the jeep before the Uzi's lethal cargo reached them. One man took the bullet straight in his head but the other managed to get a couple of rounds off before he fell. The bullets didn't come anywhere near Tanaz because the impact had spun him around before he could bring up his rifle. The gun was arcing towards the right as he fell and both bullets exploded into the windscreen of the station wagon, starring the toughened glass.

Meanwhile, inside the station wagon, Iqbal was bringing up his own Uzi to fire when the barrel snagged in his shawl. He clawed at it frantically, but by the time he cleared it and got the weapon up, the Pakistani NCO's carbine had begun to spit lead.

The NCO had been shocked into stillness when the Uzi in Tanaz's hands thundered to life. By the time his training took over, the first two soldiers in the jeep were already dead. Tanaz was realigning her weapon onto the second set of soldiers in the rear of the jeep by the time the NCO released the safety and brought his carbine into play. The sharp three-round burst slammed into Tanaz a fraction of a second after she had cut down the last of the four men in the rear of the jeep. The harsh multiple impact literally lifted Tanaz in the air and threw her backwards over the embankment into the field. She hit the ground hard and then she was still. Blood began to seep out and stain the folds of her burqa.

Before the NCO could fire again, hot lead from Iqbal's weapon turned his head to pulp and he slumped to the ground.

Iqbal managed to get off a second shot at the soldier behind the wheel of the jeep, who was sitting transfixed at the sudden turn of events, when the first PK-7 round fired by Tanaz's final victim shattered the windscreen of the station wagon. The slug slashed through the windscreen and thumped harmlessly into the upholstery of the seat beside Iqbal.

Damn! That was close...

The thought was still forming in his mind when the second rifle bullet sliced through the already shattered windscreen and slammed into him.

The heavy 7.62 mm slug travels with tremendous power; even at a range of 4400 metres it carries almost eighty joules of energy, more than adequate to deliver a crippling blow to the human body. The bullet that smashed into Iqbal had barely travelled thirty metres. It was moving with the lethality of an express train gone berserk. It made short work of his breastplate as it ploughed through his chest, throwing him backwards into oblivion.

The sound of gunfire cleaved through the silence of the night for miles around. For a very long time its echoes seemed to reverberate in the darkness. The two Force 22 commandos racing through the night barely a mile and a half away from the RV, juddered to a halt. A little ahead of them was their guide Rehmat, whose job was to get them safely across the international border.

'Bloody hell!' Tiwathia muttered. 'Is that what I think it is?'

'The first was definitely an Uzi and that's what Tanaz was carrying,' Sami replied. 'The second lot sounded like the PK-7 and... I think there was some carbine fire too.'

'Shit!' Tiwathia paused for a moment. 'Do you think we should go back?'

'What good would that do?' Sami said. 'They must be at least three miles from here. By the time we get there, so will the Paki police and their border forces.'

The two men exchanged worried glances.

'Come on, come on! Let's get going,' Rehmat hissed at them urgently from the darkness. 'We need to get out of here as fast as we can. The place will be crawling with patrols soon.'

Reluctantly, the two officers turned and began to move towards the safety of the Indian border. They knew Rehmat was right.

What the hell are we going to tell the colonel? Sami thought as he followed the guide.

Despite the rapid clip at which they were

moving, safety was still four stress-filled hours away. Standing between them and the IB was a cordon of mines, barbed wire, men, guns and electronic eyes and ears.

FOUR

'Tell me exactly what happened,' Colonel Rajan Anbu said as soon as they had settled down in the Ops Room of the Force 22 base at Kasauli. As usual, Anbu was calm and gave no indication of stress. He had already done the basic, initial debriefing as soon as Sami and Tiwathia had crossed the IB and returned to the safety of the advance ops base, so he had some idea of the events that had transpired across the IB in the hunt for Salim. But there was only so much you could say on a radio network, even a secure one.

'Okay, MS, I understand what you're saying,' Anbu had told Sami at the end of the debrief, masking his dismay. 'You guys have done a fabulous job. Get some rest now and meet me at the Ops Room at 1700. We'll go over the whole thing in detail then.'

Located one level below the ground, the Force 22 Ops Room was a large rectangular room with a single door. The back wall was occupied by a gigantic electronic battleboard-cum-screen next to which was a large-screen plasma television. Along the right wall was a row of four tables angled so that they faced the screen. Each table held a gleaming desktop computer and a bank of phones. The left side of the room was taken up by a large wooden table on which were placed two brightly coloured and somewhat bulky phones. Marshalled in front of this table, in the middle of the room, were four neat rows of chairs, all facing the battleboard-cum-screen. Anbu leaned against the solitary table to the left, facing the battleboard. Sami and Tiwathia had swivelled around two of the chairs in the centre and were seated in front of him.

'So, tell me what happened.'

The stocky forty-three-year-old colonel was the first Commanding Officer of Force 22 and a fine example of that peculiar streak of controlled aggression that makes the Special Forces man stand apart from and ahead of the pack. Anbu was known to lead from the front and never expected from the extraordinary men and women that he commanded, anything that he was not willing to do himself. And that was no mean achievement, considering his unit comprised the crème de la crème of the country.

Born from the bloody crucible of the long, low intensity conflict between the Indian and Pakistani military and intelligence establishments, Force 22 had been created to provide a rapid covert response to situations that could not – or should not – be dealt with by conventional forces in a more conventional manner.

Every officer in Force 22 was handpicked from the Indian army, navy, air force or intelligence services. Each one was a commissioned officer not below the rank of captain and was in superb physical condition, a high achiever amongst his or her peers, trained to fight over land, sea and air, skilled in most known methods of killing and motivated to the highest possible levels.

Anbu repeated his question to Sami and Tiwathia: 'Please start from the beginning.'

The two commandos in front of him looked unhappy and ill at ease. Sami, the senior of the two, automatically took up the baton. Keeping his emotions in check, he told Anbu everything – from the time they had crossed the IB and linked up with Tanaz, to the successful completion of their mission in the hill town of Murree, thirty kilometres from Islamabad, where Murad Salim and his assistant Azam Cheema had set up their operational base.

'You are sure Salim is dead?' Anbu asked.

'There can be no doubt about it, sir,' Tiwathia intervened. 'Iqbal cleaved his head off with the scimitar.'

'Scimitar?' Anbu was momentarily nonplussed. 'What scimitar?'

'During the shootout, Tanaz's weapon jammed,' Sami replied. 'She was right in front of Salim when it happened. He was about to shoot her when Iqbal snatched up this really fancy scimitar lying on the table before him and chopped Salim's gun hand off. Then – I think he was carried away by the heat of the moment – he cut off Salim's head with it.'

'Damn!' Anbu tried to visualize the scene. 'That must have been one hell of a blow.'

'It was, sir!' Tiwathia replied, suddenly animated. 'The damn thing went through Salim like a knife through hot butter.'

'Really?' Anbu nudged the story on. 'What happened then, on the way back?'

'Iqbal's wound started bleeding like crazy...'

'Iqbal's wound? You didn't tell me he was injured.'

'Yes sir, he stopped a bullet meant for Tiwathia.'

'Just raced forward and threw himself in the way, sir. If it hadn't been for him, I may not even be here today.' Tiwathia's voice throbbed with emotion. 'He was a good man.'

'Was?' Anbu interjected gently. 'You don't know for sure he didn't make it out alive.' He gave Tiwathia an encouraging smile. 'Hope for the best, Vikram. Always!'

Tiwathia smiled half-heartedly and looked away. There was an awkward pause before Sami took over again.

'By the time we reached the RV it was clear that we'd have a problem getting Iqbal back with us. Then Tanaz said she'd take care of him and Iqbal wanted to stay on with her. In any case, he needed to get to a doctor and she said there was a secure one pretty close to the RV.'

'They're like twin souls, sir. It's really strange how similar their stories are. Just like Iqbal lost his mother and sister to the terrorist bombs at Sarojini Nagar, Tanaz lost both her brothers to the jihadis. The Jaish-e-Mohammed had recruited the youngsters and sent them in to attack the police lines at Jammu. You remember the attack two years ago?' Anbu thought for a moment and nodded. 'Well, both of them were gunned down during that attack. That's why Tanaz enlisted in the RAW. She realized it was the only way to help bring peace back to Pakistan – by putting an end to these bloody terrorists and their conniving masters.' Vikram was finding it hard to keep the anger out of his voice. 'Tanaz and Iqbal took to each other like fish to water. I was... am... really happy for them.'

The sudden shrill ringing of the secure phone on Anbu's table startled the three men. Sami made to rise, but Anbu gestured to him to stay put.

'Don't worry, MS. I'll take that.' Leaning forward, he picked up the receiver. 'Yes? *What?* Okay! Let me call you back.'

Returning the handset to its cradle, he picked up the remote control lying next to the phone and flicked on the television. The three men watched in mounting horror as the bloodbath on the screen cascaded into the room.

'The first bomb went off at 7:30 p.m. at the entrance to the Hanuman Mandir in old Jaipur city. At that time the temple was packed with devotees who were leaving after the evening aarti. The explosion caused a stampede, resulting in many more casualties. In the next twelve minutes, seven more bombs went off in other, equally crowded areas of the old city. All the bombs appear to have been placed on cycles and had been carefully deployed on the various routes leading away from the temple. It's obvious that the terror module responsible for these serial blasts had reconnoitered the area thoroughly and carefully worked out the direction in which people would flee after each successive bomb blast. Details of the casualties have yet to be established, though initial estimates indicate that at least sixty-five people have lost their lives in this horrific attack and more than three times that number have been injured.'

The reporter's voice was pitched high with excitement. The camera broke away from his face to show the destruction all around – the large black crater on the road, shattered vehicles and windows, blotches of blood staining the road. Shattered limbs lay desolately here and there. Shaken, battered people could be seen stumbling around in a daze, the braver amongst them ferrying the wounded to the cluster of ambulances that darted in sporadically and sped away with blaring horns and flashing strobe lights.

'Bloody hell!' Tiwathia exclaimed. 'What's this about?'

'An email was received by all major news channels and the Rajasthan police commissioner's office just six minutes before the first bomb exploded,' the anchor's voice announced. 'The two-page email was sent by a group that calls itself the Indian Mujahideen and it challenged the police to stop the blasts and threatened dire reprisals against the state and people of India.'

Extracts from the email began to scroll across the television screen.

Hindus! O disbelieving, faithless Indians! Haven't you realized that the falsehood of your thirty-three crore dirty mud idols and the blasphemy of your deaf, dumb, mute and naked idols of Ram, Krishna and Hanuman are not going to save your necks, Inshallah, from being slaughtered by our hands? Never again will we let you sleep in peace. Never again will you step into a market without fear clutching at your heart. Never again will you leave your house without the fear of not knowing if you will return alive. We will ensure that the dust will never settle...'

FIVE

'What the bloody hell are we doing, sitting on our hands while those bastards go around killing scores of innocent men, women and children everywhere? We should just...'

'We should just what, Vikram?' Anbu asked quietly.

'We know who is behind this, sir.' Tiwathia looked agitated. 'The Indian Mujahideen is just a front for the YPS. And I am sure there is no doubt in anyone's mind that the YPS is yet another tool being used by the ISI.'

'No, Vikram, I am not saying there is any doubt. We all know that Pakistan is using the jihadis to bleed us white.' Anbu didn't elaborate since both his officers were already conversant with the facts. After the debacle of two failed operations, Gibraltor and Grand Slam, and the comprehensive defeat handed out to them by the Indian forces in all the wars they had fought, the Pakistan Army had realized they had no hope of matching forces with their neighbours. And so, in 1988, General Zia launched Operation

TOPAC, a proxy war initiated and supported by the ISI, which was aimed at balkanizing India. 'This latest Indian Mujahideen stunt is their attempt to prove that this is a domestic Indian problem and that Pakistan has nothing to do with it.'

'Aren't they serious nutcases?' Sami couldn't contain himself. 'Their economy is in shambles. Their economic growth rate is down from 6 to 0.6 per cent, inflation is soaring over 25 per cent, and unemployment is growing on a daily basis. They barely have enough to eat and yet they're exhausting all their resources either trying to balkanize India or talibanize Afghanistan. If the IMF had not given the Pakis over 7 billion dollars in aid last year and the Americans were not pumping in over 1.5 billion dollars every year, Pakistan would have crumbled and fragmented long ago.'

'I don't understand how there can be any Indian support for these conniving, deceitful bastards.' Tiwathia slammed his fist on the table angrily.

'Vikram, it's always easy for terrorist groups to recruit criminals or otherwise disgruntled and disillusioned people. Anyway, I think this is a question MS will be able to answer better.' Anbu gave Sami an encouraging look.

'Well, sir, we all know that politicians will do anything to exploit the minority vote bank. And there have been several incidents that left many Indian Muslims feeling persecuted. These are the people the ISI is using to carry out terror strikes in India.'

'But don't these guys realize they are being used as pawns by the ISI?'

'It's not that simple, Vikram. Let me give you a potted history first, okay? Like every socio-religious group, Muslims are also divided into various groups – Sunnis, Shias, Brelvis, Hanafis, Sufis, Deobandis, Salafis, and other, more radical ones like the Wahhabis.

'Both Sunnis and Shias agree on the Five Pillars of Islam: Shahada, the profession of faith; Salat, the prayers; Zakat, the giving of alms; Sawm, fasting during Ramadan; and Haj, the pilgrimage to Mecca. However, Sunnis feel that Shias are more focused on the martyrdom of Ali and Hussein and less on the fundamentals of Islam. Shias also have a different call to prayer and often combine prayers, thus sometimes worshipping only thrice instead of the five times that Sunnis insist on. They even perform Wudu, or washing, and Salat differently and place their forehead on pieces of hardened clay from Karbala rather than on the prayer mat directly. Clear so far?'

Tiwathia nodded.

'Sunnis, on the other hand, believe that the first four Caliphs rightfully took Mohammed's place as the leader of the Muslim world and they recognize their heirs as legitimate religious leaders. Also, Shias and Sunnis have very different views or interpretations of the Sharia, which literally means the path to the water source and is the body of Islamic religious law, which if followed will lead to salvation.' Sami stopped and looked at them expectantly.

'Okay, I think I got that,' Tiwathia said, after he had mulled it over for a moment. 'Now tell me about the radical sects you mentioned earlier.'

'The fundoos are the ones who seek to establish a global Islamic state and want all Muslims to return to pristine Islam as it was practised in the early period. These so-called purists take a very stringent view of the Sharia and are dead against any deviations from the Islam that was practised by the Prophet, his companions and their immediate followers. That's why they take a very dim view not only of non-Muslims, but also of other Muslim sects – particularly the ones that take a more liberal view of Islam.'

'I see... go ahead.'

'Okay, so just like Muslims everywhere else, the Indian Muslim has also been influenced by various schools of Islamic thought down the ages. In India, in the eighteenth century, there was Shah Waliullah, who tried to address every section of Muslim society and get them to revert to pure Islam. He didn't have much success but his views exert considerable influence even today. In fact, it's unfortunate that several sections of the ulema study his teachings just to try and prove his Deobandi or Brevli roots.'

'Why is that unfortunate?'

'Simply because both those sects originated long after Waliullah's death.'

'So, basically they are just trying to capitalize on his name.'

'Exactly.' Sami nodded and resumed, 'The second person who tried hard to revive Salafism in India was Shah Ismail, the grandson of Shah Waliullah. However, like his grandfather, he didn't make much headway; nevertheless, he is viewed by the modern Islamic fundamentalist as a role model.'

'So how relevant is all this to what's happening in India today?'

'I'm coming to that, but first let me take you back to Saudi Arabia for a moment. In the eighteenth century, there lived a man named Muhammad Ibn Abd al Wahhab. Wahhab was another purist who formed an alliance with the House of Saud, the ruling family of Saudi Arabia, to try and eliminate all deviations from the practice of Islam. He was by all accounts very successful in this alliance; even today, the Saudi ulema is very closely associated with the House of Saud. In fact, now the Wahhabi writ runs large not just in Saudi Arabia but also in parts of Yemen, Qatar, Kuwait and Bahrain. They also have considerable influence over large parts of South Asia.'

'And what about India?'

'Well, with Saudi aid, the Salafis flourish in India even today. However, you must understand that historically the Indian Muslim is secular and by now totally sick of the way our religion has been maligned by these jihadis. We're tired of being viewed with suspicion by everyone because of the actions of a handful of fundamentalists.' He spoke bitterly. 'By now, the world over, most people only associate terrorism with Islam; they don't realize that Islam is the second largest religion in the world and as beautiful, deep and strong as any other.' There was complete silence when he stopped.

'It's complex, I know.' Sami gave a small smile. 'It can be a bit confusing, especially if you understand that what I am saying is merely my interpretation of events; there are many who have differing views on all this.' He shrugged. 'Anyway, to round off, in India, Waliullah's followers founded the Dar-ul-uloom at Deoband with a view to propagating the return of Islamic puritanism in India. For the Deobandis, the guiding principles remain the goals of Waliullah. In India they exercise considerable influence through a network of madrassas.'

'So it's basically Waliullah's legacy that we are suffering even to this day?'

'Well, that's not quite how I would put it, but you're not incorrect in saying that.'

'And the ISI simply uses this segment to unleash terror in India!' Tiwathia shook his head gravely. 'Don't the Pakis realize how badly all this shit is going to boomerang on them?'

None of them offered an opinion since they all knew from watching the news that most of Pakistan was in flames. The Swat Valley was already under Taliban control, Peshawar teetered on the edge, and now even the major Punjabi and Sindhi cities were under threat. Despite the elaborate denials issued by the civilian government ostensibly in control of Pakistan, it was no secret that in the NWFP, which in geographical terms was about one-sixth of Pakistan, women had already been forced back into the burqa, over two hundred girls' schools had been destroyed, music was banned and barbers forbidden to shave beards. In an almost exact repeat of the scenario that had earlier played out in Afghanistan when the Taliban moved in to seize control, the beard patrols were out and the slightest infraction invited brutal, primitive punishments like flogging and stoning.

'Everyone realizes that, Vikram,' Anbu finally spoke up. 'There has hardly ever been a terrorist incident anywhere in the world that hasn't implicated Pakistan in some way or the other. Either there were Pakistani nationals or people of Pakistani origin involved, or the attackers had spent some time in Pakistan in the period preceding the attacks. And all the organizations that perpetrated these attacks continue to function with total impunity in Pakistan, though in some rare cases they have made some trivial, cosmetic changes to their names. In fact, just recently the British prime minister went on record to state that over 75 per cent of the terror attacks against Britain originated in Pakistan.'

'Why is that surprising?' Tiwathia flared up. 'We all know that regular Pakistan Army troops and ISI paramilitaries were fighting alongside Al Qaeda when the Americans attacked Afghanistan. That's why they even had to beg the Americans to give them a few hours' window to get their troops out when Khost was attacked.'

'The irony is that it was the CIA who helped Osama to build that massive complex of tunnels at Tora Bora.' Sami gave a grim smile. 'Then they had to expend so many American lives to capture it back.'

'Well, serves the fools right. We warned them about this all along, but they never paid any attention to us, and now every bloody Al Qaeda idiot is either hiding in Pakistan's Tribal Areas or being given safe sanctuary there. Funnily enough, the Americans had used these identical hideouts to launch mujahideen operations against the Russians in the eighties.'

'And don't forget how the Pakis kept Osama Bin Laden and about fifty of his Taliban fighters at the Chirat commando training facility in northwest Pakistan, in August 1998, when the Americans were pressurizing Mullah Omar to give him up.'

'What else could they do? They could hardly leave their old Taliban buddy in the lurch. They hid Osama in Chirat so that Mullah Omar could tell the Americans he was not in Afghanistan.'

'That's the nub of the problem, Vikram.' Anbu stepped into the discussion. 'After creating this monstrous lot of terror organizations and supporting them all these years, the Pakis suddenly realized that they would have to turn on them or at least appear to turn on them when old George

Bush gave them the "are you with us or against us" ultimatum after 9/11.'

'They couldn't turn on them even if they wanted to, sir. There's no way in hell the Pak Army or the ISI will allow that to happen. Not after the massive Islamization programme that they went through under General Zia. Now they're not only sympathetic towards the Taliban and Al Qaeda, they actually applaud their rabid ideology and support it fully. In fact, they regard these terror groups as strategic assets.'

'Although that's what the Paki general said in his famous memoirs.'

'Yeah, right! Don't you know that in 1999, RAW released a recording of the same guy talking with his Chief of Staff – the COS was assuring him that they had the jihadi groups by their tooties!'

'Oh well, we know who has got whom by their balls.' Tiwathia laughed sarcastically. 'I've always wanted to know why the general called the book a memoir because I think it's one of the best works of fiction I've ever come across.'

'The fact is, there was no way in hell that Pakistan could afford to antagonize the Yanks by openly refusing to take on the terrorists. And they needed that "frontline state in the war on terror" tag so they could continue to milk the Americans of billions of dollars, save their economy, and avoid being declared a failed, terror-sponsor state by the international community. In any case, just to stay afloat they need the billions of dollars the Yanks have been doling out to them all these years.'

'That's exactly why, every once in a while, the Pakis catch a few low-level Al Qaeda terrorists and throw them at the Yanks to appease them. The only two or three senior Al Qaeda commanders who have been killed or captured so far are the ones who started refusing to toe the Paki line or those the drones took out.'

'Don't the Americans have any sense? Can't they see how the Pakis are leading them up the garden path? Their own economy is staggering and yet they're pumping billions into Pakistan. And all the while, a handful of Pakis are coolly diverting this money into Swiss accounts. None of it is reaching their economy, that's for sure. No money has gone into infrastructure, social services, healthcare or education, otherwise they wouldn't be in the sad shape they are in today.'

'As for the military hardware that America has been giving them to fight the terrorists, they're either using them to arm the terrorists in Kashmir or to strengthen their line-up against India,' Sami said angrily. 'The Americans must be really dumb not to know this!'

'No, MS! The Americans are aware of it, especially after what Salim's lashkar did at New Orleans and San Francisco last week. God knows how many died and how many more will die in the days to come. Believe me, there's nothing like having a few thousand of your countrymen killed to give you a rude wake-up call.'

'Yes, that certainly got them by the short hair,' Sami agreed. That's why they've now stepped up the pressure on Pakistan to turn off support to terrorists all over the place, including Kashmir.'

'Which brings us right back to the point I was making, Vikram. The Pakis are turning cartwheels trying to prove that terrorism in India is a homegrown freedom struggle rather than Pak-sponsored terrorism. That's precisely why we see previously unknown groups like the Indian Mujahideen suddenly emerging on the scene. That's also why they're now busy urging militants in places like Assam to carry out terror strikes.'

'That's precisely the point I've been trying to make, sir,' Vikram interrupted. 'When the cops, the Intelligence Bureau and RAW have clear proof that the YPS and the Indian Mujahideen are two sides of the same coin, why don't we just cut them down and put an end to all this?'

'That's assuming we know who *they* are. And even then, what you suggest is very simplistic, Vikram. Terrorism can never be resolved only by the application of military might.'

'I beg your pardon, sir, but are you trying to say that we should just sit back and allow these crazy bastards to bomb innocent men, women and children whenever and wherever they choose to? Are you...'

'No! That's not what I am saying, but the fact remains that fighting terrorism calls for a well-defined offensive-defence, a definite counter-insurgency strategy and constant innovation by security forces. There is no single strategy that we can use to successfully combat it. Any strategy we adopt will have to be a use-and-throw one. In fact, in this battle, the winner will be the one who keeps the basics in mind, but innovates constantly.'

Anbu paused momentarily, recognizing the need to drive home some ground realities to the young officers he commanded.

'Diplomatically, we have to attack the terror sponsor states. Politically, we have to stop vote bank politics and ensure that economic development is equitable and addresses all sections of society. Our leadership has to work on the root causes of alienation, which allow terrorists to recruit and subvert easily swayed youth. We have to make sure that local support to the terrorists is cut off since without that, they're dead in the ditch.'

He raised his hand to prevent Tiwathia from interrupting.

'On the intelligence front, we have to make sure we have our eyes and ears to the ground at all times so we can see an attack coming. Simultaneously, our security forces have to be ramped up to contain the attacks that get through because, despite all our efforts, some certainly will succeed. Militarily, we have to use force to cut down the attackers and force the terrorists to the negotiating table. And legally, we have to bring terrorists, their supporters and financers to book.' There was another pause as Anbu allowed his words to sink in. 'You see... it has to be a comprehensive package if we are to deal with this menace successfully.'

'So, what I understand is that for us – the security forces – the main plank of the war on terror is good, timely intelligence.'

'Bang on target! *That* is the key. As we all know, there are only three basic ways to gather intelligence – observe it, buy it or steal it. However, in such a fluid and geographically unconfined war, the way to get timely intelligence is either by subverting some terrorists and turning them into informers or sending in our own people to infiltrate the terror groups.'

'I don't know how easy it will be to subvert these crazies,' said Tiwathia. 'Most of them have been brainwashed so thoroughly that they can no longer differentiate right from wrong. I was going through the Al Qaeda recruitment manual the other day and it exhorted the recruiter to keep the recruit busy with lectures and religious pamphlets, especially those that discuss heaven and hell.'

'Yes, the recruiter will always try to play on the aspects of Eternal Paradise or Eternal Damnation. This works especially well with new religious converts or those who are not very conversant with the scriptures and can be browbeaten easily. But there will always be people who have become disgruntled with the uncertainity of life as terrorists, or realized they are being misguided and misused in the name of religion... or someone who can simply be bought over with more money.'

'But I thought these days the typical terror recruit is far more literate and savvy than before, when they were mostly poor, uneducated youngsters who had been lured in.'

'Obviously! They need savvy terrorists because the uneducated ones wouldn't last very long against modern security forces. But this is also a major chink in the terrorists' armour, since the literate ones are also going to be able to see through the hidden agenda and realize they are only being used.'

'Isn't that what happened with Iqbal?'

'Precisely! However, we have to be very careful that the guys we subvert don't turn on us – or they could cause a lot more damage.'

'Yes, they could,' Anbu agreed. 'In this battle, as in every battle, the key is not allowing the enemy to know what we know.'

'So subverting one of their guys may be far more complicated and troublesome than the results it may yield.'

'True, but also remember that trying to send an infiltrator into any terror group is not only a difficult and time-consuming process, it is extremely dangerous for the person trying to do so. They will show absolutely no mercy if his cover breaks for any reason whatsoever.'

'That goes without saying, sir. It will have to be someone who is highly trained and motivated; someone who can stay the course for a long, long time on his own resources and, more importantly, with inner confidence.'

'Pity we don't have James Bond on our side.' Sami gave a half-hearted laugh.

'Or Jason Bourne.'

The three Force 22 officers were silent, their eyes again drawn to the terrible scenes being telecast on the screen in the far corner.

'Or Iqbal,' Tiwathia said softly. 'He had the motivation and the training... he was even the right age to have infiltrated the YPS.'

'More importantly, Vikram,' Anbu added, 'Iqbal had already seen through the lies and the deceit. He was fully aware of the dark underbelly of terror and he knew it had nothing to do with religion.'

'We all know that he was mentally strong...'

'Yes. Remember how he went back across the LOC alone and took down Maulana Fazlur Rehman at Muzzafarabad? Can you imagine the guts that must have taken?'

Another long silence fell upon the three men. It ended only when Vikram whispered, more to himself than anyone else, 'Damn! I really wish we had brought Iqbal back with us. Then he would not...' His voice trailed away. Even the battle-hardened commando was unable to voice the thought that the man who had saved his life was probably dead.

SIX

For a long time Tanaz couldn't believe she was alive. The first two bullets fired by the Pakistani NCO had slammed into the stock of the Uzi in her hands, reducing it to a useless piece of mangled metal. The third had clipped the back of her hand. It had raced along the length of her arm, leaving a long, bloody furrow right up to her shoulder. The wound itself was neither dangerous nor fatal, but the loss of blood could be both. Shaking her head to rid herself of the wooziness, Tanaz sat up groggily. Gritting her teeth, she tore a long strip of cloth from the hem of her burqa and wrapped it tightly along the length of her arm. The biting pain sent a wave of giddiness through her. She pulled herself together with an effort and looked around for Iqbal.

Then she saw the station wagon with its opaque windscreen.

'Iqbal!' Tanaz cried out in alarm, her pain forgotten as she ran to the vehicle. Iqbal lay slumped to one side. Through the folds of his shawl, the hole punched into his chest was clearly visible. Fresh blood oozed from it in a shocking, never-ending stream. Tanaz reached out and felt the warm stirring of Iqbal's breath on the back of her hand; the pounding in her heart receded slightly as she realized he was still alive.

She knew it was imperative that she stop the bleeding and get Iqbal away immediately. It was only a matter of time before someone landed up to investigate the gunfire. Working as fast as she could, Tanaz snatched up a fresh field dressing from the rear seat of the station wagon and used it to staunch the bleeding from Iqbal's chest wound as best as she could. The sight of the open wound and so much blood sent fresh waves of nausea through her.

Stop it! her mind screamed. She knew they would not get out of this alive if she did not take charge of the situation immediately. Gradually, reason and training seized control, forcing her mind into overdrive as her hands began to mechanically finish applying the bandage.

The station wagon is finished! Even if it's not, do I have time to change the tyre? How long before someone else lands up? Should I use the army jeep?

She was still struggling with Iqbal's makeshift bandage when she heard the deep, guttural sound of engines. Grabbing the Uzi from the floor, where it had fallen when Iqbal had passed out, Tanaz jumped out of the station wagon and spun around to face the new threat coming round the bend.

The four vehicles thundered down the track, carrying a wreath of dust with them. They came to a halt just short of the station wagon. The first and fourth vehicles in the mini convoy were Toyota Landcruiser SUVs and the two in between were the Toyota Hiace minibuses that are so common in Pakistan.

There was a long pregnant silence as the unseen occupants of the dust-laden convoy surveyed the gory scene of the shootout. Tanaz's breath seemed to stop and she gripped the weapon tightly with both hands. Every fibre in her body screamed at her to lunge into action.

But at what? Whom?

The answer to her questions emerged as the doors of the lead Landcruiser opened in tandem and four men stepped out. They were all heavily bearded and dressed in identical dark Pathani suits. All four carried 5.45 mm AK-74 assault rifles in their hands.

With a sinking heart, Tanaz saw the rifle muzzles train on her. There was no way she could match that kind of firepower. The slightest move would mean certain death for Iqbal and her.

'What happened here?' the man who had emerged from the co-driver's seat called out. Marked with an unmistakable Afghan accent, his tone was devoid of emotion, as though he was inquiring about the weather.

'There was an... an altercation.' Tanaz tried to

keep all traces of fear and nervousness out of her voice.

'Step away from the vehicle and drop the weapon in your hand,' the man said, again in the same flat tone.

'I'll step away if you want, but I won't drop my weapon.' Tanaz made sure she remained perfectly still as she spoke. 'Not until I know who you are and what you plan to do with us. If you mean us harm, I promise I'll take at least a few of you...'

Her words brought a faint, derisive smile to the impassive faces of the quartet facing her. 'Who are you, woman?'

'I am a believer... a mujahideen.' Tanaz's intuition guided her reply.

'What happened here with them?' He pointed at the dead army men strewn around.

'They saw my husband was wounded... they thought I was a helpless woman all alone and...'

'Where is your husband?'

'In there.' She gestured at the station wagon with her weapon.

'Is he still alive?'

'Yes, he is, but he is badly injured. I need to get him to a doctor quickly.'

'Where were you two headed?'

'We've just returned from a mission from across.' Tanaz gestured vaguely towards the Indian border. 'We were on our way back to rejoin our group when this happened.'

'Which group?'

'The Lashkar,' Tanaz replied without hesitation, knowing it was the safest one to name since it was large enough to accord them the anonymity they desperately needed right now.

'Wait!' the man commanded. 'And don't make any sudden moves.' He turned and walked back to the Hiace minibus. He opened the door and leaned forward to talk to someone, his demeanour clearly deferential. A long moment later, he shut the door and began to walk towards Tanaz. He must have muttered something as he passed the other men because they all shouldered their weapons.

'Come on, woman. Let's get the two of you out of here.'

Aware that her options were limited, Tanaz lowered her weapon and asked, 'Who are you? Are you also mujahideen?'

'What did you think? The Salvation Army?' the leader grunted sarcastically, his words eliciting a short, barking laugh from the other men. 'Come on. Let's get a move on. We need to get clear of this area before someone else lands up.'

Two of them reached inside the station wagon and hauled out the still unconscious Iqbal. The other two quickly gathered all the arms and ammunition they could lay their hands on from the fallen Pakistani soldiers. Tanaz hurried behind them as they carried Iqbal and laid him on the rear seat of the second Hiace minibus.

'He has been shot badly,' the man carrying him said to Tanaz as he put Iqbal down. 'Try and keep him as still as possible. If he loses too much blood...' The man shrugged.

'How long before we can get him to a doctor?' Tanaz asked worriedly.

'Not long,' he muttered, 'maybe an hour at the most. He'll take care of him meanwhile.' He gestured at the man who had just alighted from the other Hiace, toting a large black medical bag. The newcomer was short, though equally heavily bearded and sported a pair of thick horn-rimmed spectacles. He ignored Tanaz as he got into the vehicle beside Iqbal.

As the convoy started up again and carefully nosed its way past the shot-up vehicles, the bespectacled man removed the blood-soaked bandage and began to check Iqbal's wounds.

'Are you a doctor?' Tanaz asked anxiously.

'Keep quiet, woman, and let me do my work,' the man said harshly without looking at her. He had a strange accent that Tanaz was unable to place. 'And keep yourself covered! Have you no shame? Showing your face like that!'

Tanaz suppressed an angry retort as she threw the veil of the bloodied burqa over her face. She kept her mouth shut as she watched the man get rid of the field dressings and clean up both the wounds. The minute the bandages came off, blood began to spurt out again. He reached into his bag and hauled out two silver-green rectangular packets with QuikClot printed on them in large red letters. Slitting them open one by one, he began to sprinkle sand-coloured granules onto the wounds. Tanaz had heard about this wonderous haemostasic agent but this was the first time she was seeing it being used.

She watched in open-mouthed admiration as the thirsty, sand-like granules soaked up moisture from the blood and began to coagulate into a thick clot that completely covered the wound. Amost instantly, the flow of blood ebbed to a trickle and then stopped altogether.

'What is that? Will it staunch the bleeding?' Tanaz couldn't stop herself from asking.

'Of course it will.' Perhaps the man was so used to being asked about the miracle powder, as the less literate jihadis were wont to call it, that he forgot he had told her to keep her mouth shut. There was a distinct note of pride in his voice as he explained, 'The clot is strong enough to withstand high pressure, including blood transfusion. It will even stop blood loss from high volume arterial and venous bleeds. It's a real life-saver.' He waved the now empty packet at her before chucking it down. 'In fact, had it not been for this, the goras would have lost many more lives in Afghanistan by now. Every damn NATO soldier carries one these days.' Then, just as suddenly as he had begun to talk, his surliness reasserted itself and he clammed up. He gave Iqbal a shot and then jabbed an IV into him, hooking the bottle to the handle above the door.

Still marvelling at the clot, Tanaz refocused on Iqbal, trying to keep him as comfortable and still as possible. Maybe it was her imagination, but she thought he was breathing a lot easier by the time the vehicles halted an hour later.

SEVEN

The place they stopped at seemed to be a small village, or a suburb of the town looming large in the distance. From whatever little she was able to make out, they seemed to be near Faisalabad.

Not that it mattered. Tanaz knew she had no option but to go with the flow, at least until Iqbal was fit enough to travel.

The opening of the vehicle door put an end to her thoughts. The two burly mujahids who had carried Iqbal into the Hiace lifted him out and carried him into the compound.

The compound comprised several small houses, most of them mud-walled, though there were a few brick ones too. A shoulder-high mud wall encircled the entire cluster. Cowdung and debris littered the area. Broken furniture was strewn around on the flat roofs of most of the houses. It had the peculiar, unkempt feel of a place that was largely inhabited by men whose minds were occupied with things more important than cleanliness.

Either that, or this place is mostly used by transients who are merely passing through.

Hurrying along behind the two men, she asked, 'Where are we?'

'At a safe place,' the same man who had spoken earlier replied.

'Safe from the army?'

'The army? The Pakistan Army?'

'Which other army is there in this country?'

'Well, no one talks about it openly, but the American Special Forces slip in and out, conducting raids inside Pakistan. Don't you know?'

'Really?' Tanaz showed an appropriate degree of surprise and anger. 'Why do we allow it?'

'Exactly!' He gestured vehemently. 'As for the Pakistan Army, I wouldn't worry too much if I were you.' He looked at her and laughed. 'This compound belongs to the local ISI commander. No one is likely to bother us here.'

The room they entered would have been known, in a more organized place, as the medical room or the sick bay. Placed squarely in the centre was a steel operating table. Above it hung four large, naked tubelights. To one side was a tall steel cabinet with glass shutters that held an assortment of medicines and supplies. A rudimentary effort had been made to keep the room cleaner than the area outside. A faint but distinct hospital-like smell of disinfectant hung in the air.

They had just finished laying Iqbal down on the operating table when the man who had tended to him in the van strode in. Behind him came a thin, gawky man with a harried air about him.

'You wait outside, woman,' the man ordered Tanaz in the same curt manner in which he had spoken to her earlier. 'We have to operate on him.'

'No,' Tanaz replied softly, but firmly. 'He is my husband. I will stay with him.'

'Okay, then you will help,' the man replied with a dismissive shrug. 'Take these and boil them.' He pulled out a tray of operating instruments from the corner cabinet and gestured to the cooking gas alongside it. 'And don't say I didn't warn you. It's going to be bloody and painful.'

'I won't complain,' Tanaz countered, though her heartbeat escalated and she could barely contain her anxiety.

There was a glint of admiration in the man's eyes as he looked at her. 'I hope you're strong.' He paused. 'Bear in mind that we have run out of anaesthesia. Your man will have to bear the pain on his own.'

'No anaesthesia! Allah have mercy!' Tanaz tried to shut out the thought of the knife cutting into Iqbal's flesh. 'How will he bear the pain?' For a moment she felt her will weaken. Then she shut down her mind and began to focus on the task given to her. Of their own accord, her lips began to move in silent prayer.

Iqbal's body jerked awake as the knife sliced open a neat valley in his chest. Then the doctor dug in, searching for the 7.62 mm slug that had shattered Iqbal's chest. Seconds later, the scorching pain hit him and Iqbal began to scream. His legs thrashed wildly and the men had to exert every ounce of their energy to keep him down. The more he screamed and thrashed about, the more the doctor scrambled inside, unable to achieve a clean removal of the slug. Finally, Iqbal's voice deserted him and then, eventually, so did consciousness.

It was some time around then that Tanaz fainted.

When Tanaz came to, she found herself alone in the room, still lying on the floor where she had fallen. Iqbal's screams echoed in her head, blanketing it with pain, that helpless, endless pain we feel when someone we love is being hurt. Large ugly drops of blood were splattered all around her on the floor.

She sat up hesitantly and saw Iqbal lying still on the operating table. His face was pale and his breath was running shallow. But his heavily bandaged chest heaved rhythmically and he appeared to be in better shape than when they had carried him in.

'We managed to get both the bullets out of him.' The sudden, surprisingly squeaky voice from the door startled Tanaz, making her jump. It was the gawky, nervous-looking man who had assisted the doctor in the surgery. 'He should live, Inshallah... if he doesn't catch an infection...'

'He *will* live,' Tanaz retorted, more sharply than she had intended. 'He has to.'

'Inshallah!' the man repeated simply, raising his hands heavenwards. 'So, Ghazi was saying you had a shootout with the army?'

'Yes.'

'That's strange... very strange. They never bother us – at least not in this part of the country.' There was a hint of suspicion in his tone, or so it seemed to the ever watchful Tanaz.

'Maybe they thought I was helpless,' she replied, sticking to the version she had given earlier, 'because my man was injured.'

'Maybe!' The man watched her unblinkingly. 'Where are you two coming from?'

'Across.' Tanaz's answer was monosyllabic.

'What did you go there for?'

'We were sent for a task.'

'What task?'

'If you were meant to know, you would have been told.' Tanaz's eyes dared him.

'Bitch!' he spat out. 'Why don't you just clean him up instead of chatting me up?'

Tanaz turned away silently, relieved the inquisition was over, at least for the moment. She filled the metal basin lying in the corner with water and taking a wad of cotton from the cabinet, began to clean Iqbal, starting with his face, working her way down his body, careful to keep away from the bandaged parts.

'Where are we now?' she asked after a while.

'It's a safehouse given to us by the ISI,' he said. 'But it's mostly the Arabs and other foreigners who use it.'

'Arabs?' Tanaz couldn't keep the surprise out of her voice. 'What are they doing in these parts? I thought they kept to the north.'

'For a woman, you seem quite well informed about these things.' The man gave her another keen look.

'Why shouldn't I be?' Tanaz retorted belligerently. 'So what if I am a woman? Does that make me any less a mujahideen?' She turned to face him. 'Don't you know I've sacrificed both my brothers for the cause... not to mention three years of my life?'

'All right, all right! Don't get so worked up. I just asked. You know how troubled these times are; one has to be careful and question everything.'

'I understand.' Tanaz discarded her belligerence, eager to have him talking again. 'I know exactly what you mean. These days you can never take anyone at face value.'

'Well, the Arabs, in fact all the outsiders, began to move out once the goras started sending their drones across the borders on search-and-destroy strikes. Especially the important ones... they are extra careful these days.'

'The important ones? You mean like those who brought us here?'

'Those who got you here?' The man gave a sardonic laugh. 'Hardly! But the man they are escorting certainly is.'

'Which one is that? I didn't see him.'

'The Ameer is only seen by those he wishes to be seen by.' He gave another knowing, almost condescending laugh. 'In fact, you are lucky he even stopped to pick you two strays up...' The man's voice trailed away, as though suddenly aware that he was talking too much.

'The Ameer? Is that his name? Who is he?'

'There you go again, with your questions!' the man retorted brusquely, his tone dissuading Tanaz from asking any more questions.

Three grim days later, Tanaz was coming out of the hospital room in the morning after checking on the still weak, but now sporadically conscious Iqbal when three men emerged from a hut across the compound, about fifty feet away. Although all three were dressed alike, the one in the centre caught her attention immediately.

Tall and built like a Patton tank, the man had a long, angular scar running across the right cheek of his gaunt face and a strange glow in his eyes. A chill ran down Tanaz's spine as their eyes met. She looked away hastily and bowing her head, scurried away as she had seen the one or two other women in the compound do.

Almost simultaneously, a posse of men erupted from the huts around and began to make their way towards the mini-convoy of vehicles that had brought Tanaz and Iqbal here. The man she now knew as the Ameer walked into the Hiace van with darkened windows positioned behind the leading Landcruiser. Engines revved to life and moments later, the convoy was moving. Within minutes it had disappeared into the swirling desert sands, heading north.

'So you have finally seen the Ameer!' said a reedy, nasal voice just behind her. She turned with a start to see Pervez, the doctor's assistant.

'You startled me,' Tanaz said accusingly.

They stood there, watching the dust settle on the horizon. 'Where has he gone?' Tanaz asked.

'The Ameer? Who knows! He never stays anywhere for more than a day or two.'

'Really? That's strange.'

'Why? It makes perfect sense from the security point of view. Most of the other leaders follow the same rule and the Ameer ul Momineem is, after all, the most important of them all.'

'Ameer ul Momineem? The Commander of the Faithful?'

'Yes, woman, that's who he is!' Pervez looked at her disdainfully. 'Not many know of him today, but what he is doing will soon surpass anything even the Sheikh had visualized.'

'Oh!' Tanaz purposely kept her tone a little stupid, hoping the man would keep talking, but it didn't work this time, possibly because he had other things on his mind.

'How is your man now?' Tanaz was about to reply when Pervez continued. 'I may have to move him today. We're expecting a couple of other patients soon.'

'But he is not okay yet,' Tanaz protested. 'We must keep him in an area as free from infection as possible.'

'There you go again, trying to tell me how to do my job.' Pervez looked angry enough to strike her. Tanaz tensed, but the moment passed and he said tersely, 'Just get him ready to be moved out in an hour or so... take him to that one.' He pointed to a tiny, abandoned hut on the edge of the compound. 'And from now on, you look after him yourself.'

Tanaz bit her tongue, knowing this was not the time or place for aggression, certainly not until Iqbal was back on his feet.

All thoughts of the Ameer faded from her mind as she began to prepare Iqbal for the move. *I might as well change his bandages again. I don't know when I'll be able to get hold of fresh ones.* Doing exactly as she had seen Pervez do over the past two days, she changed Iqbal's dressings and hid a clean set of bandages in her burqa.

Perhaps because of a resurgence of pain, Iqbal wandered into wakefulness as she finished knotting the bandage on his shoulder. For a long moment he lay still and watched her. 'How are you, Tanaz?' His voice was a whisper, forced out by muscles beginning to rust with disuse.

Tanaz looked up in delight. Taking a quick look around to ensure they were alone, she threw back her hijab.

'How are you?' she whispered back. 'How is the pain now?'

'Better.' Iqbal's eyes were fixed on hers. 'I feel stiff, but I'm better.'

'Good!' Tanaz said reassuringly. 'That's what the doctor said too. They've decided to move you to another hut to recuperate.'

'I don't care.' Iqbal gave a weak shrug. 'As long as you are with me.'

'I am!' She caressed his cheek lovingly. 'I will be there... always.'

'Mashallah!' Iqbal could not prevent the weak sigh that escaped him; even this brief effort had tired him out.

'Don't worry, Iqbal, you'll be up and about soon... as good as new.'

But on this count Tanaz was wrong.

Iqbal's return to health was a slow and painful process. A full fortnight passed before he could get up to relieve himself. Even then, he needed Tanaz to support him. It was over a month later that Iqbal was finally able to slowly walk around the compound. From that point on, his recovery was swift, if not miraculous. Tanaz's constant nursing and feeding ensured that Iqbal was soon stepping out of the hut and slowly clocking at least a mile each time; once, twice and soon, thrice a day. Tanaz was constantly by his side. Every painful grimace as his stiff limbs and muscles ached back into use elicited a sharp look of concern from her.

'I'm all right, Tanaz. Don't worry, nothing is going to happen to me now.'

'Ameen!' Tanaz threw a grateful look heavenwards.

'Nothing can happen to me now,' Iqbal murmured, 'now that I have a reason to live.'

Tanaz threw him a playful, quizzical look. Emboldened by the dusk falling around them, Iqbal reached for her hand under the burqa and gave it a long squeeze. By now almost everyone in the compound was used to seeing the two of them walking around every morning, afternoon and night. Even so, they kept a low profile and spoke to the others only when it was essential. More contact meant more questions. It was only because the Ameer himself had delivered them to the compound that they had not faced closer scrutiny so far.

Iqbal broke the silence between them.

'I can't wait for us to get back...'

'Get back?' For a moment Tanaz was perplexed.

'Back across the border. Back home so that we can...'

'Home?' Tanaz asked, suddenly engulfed by sadness. 'I've forgotten what a home feels like.'

'Don't worry, Tanaz.' Iqbal wanted to take her in his arms and brush away the pain on her face. 'Together we'll make a home. You, me and... one day, our children.'

'Hush!' The smile returned to Tanaz's eyes, though Iqbal could not see it because of her hijab.

'Yes, we will, Tanaz,' he promised. 'I can't wait for us to return and get married.'

'I'm already yours, Iqbal. You know that. As for the wedding ceremony... if it's important to you...'

'It isn't, but I want everything to be perfect for you,' Iqbal murmured.

'It already is.'

Even the bleak, ill-kept compound was filled with vibrance as the red embers of the setting sun bathed it in a tranquil glow. They sat outside their hut, watching the sun go down. The place was shrouded in silence since most of the temporary inhabitants had left the previous day. Perhaps an operation was in the offing, though neither of them knew for sure.

As he looked around the deserted compound, Iqbal was reminded of the time he had travelled through Pakistan on his way to the training camp at Muzaffarabad. It all seemed so long ago, but the memory was as strong as though it had happened yesterday.

'Tell me, Wasim,' he had asked their guide, 'how come all the places we stay in are deserted? Where is everyone?'

Wasim had given Iqbal a long look before he replied, 'They're not abandoned or empty. We have to be careful and ensure external trainees don't mix with the others... Salim sahib is very strict about that.'

'I don't understand... which others?'

'The locals, primarily.'

'Why?'

'Not everyone here supports the jihad. There are some who feel that Pakistan should worry more about itself and its economy than expend time, energy and resources on external problems.'

'I thought the people of Pakistan were solidly behind us... behind the jihad.'

'The people of Pakistan?' Wasim said. 'People are people... they tend to worry about basic things like food, shelter and clothing. Everything else is secondary.'

Shrugging away the memory, Iqbal turned to Tanaz. 'The less contact we have with the others, the less chances of us making a mistake and giving ourselves away.'

'I suppose so.' Tanaz nodded. 'We must take each day as it comes... till you are strong enough for us to move out.'

'I know.' Iqbal looked at her steadily. 'I just wish

we could be home now. The two of us... and nobody else.' His voice had fallen to a low whisper.

In the fading light, Tanaz reached out and took his hand. Her touch was electric and Iqbal felt his breath catch. Silently, he got up and led her into the hut. The time for words was past.

Iqbal's hands were trembling as he latched the door and leaned back against it. Then Tanaz was in his arms and their lips sought each other's hungrily. She shuddered as his teeth caught her lower lip and sucked on it, gently, then hard, until she moaned in pain. He drew back then and his lips explored her face, caressing her eyes, her cheeks, her forehead, the lobe of her ear, down to the side of her neck. They returned to coax her lips apart again and she pulled him closer until their bodies clung to each other.

Stepping back a little, Iqbal freed the burqa from Tanaz's body. It crumpled to the floor and the rest of their clothes followed, pulled off by shaking, frantic hands. Without letting go of her, Iqbal manouevred Tanaz back until she lay on the mattress, her naked body a burnished brown in the twilight. His hands glided down, lingering to stroke, lift, caress, his fingertips rough on her soft skin. His lips followed, his beard grazing her neck, her breasts. She moaned as he took her hard, erect nipples into his mouth, tugging at them, biting them. She arched as he moved down, his lips and fingers restless in the hollow of her navel, the shadow between her legs. Her body froze as her mind struggled to comprehend what was coming, but he moved up again to kiss her lingeringly on the lips and she curved into him, trusting again, her hands tentatively exploring the scarred skin on his back, the lean line of his spine. He turned over then and pulled her on top of him, his eyes laughing as she cried out in surprise. Eyes still locked into hers, he took her hands and raised them to his face, then downward. Her fingers traced his shoulders, his arms, his chest, then moved down over his stomach, uncertain but determined. He gathered her to him then, with a strength that had eluded him all these days, and she exclaimed as he pushed her onto her back and parted her legs. His fingers were gentle as they touched her, then his tongue replaced them with its questing, probing quickness. She moaned, unable to hold back the words, the endearments, the entreaties.

He pulled himself up and looked at her, his body poised above hers for a moment before coming down hard. Her hands came up to push him away as pain lanced through her but it was only for a moment and he stilled, waiting for her to calm before beginning to move again, slowly at first, then fast and unstopping, his eyes watching the play of expressions on her face. She moved with him, her arms holding him tight, her teeth biting down on her lips. When the orgasm caught her, lifting her and spiralling her outwards in a moment like no other she had known, she cried out and he tensed as her nails sank into the newly healed skin on his back. Then he, too, was beyond any pretence of control as he thrust into her repeatedly and without thought until he came, his body shuddering as he collapsed on hers, his eyes shut and his breathing shallow.

The following month, Tanaz missed her period.

'Are you sure?' Iqbal asked her again and again, unable to contain the joy that almost threatened to unseat his mind.

'How could I not be sure, Iqbal?' Tanaz asked in mock exasperation.

'Okay, but we need to get you to a doctor and make sure.'

'And that's not going to happen here for sure.'

'I know.' Iqbal nodded. 'But I'm quite all right now. We can tell them we are off to rejoin our group and move on. In any case, we can't stay here much longer. They'll start asking awkward questions sooner or later.'

'You're right!' Already, some of the permanent inhabitants who manned the compound had started making discreet but persistent enquiries. It was only a matter of time before the curiosity spread. 'Let's do it first thing tomorrow morning.'

'Perfect!' Iqbal leaned back against the wall. 'It will be good to get back home. Abbu and Ashraf will be thrilled to meet you and welcome you into the family.'

'You think so?' Tanaz asked dubiously.

'I know so. I also know that Colonel Anbu and the others in Force 22 will be happy to see us again.'

'How can you be so sure? They are professional soldiers. For them the mission is the only thing that matters.'

'Maybe, but my instincts tell me that this man... this Colonel Anbu is different. There's something special about him. Trust me.'

'I do trust you, Iqbal, you know I do.' Tanaz looked away uncertainly. 'But why do we need to go back at all? Why can't we just stay on here? We could return to the desert. I have family there... whatever little is left of it.'

'And then?' Iqbal asked her gently. 'After all that has happened, how do you think we'll live? Always looking over our shoulders? With the perpetual fear of not knowing who might recognize you... or...' Iqbal's voice tapered off. 'How long do you think it will be before the hardliners take over Pakistan? Can you imagine what the situation will be once that happens? The country will lapse into the dark ages for all you know. Is this where we want to bring up our child?'

Tanaz knew Iqbal was right, but her fear of what lay across the border held her back. Iqbal tried to calm her.

'Tanaz, we know what these jihadis are capable of. We've both lost so much to them. And they haven't spared our god or our religion either. Is it right to give up the fight halfway? Will you be able to rest peacefully afterwards?'

Tanaz did not reply for a long time. Finally, when she looked up, it was with a steely resolve. 'You are right! We have a duty to stand up and be counted. These maniacs cannot be stopped until every one of us decides it's time to take them on.'

'I knew you'd feel like that!' Iqbal's smile was triumphant as he pulled her into his arms.

Neither of them had an inking of what the 'maniacs' had let loose on the streets of India, even as they stood there dreaming of their future.

EIGHT

A few hundred miles to the south, the 1096 Ahimsa Express from Pune pulled into Ahmedabad Junction railway station. The six men who alighted from it had occupied different second-class compartments in the train. They had chosen to travel second class not because they lacked money – their supporters ensured they always had plenty – but because the crowded compartments accorded them a greater anonymity than the first-class or air-conditioned sleepers.

Moving with planned deliberation, the six men weaved through the crowds on the platform and converged near the entrance to the second-class retiring room. Waiting for them were four men dressed in the low-cost casuals typical of the small-town middle-class student. All ten were in their early twenties and all were clean-shaven. No words were exchanged as one by one, they followed the man who appeared to be their leader, to the exit. They separated then, a few hailing autorickshaws and taxis while the others headed towards the bus depot. They were soon swallowed up by a city settling down to the business of a new day.

An hour or so later, the ten men were together again, at a two-bedroom apartment a short walk from Ahmedabad Civil Hospital. The apartment was tiny and sparsely furnished, as most student accommodation is; the paint was peeling off the walls and large splotches of damp stained the ceiling. A large double mattress was propped up against the wall for more floor room.

Asif was already there, talking in low tones with three other men. Their conversation stopped the minute the first of the newcomers walked in. Asif waited for the other nine to arrive before he began to speak. The well-rehearsed, hour long briefing was carried out with stark, almost military precision.

'Any questions?' he asked when the briefing was over.

'No, Asif bhai,' was the murmured, unanimous response. Most of them could have recited the instructions and warnings even in their sleep. They had all been through the trial run carried out a fortnight ago.

'Good!' Asif seemed pleased. 'Then let's synchronize our watches. The timing is very important, otherwise we won't be able to...'

'...capture the flow of people,' the youngest of the lot, an eighteen-year-old school dropout named

Ashraf, finished with a cheeky grin. 'Don't worry so much, bhaijaan. Nothing will go wrong.'

'It better not!' Asif said sharply. 'There's no margin for error, and remember, if even one of us slips up, we all go down.' His remark ensured that the mood was sombre as he wound up: 'Okay everyone, I want you to eat and get some rest. We move out at five o'clock sharp.'

The first man left precisely at five. The others followed at two to three minute intervals. Each of them carried a large steel tiffin-box. Only Asif appeared with a large hard-shell suitcase. And he was the only one who didn't have a bicycle waiting for him below. Hefting the suitcase, he began to walk briskly towards the Civil Hospital.

Meanwhile, the others had fastened their tiffin-boxes securely to the rear carriers of their bicycles and pedalled away towards their different destinations.

The man in the lead stopped at Maninagar and parked his bicycle among the others that crowded the side of the road. He padlocked it carefully and hailed an autorickshaw to make his way back to the apartment.

As he got into the autorickshaw, Asif opened the boot of a stolen Ambassador car that had been left in the parking lot of the Civil Hospital the previous day. He put the suitcase in, relocked the boot and made his way back to the apartment. He was halfway across the hospital compound when his mobile phone beeped.

Item delivered.

The message was short and cryptic, as were the ones that followed. One by one, as Asif walked back to the apartment, they all checked in.

With a quiet gesture of satisfaction, Asif dialled a number from memory.

Far away in Mumbai, the call was answered by a slim young man in the backseat of a maroon Ford Endeavour SUV which was snaking its way through the evening traffic. The laptop on the seat beside him radiated a soft white glow. He watched the screen intently as the NetStumbler software installed on the laptop reached out in the gathering gloom of the evening, searching for an unsecured wireless Wi-Fi network to latch on to.

'There! That's it!' he exclaimed suddenly. 'Stop somewhere here. The signal strength is good.' Even before the vehicle had pulled over to the side of the road, his fingers were flying across the keyboard. He logged into a newly created email account on yahoo, clicked on the drafts folder and eight seconds later, a two-page long mail was on its way. It was addressed to over a dozen recipients, most of them senior managers in various media houses. A copy was also marked to the police commissioner of Ahmedabad. The minute the emails left his account, the man logged out, shut down the laptop and barked urgently at his driver, 'Let's go!'

Pulling into the traffic again, the Endeavour sped away as fast as it could. It was soon zipping down the expressway towards Pune, from where it had driven up earlier that afternoon.

The first of the addressees stared in shock at the email on his computer screen. By the time he finished reading it, his hands were trembling and his breathing was uneven. He reached for the phone lying next to him but it was already too late.

The bombs had begun to explode.

Eight of the ten men had returned to the apartment and were seated in front of the television when the first tiffin bomb kept on the cycle at Maninagar exploded. Almost immediately, a second one exploded at Saraspur. By the time the third bomb went off at Hirabazar, television crews had descended. Like vultures circling their prey, the perpetually news-starved media swung into action, beaming the carnage across the country.

'You only got three!' Ashraf crowed at the man who had planted the bomb at Maninagar. Some of the others laughed. 'I keep telling you that you don't know how to...'

'Shut up, Ashraf!' Asif hissed. 'Leave Sajid alone and let's hear what they are saying.'

Ashraf subsided sheepishly and they went back to watching the screen.

By now the eighth bomb had gone off and the city was bleeding.

'I want to see what happens at the last one.' Asif checked his wristwatch and got up.

'May I come with you?' The ever excited Ashraf jumped up. 'Please?' He pleaded like a schoolboy, shifting eagerly from one foot to the other.

'Okay, but wipe that silly grin off your face,' Asif said roughly. 'And keep your mouth shut.'

The two men walked back to the Civil Hospital at a brisk pace. All around them people were elbowing their way through the crowds, most heading away from the hospital. As they reached the hospital, the duo was met by the collective wail of a long line of ambulances that off-loaded casualties and then screamed off to bring more. The compound in front of the hospital was packed with people.

Asif and Ashraf leaned casually against the closed shutters of a shop across the street and watched the hospital from a distance. There were several other morbid souls like them scattered around, watching the drama unfold.

It didn't take long.

Asif was glancing at his watch for the third time when a black cloud billowed up from the Ambassador. A split second later, a giant roar shattered the air. Even from a distance, the explosion shocked them into a stunned silence.

Though they were well out of range, both ducked instinctively as metal shrapnel burst out of the now decimated car and scythed into the people around. A cloud of dust swept through the hospital compound, enveloping everything it touched. For a moment, there was a stunned silence. And then the screams began.

Asif saw the smirk on Ashraf's face. He nudged him sharply and the two of them peeled away from the crowd that was growing with every passing moment.

Ashraf gave a gleeful shout of laughter as soon as they entered the apartment. 'You all should have seen...'

Asif cut him off with a thump on his back. 'Shut up, you fool!' he hissed venomously. 'If someone hears you, we're all dead. They'll bloody lynch us. How many times do I have to tell you to control yourself?'

'Sorry, Asif bhai. Very sorry.' Ashraf gave a weak grin, sobering up immediately. 'It will not happen again.'

'It had better not! Arsehole!' As Asif turned to the others, a flash of defiance, almost hatred, blazed across Ashraf's face. Asif nodded at the men who had come with him by train. 'Okay, it went off fabulously. I want all of you to leave the city immediately. Leave the house one at a time. I'll see you in Pune next Monday.

'And you,' he said to the second group that had

met him at the station, 'head back to your home stations and stand by till you hear from me.'

One of the men from the second group asked, 'What's next on the agenda, bhai?'

'You'll be told when the time comes, miyan. I'm sure you know the rule by now. No operation is discussed till we are all together and everything is in place to execute it. That way, there is no chance of a leak.' Asif's tone was curt and final.

'Come on, bhai!' the man protested. 'By now I'm sure you trust us.'

'I do! But that doesn't mean one of us will not slip up and get caught.'

No one said anything. By now most of them had become used to Asif's cagey ways.

'But don't worry,' Asif said, trying to ease the atmosphere a little, 'it won't be long now. Before they recover from one strike, we'll be hitting them with another, and another. Remember the promise we made – we will never allow the dust to settle.'

His words were greeted with smiles and nods.

'And before you leave, remember to collect your cash from me.'

The grins broadened. Despite being extremely secretive and a very tough leader, Asif was always easy with the money, especially when a job had been done well.

One by one they collected their share of the money and moved out.

An hour later, barring the three students who had

leased the apartment a few weeks ago, no trace of the bombers remained. These three sat glued to the television, lapping up the details of the deaths they had caused, the long list of people killed or injured – kafirs and non-kafirs.

It was not for nothing that Asif had been codenamed The Recruiter by his controller.

NINE

The National Intelligence Advisor (NIA), G.K. Rao, was the first to reach the conference hall where the Core Crisis Committee was scheduled to meet that morning. The prime minister had called the meeting late the previous night, barely a few hours after the serial bombings at Ahmedabad. Since only the core group was involved, setting up the meeting took no time.

He is going to be really worked up, Rao thought. *I feel sorry for the home minister... but he's such an incompetent arsehole*. A tired, exasperated sigh escaped him. *Most politicians are plain idiots, a large number of them criminals. God alone knows why and how they get elected.* Rao shook off the futile thought as he began to look through his notes in preparation for the questions that were likely to come up.

Rao was one of the first agents to have joined RAW. He was in his mid-fifties, short and portly, and wore round black horn-rimmed spectacles that had gone out of fashion a few decades ago. He was one of the few who understood the true state of

Indian Intelligence and had to his credit several daring and critical operations, none of which would ever be publicly acknowledged. His biggest strength was his total lack of political bias or mentors. This, more than anything else, had made him acceptable across the political spectrum when the PM decided to set up the National Intelligence Command (NIC) some months ago and appointed Rao at its head as the NIA.

The tiny conference room was located just down the corridor from the PM's offices in South Block. A large U-shaped mahogany table that could seat a dozen people dominated most of the room. At the open end of the U was a wall with a large plasma screen. Every person seated at the table could plug in his laptop and use the screen to project information onto it.

Rao had just finished hooking up his laptop when the Core Team members began to arrive. As expected, Narayan, the National Security Advisor (NSA), arrived first. He greeted Rao with a grim nod as he moved to the chair on his right.

Like Rao, Narayan was an old intelligence hand. A die-hard professional, he had survived a tumultuous four-decade long tenure without any political mentors, on the strength of his competence. Tall and elegantly dressed, he was a man of few words. But when he did speak, he chose his words with great care. Except for their capabilities and efficiency, the two men had less than nothing in common.

The door swung open again and the ministers of defence, home and external affairs entered. For a change, there was no small talk, only muttered greetings. An uneasy silence gripped the room. It only deepened when the doors flew open yet again and the prime minister walked up to his seat at the head of the table with a firm, almost angry gait.

He got straight to the point as he turned to the home minister with a question: 'What have you got to say about the terror strikes in Ahmedabad?'

The home minister was about to respond when the PM cut him off. 'The way we have bombs exploding all over the country, it's almost as though we are at war.'

'We *are* at war, sir!' Rao's voice was quietly emphatic. The PM gave him a cold look but Rao continued, unfazed. 'Sir, we have been at war every single day since partition. In addition to the full-scale wars that have been thrust upon us, the Pakistanis have made sure we are perpetually engaged in endless conflict.'

'Aren't you overstating it a bit, Rao?' The home minister seemed relieved as the focus shifted away from him.

'Am I, sir? Why don't we step back and look at the facts?' Rao replied in a measured tone. 'Is there any denying that Pakistan is a laboratory for radical Islam? Or that it's in cahoots with our other neighbours?'

'Our other neighbours? Aren't you getting a bit paranoid?'

'Are we?' Narayan came smoothly to Rao's rescue. 'China would love to see a weak, tottering India. It could then retain topdog status in Asia and remain the world's fastest growing economy and the first choice for foreign investments.'

'And how exactly is China planning to do us in?'

'Planning to?' Narayan's grim laugh was neither pleasant nor polite. 'They're already doing it. India is possibly the only country with whom they've made no real effort to resolve border disputes. They have supported Pakistan with military hardware which they know will be used against us. And they've blocked every move within the UN to ban Pakistan-based terror groups like the Jamaat-ul-Dawa... and of course, we all know who has been helping Pakistan with testing and developing nuclear weapons.'

'As for our other neighbours,' Rao took over again, 'Nepal is firmly in the grip of the Maoists. They favour China and will follow its dictates since the Maoists receive extensive moral and material support from China. And Bangladesh marches to much the same beat as Pakistan.'

'I fully endorse that,' Narayan said. 'All these countries pretend to work in isolation, but the subtle alliance between them has tied up India's security forces in knots all these years and cost us millions by stunting our economic growth.'

'The Pakistan Army and the ISI are spearheading this battle,' said Rao. 'They want to radicalize the

Indian Muslims and incite the Hindu majority to lash back at them until there is complete chaos. Our security forces get tied up in meaningless internal duties and soon, war fatigue will set in and completely demoralize them. I'm sure you know that in all these years, there hasn't been a single day when the Indian Armed Forces have not been engaged in combat.'

'Okay, now if the history lesson is over,' the external affairs minister cut in impatiently, 'can you tell us who is responsible for these serial bombings?'

'I think we all know we can safely attribute the terrorist problems we face to Pakistan,' said Rao gravely. 'After all these years, despite dozens of accords, treaties and promises, Pakistan has not relented in its efforts to balkanize India. Our problem is not so much the Islamic purists calling for a return to the original practices of Islam, it is the ISI with its subversive tactics, using disgruntled and criminal elements in India to wage a low-intensity conflict against us. This war of a thousand cuts aims to bleed our economy, fragment our society and keep international attention focused on the conflict in Kashmir, which they have always tried to pass off as domestic militancy.'

'Not to mention the fact that this simmering problem with India enables the Pakistani Army to retain control over Pakistan. It also ensures they get unstinted support from countries like China.'

'That's absolutely correct,' Rao said. 'In fact, the terror attacks they sponsor against India are mainly aimed at provoking an armed response from us, a response that will give the Pak Army an excuse to pull out their troops from the NWFP area and thus reduce pressure on the Taliban and Al Qaeda. The army is deeply unhappy about the operations they are being forced to conduct against the Taliban due to American pressure. They would love to have an excuse to get out of that.'

'But isn't it in their own interest to fight the Taliban? Doesn't Pakistan suffer from terror attacks too?'

'Yes, but there are many in the army and the ISI who want the Taliban to take over Pakistan. They want the Islamic caliphate to expand and take control of maximum territory. In fact, this lot views everything in terms of a jihad against what they call the Crusader-Zionist-Hindu nexus.'

'All that's fine, Rao, but who specifically was responsible for these bomb blasts in Ahmedabad – and why are we not able to prevent such attacks?' The prime minister's tone was curt.

'The investigations are still on, sir, but it's almost certainly the handiwork of the YPS.'

'I thought the Indian Mujahideen claimed responsibility for the bombings.'

'They did, sir, but the Indian Mujahideen is merely the action arm of the YPS. The name has been chosen because they want to portray it as a homegrown terror group.'

'They think they can get away with that?'

'Well... ever since the Supreme Court banned the YPS as a terrorist group, they have been trying every trick in the book, including the use of some dubious political patrons, to get the ban lifted. If they manage that, they'll be able to re-establish their over-the-ground network and actively promote their brand of extremist Islam, while simultaneously carrying out terror strikes as the Indian Mujahideen. This model – of a legitimate political movement or welfare organization as the front with an underground terrorist arm operating in its shadows – is being used by several terrorist organizations in many democratic countries.'

'You mean, like the Jamaat-ud-Dawah and the Lashkar-e-Toiba in Pakistan?'

'Exactly, sir. It makes it really hard for security agencies to act.'

'Is it true that the founders of the YPS are influenced by Deobandi Islam – just like the Taliban and several other right-wing terrorist groups?'

'It is,' Rao confirmed.

'How in hell has the YPS suddenly become so organized? They were just a ragtag bunch till recently.'

'Sir, though the YPS started as the student wing of the Jamaat-e-Islami, which itself was inspired by

Iran's Islamic Revolution, the JIH distanced itself from the YPS when it started inciting people to wage war on the Indian state. However, by then the YPS had been identified by the ISI as a valuable tool for use against India. They helped it to link up with the Lashkar-e-Toiba, Jaish-e-Mohammad, Harkat-ul-Jihad al-Islami and other such groups and this enhanced their resources and strike capabilities considerably.'

'I'm glad you've done your homework so thoroughly,' the PM said brusquely, 'but what I want to know is why we've been unable to prevent these bomb attacks.'

'Sir, no country in the world can be on guard all the time, everywhere. A few attacks will always get through, no matter how strong our defences. There is no single battlefield here, no enemy, and no obvious target to protect.'

'Are you trying to tell me, Rao, that there is nothing we can do? Are you saying that we simply have to live with this, accept it as yet another unpleasant reality?'

'No, sir, I'm not saying that, but there is no simple solution.'

'I'm aware of that, Rao,' the PM said wearily. 'Tell us what we can do.'

'Well, sir.' Rao took a deep breath. 'Military operations must always be conducted speedily to ensure the objective is attained in the shortest possible time with the least possible resources. Delhi must acknowledge that Pakistan is a failed state and talking peace with it will just not work.'

'What nonsense!' the external affairs minister exploded.

'I agree with Rao,' Narayan intervened. 'We must understand that in Pakistan the power and pervasiveness of the army and the ISI is built on hostility with India and their success in anti-India operations. Why will they ever give it up?'

'Pakistan is more than just an army and the ISI. What about civil society?'

'Well, as far as that goes, sir, the Taliban is not the cause, it is in some measure the result of the talibanization of Pakistan's society,' Rao explained. 'In 1947 there were less than 250 madrassas in Pakistan. At the end of last year there were 23,000 and they churn out 1.2 to 1.7 million students annually.'

'So what?' the external affairs minister said. 'Madrassas need not impart only fundamentalism. Sometimes they are required to fill the gap in the absence of state schools.'

'Well, in the case of Pakistan, the government's failure to invest in education has been systematically exploited by the Wahhabis, who use Saudi-supplied petro-dollars to control these madrassas. They've been subverting entire generations of children and putting them firmly on the path of the jihad. Look at this.' Rao switched on his laptop and opened a slide. The words scrolled down: *Right from kindergarten, when a child is just five or six years old, he shall be judged by the fervour with which he gives speeches on jihad and shahadat.*

'These instructions have been issued by the Central School of Secondary and Primary Education in Pakistan,' Rao continued. 'This, sir, is the society you wish to engage with diplomatically.'

'So you're saying that diplomacy is not a solution?'

'Yes, sir. First, there's the problem of who we should talk to; the civilian government has no real say in anything and the army has its own axe to grind. To my mind, the only way we can win peace is by taking the battle deep into the Pakistani hinterland.

'To begin with, sir, we need to declare Pakistan a terror state and snap all diplomatic, commercial, sport and cultural links with it. All planes, trains and buses should be stopped and overflight permissions withdrawn. We must also renegotiate treaties like the Indus water treaty and install new waterflow control procedures.'

'Do you have any idea of the effort it took to negotiate these treaties?' the external affairs minister asked irritably.

'I think so, sir. I also know for a fact that most of these treaties favour Pakistan over India.'

'What nonsense, Rao! Are you saying they were fools, the people who negotiated these treaties... or are you accusing them of consorting with the enemy?'

'Neither, sir. We've been so busy trying to prove we are not the neighbourhood bully and are serious about the peace process, we've bent over backwards to give them more than their fair share. They, on the other hand, have always taken this kindness to be our weakness.'

'I'm so glad you're not a diplomat, Rao,' the external affairs minister remarked.

'Me too, sir,' Rao replied evenly. He knew he had crossed the line and focused on hammering out his final points with clarity. 'We must immediately seal the Indo-Nepal and Indo-Bangladesh borders. These open borders help no one but the ISI. India has gone out of its way to woo Nepal and Bangladesh while Pakistan takes advantage of the situation.'

'Go ahead, Rao,' the PM said thoughtfully.

'Sir, Pakistan has to be kept busy with its own problems so it can't inflict so many on us. That's why we must offer troops to the International Security Assistance Force in Afghanistan and help them finish off the Taliban and Al Qaeda. The presence of Indian troops in Afghanistan will prevent attacks like the one on our Kabul embassy and it will force Pakistan to deploy troops on that frontier, thus reducing the pressure on the Indian borders and diluting their focus on Kashmir.'

'Have you gone crazy, Rao?' the defence minister exclaimed. 'How do you think the Indian Muslims will react to our sending forces to Afghanistan?'

'There may be an outcry at first, but they will understand when they start to see some measure of peace return to India.'

'Easy for you to say, Rao, you don't have to stand for elections.'

'No, sir, I don't. But the fact is that until we stop playing vote bank politics and get down to the business of serious governance, we can't get off the road to eventual disintegration.'

'So you think we should just pull the plug on Pakistan...'

'Of course! It's common sense. Wars are not fought half-heartedly or with minimal force; every possible lever must be employed to break the enemy's will and capability to fight. Unless India's political leadership has clarity and determination, we'll always remain a soft state and continue to bleed... the way we've been bleeding for the past three decades.'

There was an immediate outbreak of angry comments and expletives. The PM stood up and took charge. 'Gentlemen, please. We asked him for solutions. We may or may not like them, and I certainly don't find a lot of what he said very palatable, but it's only fair that we hear him out.' He turned to Rao. 'All right, so that's what the offensive part of India's strategy should be. What about the defensive measures you mentioned?'

'The defensive strategy has to be two-pronged, sir. First, we must take measures that make it hard for the enemy to strike. Second, our security forces must be geared to respond to attacks swiftly and our legal system should be able to punish those who are found guilty. Justice must be swift and the punishment harsh.'

The PM nodded. 'And how do you think we should go about making India a hard target so that terrorists are unable to operate here so freely?'

'To begin with, sir, all Indian nationals must be issued with biometric photo identification.'

'Biometric photo identification?' the home minister repeated in surprise. 'Do you have any idea what that will cost us?'

Rao appeared unruffled. 'It will certainly cost a bomb, but in the long run it will cost a lot less than the damage the terrorists inflict on us. In any case, it's a matter of time before such measures become unavoidable.'

'And just how will it prevent terror attacks?' the home minister persisted.

'Not directly, sir, but it will form the bedrock of a system that will make it much harder for terrorists to operate.'

'Explain that, Rao,' the PM said, sitting down again.

'We must ensure that biometric identification is mandatory for all activities, commercial and otherwise. Whether a person wants a college admission or a library membership, whether he wants to rent an apartment or buy a vehicle – any vehicle, even a bicycle – or purchase a telephone or mobile connection, buy or sell property, start a business, apply for a passport, book a room in a hotel or a guesthouse, even use a cybercafé, he has to first produce his national identity card. That way, we can keep tabs on anyone and also track the movement of dangerous goods. It will also enhance our post-incident investigation capability considerably and make it easier to track down the culprits much faster.'

'I still don't see how it can be justified,' the home minister protested again.

'Neither would a lot of other politicians, my friend,' the PM retorted, 'because it would also cut down on any kind of wrongful voting.'

'Oh yes, sir.' There was a hint of a smile on Rao's face. 'You can rest assured that a lot of illegal immigrants are going to get weeded out. We'll see huge changes taking place in many constituencies, especially in areas where so many Bangladeshis have just flooded in and are passing themselves off as Indian nationals...' Rao's voice trailed off.

'You seem to have a special problem with Bangladeshis, Rao?'

'I have a problem with anyone who is in India illegally, sir,' Rao replied calmly, too old a hand to be provoked. 'The only reason I specifically mentioned Bangladeshis is because we all know that these days the ISI is using some of them to carry out acts of terror in India.'

Narayan spoke up then. 'We need to strengthen our intelligence efforts.'

'Isn't that why we set up the National Intelligence Command, Rao?'

'The NIC has shown results even in the short time it has been in existence. We've broken at least four major terror modules in the past few months,' Rao assented, 'not to mention several dozen potential strikes that we managed to blunt before they even got off the ground. But there is a lot more to be done. We need to give more muscle to our intelligence agencies and deploy more resources, both human and technical.'

'I agree with Rao,' Narayan said. 'Isn't it surprising that for a country with a population of almost 1.2 billion we barely have 3,500 people in the IB? For many years now they've been asking for more and better quality people, but the sanctions just don't seem to come.'

'There you are!' Rao shrugged. 'The Godbole Task Force set up after the Kargil intrusion in 2000 had made some very relevant observations regarding the quantity and quality of intelligence personnel. We need to start implementing these reforms instead of debating them endlessly.'

'That's what we're working on right now,' the home minister said curtly. 'Is there anything else you have to suggest?'

'Actually, yes,' Rao continued. 'Our front line against terror is the policeman on the street. We need to modernize our police forces and ensure they are better trained, equipped and motivated than the terrorists they have to combat. Right now we have archaic 303 rifles facing up against AK-74s. We have scarcely functional radio sets trying to match up to satellite phones. That must change. We have even reduced the mandatory educational requirement for constables from class ten to class eight, and there's barely any training – so how can we expect them to stand up to well-trained and highly motivated terrorists?'

'Who else will join, considering the service conditions and the salaries we pay them?'

'Very true, sir, and this is yet another anomaly we need to redress. The police and the defence services are our weapons of first and last resort against the enemy. India has to spend more money and ensure it gets the best possible people for these jobs. Crude as it may sound, only those interested in making a fast buck are keen on the police and those who join the defence services do so because they don't have other options. And a first-class counter-terror operation cannot be fought by a third-class law and order machinery.'

'Go on, Rao,' the PM said. 'What else?'

'Well, sir, we should also ban organizations that are funded by organizations that are suspect. We must identify and shut down cash flow and support to terror groups by cracking down on hawala operators and others who are known to support terrorist activities. If we cut off their cash flow, we'll seriously restrict their ability to function.'

'All this is not going to be easy to put in place, Rao.'

'No, sir, it won't be easy at all. In fact, it will require tremendous political will and be a slow and continuous process, but the sooner we begin, the better. And we can't do this alone. We must mobilize citizen action groups and strengthen resident welfare associations and local market associations, for instance, to ensure that strangers moving into a colony are immediately registered with the local police station. They will also help to make sure that all domestic help and staff hired in their areas are subjected to security scrutiny. We can even use citizen support groups to enhance surveillance of common areas, parks and markets. This will get people more proactively involved in the war on terror.'

'Don't you think it will open a Pandora's box and just add to the confusion?' The home minister sounded unconvinced. 'Some people might get high-handed and take the law in their hands.'

'I am sure there will be some incidents,' Rao conceded, 'at least in the initial stages, but that doesn't mean we shouldn't try it. Can you imagine the pressure on a terrorist if he knows that the local RWA will scrutinize him before he can even lease a room? It will no longer be as simple as conning a gullible landlord with false documents.'

'And everyone will be so much more careful before they give out rooms,' Narayan said.

'And it doesn't end there,' Rao added. 'We have to enhance technical surveillance by deploying more cameras in marketplaces, places of worship, railway stations, airports, sensitive installations and monuments. We must also plan to cover major traffic junctions and bottlenecks as and when the resources become available.

'If we network these cameras and back them up with advanced facial recognition software, we can make life hell not just for terrorists but also for criminals of all sorts. They'll think ten times before they step out anywhere.'

'This would be hugely expensive, don't you think?' the PM asked, almost gently.

'Expensive it will be,' Rao agreed, 'but if we can find the money to build huge parks and life-sized statues of irrelevant politicians, I am sure we can find the money for such a vital project that impacts national security. I think we could easily find the funds if we focused on getting back the money parked in tax havens overseas.

'As for doability, I think, sir, that we underestimate ourselves as a nation. Projects such as these have been structured and organized by people of Indian origin the world over. I am sure that once we find the political will, we'll find the means to make it happen.'

'So you want the government to play Big Brother?'

'I believe most Indians would find it a small price to pay for knowing that their families can walk the streets without the fear of being ripped apart by bombs... and for the consolation of knowing that if and when something like that does happen, the guilty will be speedily brought to book. Don't you think so?'

The discussion windmilled on, slowly but surely growing more focused as the hours fled by. What the final outcome of this meeting would be only time would tell, but at least things had begun to move. And a few things had been said that needed to be said, to the one person who might be able to do something about them.

TEN

The loud voices brought Iqbal awake with a start.

'What's going on?' he whispered to Tanaz, who was already awake.

'I'm not sure. It sounds like security forces.'

'Shit!' Iqbal's heart began to beat faster. 'Let me check.'

'No! Don't go out!'

'Don't worry, Tanaz! I'm not going to. We can listen from there.' He gestured at the window.

Just as suddenly as they had started, the voices broke off. They heard the squeal of tyres as an unseen vehicle roared to life and raced away. They waited for a few moments; when they couldn't hear anything more, they decided to venture out.

The compound was in an uproar. 'What happened?' Iqbal asked a man who was stuffing things into a rucksack as he hurried past.

'The fucking ISI is what happened!' he said over his shoulder without breaking stride. Iqbal hurried after him.

'The ISI? What do they want? I thought this was their compound.'

'It is! They came to tell us that an army patrol is approaching, to encircle the compound. Apparently, some more jihadi hides have to be sacrificed to the goras,' the man snapped. 'The bastards know there are no biggies here, just us street soldiers. They'll take us into custody... just so those gora bastards can be told that the war on terror is going full steam ahead. In return, those white sons of bitches will throw some more dollars at our great, fearless leaders.'

'So what do we do now? Where is everybody going?'

'We get our asses out of here, that's what we do, miyan. As far from here as possible.' The man finished strapping up his rucksack and shrugged it over his shoulder as he gestured to someone across the compound. 'Come on, move it, you morons. They'll be here any moment now.' He turned to Iqbal. 'I suggest you get your butt out of here, unless you want to end up as jailbait.' He walked away, talking in rapid tones to two others who had joined him. He was a dozen yards away when he looked back over his shoulder and yelled at Iqbal, 'And don't trust anyone... not for a moment.' And then he was gone.

Iqbal was stunned. The past few weeks of inactivity had dulled his reflexes and he found himself unwilling to leave the place where he'd spent some of the most peaceful moments of his life. The more practical Tanaz was quicker to respond. He felt her shove a small duffel bag into his hands. 'Come on, Iqbal,' she hissed at him urgently. 'Let's go! That way!'

Iqbal came back to reality with a start. 'Let's head for the town.'

'Yes, but we'll get out that way, then circle around to Faisalabad from the other side. It should be safer.' She started to stride away and Iqbal followed without any hesitation.

They were about two kilometres away when they saw the clouds of dust converging on the compound they had just left. Dozens of vehicles could be seen racing in from every direction.

It was late evening when the weary couple finally found themselves on the outskirts of Faisalabad.

'We need to get to a phone and call in,' Iqbal said.

'How do you plan to do that? We don't have a paisa on us.'

'Let's fix that,' Iqbal said thoughtfully. He steered her towards a dimly lit street and they stood together in the shadows, at the mouth of one of the alleys branching out from it.

The man who rode up the street on a flashy new motorcycle had the clothes and demeanour of a small-town trader. Tanaz emerged from the alley and waved at him till he slowed to a halt at the entrance to the alley. Tanaz stepped up to him, a piece of paper visible in her hand.

'Excuse me, bhaijaan. Can you help me...' The man didn't even notice Iqbal come up to him on silent feet. By the time he felt Iqbal's presence, it was too late; the wooden slat, which Iqbal had picked up in the alley, had slammed down on his head. Tanaz caught the motorcycle by its handlebars as the man fell unconscious. Iqbal dropped his weapon and wheeled the bike into the alley with its occupant still slumped on it. Turning the engine off, he lowered the bike to the ground and quickly went through the man's pockets. With a satisfied grunt, he extracted a wallet, then removed the man's wristwatch and also the gold chain that hung heavy around his neck.

An hour later, with the comfort of a hot meal inside them, Iqbal and Tanaz found themselves outside a PCO. The rickety wooden telephone booth with its half-broken, faded signboard was deserted. A bored old man lolled on a wooden chair propped up against the booth, idly smoking a cigarette. He watched as they came up to him and gestured with the tip of his half-smoked cigarette towards the booth.

'Make it short,' Tanaz whispered as they squeezed into the tiny booth. 'You can take it for granted that calls to India are being monitored.'

'I will,' Iqbal promised as he began to dial the number that he had been told to memorize not so long ago. 'Colonel Anbu will be happy to hear from us.'

And he was right. Once he got over the initial shock of hearing from the man they had all presumed dead, Anbu could barely contain his joy. He checked his emotions with an effort and said, 'I'm so relieved to hear you're well.'

'We both are,' Iqbal said excitedly. 'In fact, it was Tanaz who...'

'Don't say anything else,' Anbu cut him off quickly. 'I want you to call me again in one hour. I'll let you know what to do then.'

'No problem, sir.' And they ended the call.

Tanaz was right. All calls to India were recorded, and someone listened to them to decide if they merited further action.

Iqbal's call came up for review by the duty analyst almost as soon as it ended.

'Did you notice that?' he told his associate as they played it back. 'Almost as though... it was so damn fauji, the way he said it. Where did it come from?'

'PCO 14,' his associate replied. 'That would be... here... this one.' He jabbed at the map on the tag board in front of them.

'Great! That's not so far from the local office. Get someone there. He's going to call again in an hour. Have them bring him in so we can have a word with him.'

Thirty-five minutes later, an unmarked security

car pulled up across the street from PCO 14. The four men inside sat silently, watching the phone booth, waiting for their quarry to turn up.

Once again it was Tanaz's RAW training and field experience that saved them.

'We're not going to make the second call from the same PCO,' she told Iqbal as they exited the phone booth. 'Let's find another one as far from here as possible.'

'Aren't you being a little paranoid, Tanaz?'

'So what? Just because I'm paranoid doesn't mean they're not after us.'

They used the hour to trudge around town. It was a depressing walk. The dirty streets, the dim streetlights, the rows of boarded-up shops and an insidiously pervasive sense of gloom spoke of the shattered state of the economy far more clearly than a newspaper headline could. The few women on the streets were all accompanied by men and were covered in burqas from head to toe. Most of the men sported heavy beards and Taliban headdresses – many more of them than Iqbal remembered from the first time he had travelled from Karachi to the Lashkar training camp at Muzaffarabad.

'Am I imagining it, you think?' he questioned Tanaz about the difference.

'Of course you're not.' Her voice was grim. 'Didn't Pervez tell us the same thing? There have been many instances of men being beaten up for not keeping a beard, or for un-Islamic attire. People are scared, especially with the government increasingly abdicating control to the mullahs.'

They were still talking in low tones when they spotted another PCO. It was just as nondescript and battered as the first one.

This time Anbu answered the phone instantly. He spoke before Iqbal could get a word in edgewise. 'Put her on the line,' he said. 'How long will it take the two of you to get to the place where Rehmat met you the last time?' he asked when Tanaz answered.

'A day at best,' she replied. 'Two if things are… not so good.'

'Fine. Get moving then. Rehmat will be waiting for you, tomorrow and the next two days.'

'We'll be there.'

By the time the call brought the counter-intelligence men to the PCO, Iqbal and Tanaz had been swallowed up by the night.

Rehmat was waiting under the same tree that he had been positioned at when Iqbal, Tanaz and the two Force 22 officers had linked up with him on their return from Murree. Tanaz shivered at the sense of déjà vu. Involuntarily, she reached for Iqbal's hand. Her eyes worked ceaselessly, surveying the landscape with nervous anxiety. Iqbal squeezed her hand reassuringly and whispered, 'Don't worry, things will work out fine this time.'

And they did. Led by Rehmat, they made their

way down the winding trail that took them across the IB, to the jeep waiting at the other end.

Iqbal grinned widely when he saw the familiar figure standing by the jeep. Captain Vikram Tiwathia strode forward and enveloped him in a tight bear hug.

'I never thought I'd see the two of you again! The Old Man was thrilled to bits when you called. Come on, he's waiting for you two. Let's go.'

Two hours later, they were in Amritsar. The waiting chopper swept them into the Force 22 base at Kasauli. Tiwathia took them straight to Anbu's office, where Sami was waiting too. It took a while for the excitement to die down but then Anbu got the whole story from Tanaz and Iqbal, from the time they had parted ways with Vikram and Sami at the RV.

'What did you say his name was?' Anbu asked Tanaz when she told him about the man whose convoy had rescued them.

'I don't know,' she said, 'but the guy who treated Iqbal referred to him as the Ameer ul Momineem.'

'That means the Commander of the Faithful,' Sami translated softly for Anbu's benefit.

'Hmmm. I see. Tell me more about him.' Anbu's attention peaked immediately when he heard the name.

'There isn't much to tell. I only saw him once and except for that brief conversation with the so-called doctor, I didn't hear anything. None of the others was ready to talk about him... either that, or they didn't know much about him. But he was clearly very important, someone really high up in the terror hierarchy. I remember what the doctor said, that the Ameer was going to do more for the cause than the Sheikh had even visualized.'

'He said that?'

'Yes! Also, that it's because of the Ameer that the Islamic crescent would rule the world one day.'

'I see. Any idea which group he was from?'

'No, sir. The compound had people from several groups in addition to the Afghans and other foreign mujahideen. There were people from the Lashkar, Hizbul, Jaish, Harkat and many smaller groups.'

'Hmm.' Anbu stroked his chin thoughtfully. 'Rao was right all along. The vultures have begun to come together. We've been hearing rumours and getting vague reports about someone like this for some time now.'

'And sir!' Tanaz interrupted. 'I remember his face vividly. It's not the kind of face one could forget.'

'Excellent! Then you can help us prepare an Identikit photo of him.'

'That's a computer-generated photograph,' Tiwathia explained. 'You describe whatever you remember and the computer draws it and keeps changing it till it matches the image in your memory. Our intel officers are real wizards at it.'

'I'm sure I can do that.'

'Perfect! As soon as we've finished, Vikram will arrange for it to be done.' Anbu smiled at Tanaz. 'I have a feeling this man is important.'

'There's no doubt about that, sir,' Tanaz agreed. 'Everyone was terrified of him. There was something... something...' she searched for the right word, 'something really powerful and... *evil* about him. It's hard to put into words, sir.'

For a while they sat quietly, sipping tea. Then Iqbal said, 'You've heard our part of the story, sir. Now tell us what's been happening here in the past few months that we've been away.'

For a moment Anbu looked at a loss for words. Then he got up and came around to put his hand on Iqbal's shoulder. 'There is something you need to know,' he said.

Iqbal eyes filled with apprehension.

'When I got your call, I inquired about your father. I thought you would wish to meet him.'

'And?' Iqbal said, his voice barely a whisper.

'He is no more, Iqbal. They say he had a massive stroke about two months ago and died in his sleep.'

For a long moment Iqbal didn't speak. 'And my brother Ashraf?' he asked finally. 'Do you know where he is?'

'They say he left Lucknow just after your father's demise and moved south. We're not sure where, but give me a little time and we'll find him for you.'

'I would be grateful, sir.' Iqbal looked away,

trying to mask the sudden sickening dread coursing through him. 'I just hope he hasn't also... like me...'

'Don't worry, Iqbal, I'm sure he's well and we'll find him soon.'

'Thank you, sir.'

There was silence for a while as Iqbal struggled to rein in his emotions. It was he who finally broke it. 'What else has been happening here, sir? How are things now?'

Before Anbu could reply, Tiwathia spoke up: 'Not so good, man. In fact, it's getting worse with every passing day.'

'Really?' Iqbal was taken aback by Tiwathia's sombre tone.

'Yes.' Tiwathia told them about the serial bombings by the Indian Mujahideen in various Indian cities. 'The number of casualties is horrendous.'

'Damn them!' Iqbal exclaimed angrily, memories of the bomb that had claimed his mother and sister searing through his mind again. 'What are we doing about it?'

'You've been down that road, Iqbal,' Anbu replied softly. 'You know we're doing all we can, but...'

'It's obviously not enough,' Iqbal completed the sentence for him. 'There has to be more that we can do.'

'There always is, and we are trying, but there is only so much the security forces can do.'

'Is there anything I can do to help, sir?'

'There is, actually.' Anbu's voice was pitched even lower now. 'But it could be dangerous... very dangerous.'

Iqbal looked Anbu straight in the eye. 'That's why we came back – so we could do our bit.'

'No, Iqbal, it's not that simple. I want both of you to give this some thought before you decide to say yes.' Iqbal was about to speak when Anbu held up his hand. 'No, hear me out. This could be very dangerous and no one will blame you for not wanting to get involved – especially now that Tanaz is expecting a child.'

'But sir...'

'Iqbal!' Anbu admonished. 'We all know how much you two have already done. In any case, you haven't even heard what I have in mind.'

'So tell us, sir.' Tanaz spoke for the first time. Her expression was calm, yet determined. 'We didn't come back to India because we wanted to sit back and relax. We want to continue the fight. If we don't defend our religion from these lunatics, who will?'

Anbu studied their faces for a moment. Then he told them what he had in mind.

There was a long silence when Anbu finshed. Iqbal caught and held Tanaz's eyes.

Then he turned and faced Anbu again.

'Tell me sir, how much damage will we be able

to do? This is just one terrorist organization among so many others.'

'True, but this terror cell is still relatively new and has yet to find its feet. Also, despite being the new kid on the block, it's proving to be one of the more dangerous ones, as we can see from the huge damage they have already inflicted on several cities. They seem to be getting better organized with each passing week and are being aggressively supported by our friends across the border. If it's not checked soon, it will acquire critical mass and spiral out of control. Taking down the Indian Mujahideen will send out a clear, strong signal to the rest.'

'I see.' Iqbal and Tanaz exchanged glances again. 'In that case, we'll do it.' He spoke quietly, but firmly.

'Are you sure?' Anbu looked at Tanaz. 'You're going to be parents soon...'

'You think Iqbal is ideal for this assignment and we need to act quickly, so where is the ambiguity?'

'That's true, but...'

'Sir, if everyone only worries about themselves, what will happen to our children? What kind of world will they grow up in – if they are allowed to grow up at all?'

'You know what will happen if your cover is blown during the operation?' Anbu persisted. 'They won't show you any mercy.'

'They never do, sir.' Iqbal's tone was final, as was their decision.

'You will have to do this one on your own, Iqbal.' Anbu nodded at Tanaz. 'I wouldn't expose her to any danger.'

'I may be pregnant, sir, but that doesn't prevent me from handling communication and other such tasks. And I won't let Iqbal do it all on his own.' She got up and went to stand beside Iqbal, her hands resting on his shoulders. 'Not today, not ever.'

'That's all very well, Tanaz, but operational decisions are not taken emotionally. There is no point in taking unwarranted risks. I don't think you really appreciate the risks involved in such an operation.'

'That may be so, sir, but I go where he goes.'

'You do realize there will be many times when you're going to be entirely on your own? We'll try to be around as much as we can, but there's no way anyone can guarantee foolproof, 24x7 support in such ops.'

'I understand, sir, and I think we can take care of ourselves and each other.'

Iqbal turned to Tanaz. 'Tanaz, maybe you should –' he began.

'No, Iqbal,' Tanaz cut him off. 'Wherever we go, we go together… especially if there is danger.'

Iqbal turned to Anbu and nodded, unable to mask the love and pride shining in his eyes. 'So be it, sir. We travel together.'

'Fine, if that's what you want,' Anbu said, still reluctant. 'Let me see how we can work this out in detail. Meanwhile, you two go and catch up on some R&R. I'm sure you're both in real need of some rest and recreation!'

'That we are, sir,' Iqbal conceded, 'but before that, there's a favour we have to ask of you.' There was a sheepish expression on his face.

'Of course, what can I do for you?'

'Tanaz and I never got the opportunity to get married, sir, so...'

'Of course!' Anbu jumped up with a laugh. 'It will be a pleasure for us to organize that. And I'll host the dinner afterwards!' He turned to Tiwathia. 'Aren't you going to help organize the first wedding on this base? After all, this is the guy who took a bullet for you.'

'I know, sir,' Tiwathia quipped, 'which is why I'm wondering if it's right to condemn him to a life sentence like this.'

'There's just one more thing, sir,' Iqbal requested when the laughter had subsided, 'we don't want any religious rites.'

'Any particular reason, Iqbal... Tanaz?' He looked at them questioningly.

'Well, sir...' This time it was Tanaz who answered. 'Let's just say that both of us seem to have lost faith in religion. Of course,' she added hastily, 'we both believe in god, but we don't have much to say for organized religion... any religion.'

'Hmm... I see,' Anbu replied. 'Okay, I guess I know where you two are coming from. Let me take care of it accordingly.'

'Thank you very much, sir.' Iqbal smiled his gratitude.

'Not so fast, young man!' Anbu grinned. 'You can thank me after you've experienced some part of married life. Come, MS, we have work to do. Vikram, the party needs to rock, don't forget!'

And it did. For the first time in all the years since the military base had been built, the hills around echoed with music, a welcome change from the gunfire that people there were used to.

Dressed in a red sari gifted to her by Captain Ankita Bhatnagar and with assistance from the lady who ran the tiny beauty parlour in the nearby town, the bride looked radiant. So, for that matter, did the groom, dressed in a sherwani that fitted him a lot better than it did Captain Mohammed Sami, who had given it to him. No doubt he would have looked a darn sight more handsome if he'd been able to keep the silly, perpetual grin off his face.

The wedding ceremony was short and shorn of all but the bare essentials. The party that followed was anything but short; it lasted almost through the night and was certainly not quiet. By the time the exhausted but happy couple managed to get back to their room, the first rays of a yet to be born sun had touched the snowclad mountaintops of the Himalayas with their fingers of gentle light.

'It's lovely, isn't it, and so peaceful,' Tanaz murmured as she stood at the massive glass window overlooking the valley.

Iqbal came up from behind to wrap his arms around her. 'It's magnificent,' he said. 'You have no idea how happy I am today. I feel so... complete.'

They stood there watching the sun come up, setting fire to the silent hills.

Tanaz leaned back into Iqbal with a sigh. 'I feel like I'm finally home.'

'Me too.' Iqbal nuzzled her neck with his lips. 'I don't know what tomorrow will bring, but I'll carry these memories with me as long as I live.'

'Hush!' Tanaz whispered, pulling his arms tighter around her. 'We're alive and we're together. For now, that's all that matters.'

Tiwathia ensured that Tanaz and Iqbal were taken care of like royalty, at least as far as was possible in the almost Spartan setting of the Force 22 base. But their honeymoon and R&R were seriously curtailed by Anbu's order that neither of them should leave the base.

'It's for your own good,' he explained when Iqbal protested. 'If we're thinking of sending you for an infiltration mission, it's better you remain under wraps as much as possible. You never know who you might meet in town and then run into again at an awkward moment.'

'That's true,' Tiwathia seconded his boss, 'some brilliant operatives have been blown by the most random encounters.'

So the duo stayed at the base while Anbu and his intelligence team spent hours collating all the information they could lay their hands on about YPS and the Indian Mujahideen. When they came up against a particularly intractable source or an unusually tangled problem, Anbu called G.K. Rao, the NIA.

'Why don't you want to disclose the identity of the operative, Colonel?' Rao asked. 'Is there anything I need to know?'

'No, Mr Rao.' Anbu was candid. 'I just don't want to take any chances. You know how it is – the more people who know, the more the chances of a mess-up.'

'That's true! But are you sure that's the only reason, or do you suspect a...'

'Nothing of the sort, Mr Rao. You'll be the first to know if my people spot anything amiss.'

'That's fine,' said Rao. 'But you do know the danger of sending in an unidentified asset? He will have no protection from the cops either... should that contingency ever arise.'

'I know, but I think it's a justified risk. We need to neutralize the Indian Mujahideen and destroy their source of funding and support before they become fully entrenched.'

'Okay, as long as you've given thought to it. When do you want to send in your man?'

'I never said it was a man, Mr Rao.'

'Nice, very nice.' Rao laughed, a low rumbling laugh. 'I like your style, Colonel. I am sure your people will pull it off with the same panache with which you've carried out your previous operations.'

'God willing! You agree about the target we've chosen?'

'Absolutely! We need to destroy it before it grows and spreads its tentacles all over the country.'

'I think so too.'

'So, when does he go in?'

'The operative,' Anbu stressed the word, 'goes in when I'm convinced that adequate training has been imparted.'

'Don't take too long, Colonel. You know how much we're bleeding on this one. They need to be finished asap.' With that, the call ended and the training began.

ELEVEN

Tiwathia was pacing the floor of the tiny but hi-tech classroom when Tanaz and Iqbal walked in. Iqbal smiled when he saw Tiwathia.

'So you're going to be the one training us? Great! It's going to be fun then...'

'Fun?' Tiwathia's voice was cold, his face expressionless. 'Don't think, even for a moment, that I'm here as your friend or that training is ever *fun*. In fact, it's because you saved my life once and I consider you a friend that I'm going to make damn sure you train as though both your lives depend on it... which they do.' He paused and took a deep breath. 'Listen, the more you sweat in peace, the less you will bleed in war. And don't ever doubt that you're going to war. It's going to be bloody and the first mistake you make may well be your last one. And this war, remember, has no rules. Bear that in mind when I push you to the very edge of your limits and then a little beyond.'

'Vikram, I...'

'Quiet, Iqbal!' Tiwathia said sharply. 'Don't interrupt me again. As long as we're in training, you'll only speak when you are spoken to. And another thing – in this classroom it's not Vikram, it's sir... always sir.' His voice softened a little. 'There will be days when you hate me, days when you curse yourself for having agreed to this, but that's all right as far as I am concerned. As long as I'm convinced here,' Vikram tapped his heart, 'that I have done my utmost to ensure you two come out of this mission alive. Clear?'

'Yes, sir,' Iqbal replied, automatically standing up a little straighter as his body responded to the Force 22 officer's commanding tone. Tanaz merely nodded, slightly overawed by the interplay.

'Good! I'm glad we have that straight,' Tiwathia said brusquely. 'And yes, there is one other thing we should clear at the outset. I want you to forget everything that was taught to you at those damn jihadi camps. Wipe the slate clean and take in what we have to give you. You won't go wrong. This unit is the best of the best in the whole damn world and we take pride in ensuring that it remains that way. Now you have the ultimate honour of learning from the best. Is that clear?'

This time both trainees nodded, the expression on their faces eager, the expression so typical of young recruits when confronted with their leader.

'Good!' Tiwathia nodded. 'Let's begin.' He

motioned to them to sit down. Just then, as though on cue, the door swung open and three officers in uniform walked in.

Ankita Bhatnagar was a flight lieutenant in the Indian Air Force. She was just over five and a half feet tall, with an athletic build and a decidedly pretty face. She made an incongruous pair with the tall, burly Captain Manoj Khare. On the face of it, the two appeared to have little in common. However, both were capable of doing things with computers that would have given an Intel chip an inferiority complex. If Anbu had not pulled them out of the humdrum of regular army life, they would almost certainly have been seduced by some willing computer corporation.

They were also fitness freaks, adept at a variety of martial arts and unarmed combat, and they craved a life beyond the ordinary. No one could be certain whether it was this obvious compatibility or their common love for computers that had drawn them together, but they were now inseparable and had been humorously nicknamed 'Beauty and the Beast' by their comrades in Force 22.

Anbu had put the pair's special computer and analytical skills to good use by appointing them as the Force 22 intelligence team. Over the years, Bhatnagar and Khare had evolved into dedicated intelligence junkies who had the drive and the capability to locate just about any kind of information and weed through any kind of evidence.

Their stint with Rao when he was setting up the NIC had honed these skills considerably.

The third officer, Lieutenant Commander Ranjit Dhankar of the Indian Navy, was also on attachment with Force 22. Hailing from a small village in Haryana that had for many years lent one son from every household to the Indian Armed Forces, Dhankar looked like the archetypal Bollywood villain – hulking body, hard eyes. He was definitely not the kind of person you would like to pick a fight with, even on your best day. Though an active Navy SEAL, Dhankar was just beginning to feel frustrated with his career when Anbu proposed that he join Force 22. He snapped up the offer immediately since, as far as he was concerned, there was no longer anything special in the Special Forces. If ever there was an officer in Force 22 who had exceptional mastery over every possible weapon and a doctorate in every known method of killing, it was Dhankar. During the November 2005 strike in Pakistan, it had been Dhankar with his tenacity and resourcefulness who had got his badly wounded buddy Deopa back from Karachi after they had executed their target.

The trainees watched the trio of newcomers with interest, but before any of them could speak, Tiwathia gestured to the officers to take their seats and continued, 'In the next few weeks, we'll take you two through the entire gamut of physical training, weapon handling, bomb making, covert communications and basic field craft. In the beginning, of course, the focus will be on physical fitness since that is the bedrock of your training. That and the unarmed combat training will be handled by Lieutenant Commander Ranjit Dhankar.' Tiwathia gestured towards Dhankar who was sitting coiled on the edge of his chair, as though ready to spring to action at the slightest provocation. The almost sadistic smirk that briefly showed itself on Dhankar's already forbidding countenance made the two trainees exchange nervous glances. 'Of course, due courtesy and care will be shown to you,' Tiwathia threw a quick, somewhat uncertain glance at Tanaz here, 'considering your... er... delicate condition. So you will be excused from all physical training, barring some basic weapon handling that you may like to do – only if you wish to, of course.' For the first time a trace of embarrassment creased Tiwathia's face, as the hardened combat veteran crossed into unfamiliar terrain. Across the room, Ankita tried to keep the grin off her face as she watched Tiwathia struggle to keep his expression stern and professional.

'Thank you, sir.' Tanaz caught shades of Ankita's mirth and could not control her smile. 'Things are not so bad, at least not in the early stages.'

'Yes, yes, of course.' Tiwathia raced on hurriedly, eager to get away from the subject. 'Keeping in view your insistence on taking care of comm and intel functions, Flight Lieutenant Ankita Bhatnagar here will bring you up to speed on all aspects related to communication, various intelligence functions and related tradecraft.'

Ankita bestowed a brief, pleasant smile on the trainees.

'Captain Manoj Khare will cover basic fieldcraft. And Dhankar and I will teach you weapon handling, and bomb making and handling.' He paused, slightly out of breath after the long speech. 'Any doubts?'

The trainees replied with silent shakes of the head.

'Good! Then we start the actual stuff at 0400 tomorrow.'

'0400?' Iqbal gave him an incredulous look. 'That's like four in the morning! Damn! Even the jihadis were not that bad – sir.'

'And they are not half as good either, Iqbal,' Vikram shot back. 'Yes, four in the morning, and I expect you to be on time. Tanaz is exempt from that part of the training, so she can join us after breakfast, at 0800.'

'Sir, yes sir!' Tanaz couldn't keep the grin off her face as she saw Iqbal's crestfallen expression.

'And now I'll hand you over for the rest of the day to Captain Manoj Khare.' With that, Tiwathia and the others left, leaving Khare alone with the trainees.

'Tell me,' Khare said as he came up to the front of the classroom. With his quicksilver smile and subtle sense of humour, Khare was an excellent instructor and a fluent speaker. 'What do you think is the most important survival skill for an undercover operative?'

'Presence of mind?' Tanaz offered tentatively.

'Yes, presence of mind is imperative,' agreed Khare, 'but even more important, or should I say, a forerunner to that, is observation. The trained operative is able to observe keenly, be fully aware of everything around him at all times and he – or she,' he added hastily, 'has to be able to do this without appearing to do so.' He saw the puzzled look on the faces of his trainees. 'Come, let me explain.'

The duo trailed behind Khare as he exited the classroom and went to another room across the corridor. It was done up like the living-cum-dining room of a regular middle-class home. Halting at the far end, he waited till they were in the middle of the room and then asked, 'What is around you here?'

Iqbal and Tanaz surveyed the room, mentally inventorying it. After a few minutes, Iqbal began to name the items. Khare allowed him to finish.

'That's good, Iqbal, but you missed the apples in the fruit bowl on the dining table and the knife kept beside it. You missed those two chairs there and the set-top box below the television. You also missed…' He listed nine other things that Iqbal had missed.

'But how are they relevant?'

'They are! Everything is relevant. That's the point I'm trying to make,' Khare stressed. 'No matter where you are and what you are doing, you need to be fully aware of everything around you. That's the most basic thing.' He saw the bewildered expression on their faces and added a little more gently, 'Trust me guys, it's not that hard. You just have to train your mind to stop merely seeing things and actually start noticing them. Once you start doing that, it'll soon become a habit and that's what we want to achieve.' He paused. 'Always remember rule one – an undercover operative perpetually functions in a potentially hostile environment and has to be on guard at all times.'

Khare waited till both of them had assimilated this before continuing, 'That brings me to rule two – everything around you is a weapon, which is also why you need to be totally aware of everything.' While Khare was speaking, his hands casually reached out for a matchbox that lay on the table next to him. As they watched, he crushed the matchbox with his fingers until one side protruded sharply. 'This,' he held it between his fingers, 'is adequate to slice open the eye of the enemy and give you the moment's respite you need in order to fight back if you are cornered.'

His hand slashed out in a vicious arc, coming dangerously close to Iqbal's face and making him wince and jump back.

'The golden rule – to be aware is to be alive.'

Satisfied that he had driven home the desired lesson, Khare dropped the crushed matchbox back on the table and said, 'We will now start practising the art of observation. Today we'll go through a series of rooms and you'll start taking note of your surroundings.' He led them out of the room. 'And don't worry, it may seem hard in the beginning, but as the days go by, your mind will start doing it automatically.'

Khare was a calm and confident teacher. Over the next two hours he walked them through several rooms, talking to them, training their minds to start thinking along the desired path. By the end of the session, he was satisfied.

'They are quick learners,' he told Anbu after he had handed them over to Ankita. 'I'm confident that in a couple of weeks they're going to be as good as any of us or, at least, the best they can be at the end of such a limited training period.'

Ankita Bhatnagar was waiting for them in a room that resembled one of those tiny shops that specialize in the repair of electronic appliances.

'I gather from Captain Tiwathia that both of you have already undergone basic training in radio telephony,' she began without a preamble the moment they were seated. 'Is that right?'

'I was trained by RAW,' Tanaz replied. 'I can handle most radio sets that are commonly used by the military.'

'Me too,' Iqbal added, 'though it has been quite some time and I could do with a refresher.'

'Don't worry, guys, you're going to get a lot more than a refresher,' Ankita assured them. 'By the time I'm done, both of you will be fluent in most known methods of communication and some pretty esoteric ones too. However, our primary aim is to ensure that you are able to use covert communication methods efficiently since they are the only ones we can rely on during a mission.'

'Covert communication?' Iqbal was nonplussed.

'Stuff like dead letterboxes, coded messages, embedded messages,' Ankita explained. 'So that even if you are cut off from all normal modes of communication, or are under watch and unable to use them, you can still get a message out as and when you need to.'

'Right.' Both trainees nodded, quite impressed.

'Good! Let's begin with basic radio telephony.' She handed a radio set each to them and sat down behind a third. 'Your call sign will be...'

'Babur,' Iqbal said immediately. 'That was the code name they gave me when I went with Sami and Vikram to get Salim.'

'Fine! Babur it is. And you,' Ankita turned to Tanaz, 'your call sign will be...'

'Anarkali,' Tanaz said with a smile. Seeing Ankita's quizzically raised eyebrow she explained, 'When these guys came over to hunt down Salim, they had been codenamed Humayun, Akbar and Babur, so I figured I would be Anarkali. Fits, don't you think?'

'It sure does.' They all laughed. 'Just make sure the three horrors don't bury you alive too.' They laughed again.

The training began, and continued right through to lunch.

'You report back here at 1530,' Ankita said as she dismissed them. 'Vikram will be taking you out to the firing range.'

Iqbal threw a quick look at his watch. It was already 1455 hours. Right! So they could look forward to a nice leisurely lunch.

Tanaz noticed his expression. 'We live in interesting times,' she muttered as they headed out for lunch.

'Yeah, sure,' Iqbal murmured back. 'And if this is just the beginning, I can't wait to see what happens next.'

Ankita saw them off before she went back to Anbu's office. 'We won't have any problem with either of them,' she reported. 'Tanaz is already pretty clued in and Iqbal seems to have a knack for it.'

'So far so good!' Anbu replied. 'Let's see how they fare with the others.'

It was on the firing range that Tanaz really blossomed. Iqbal, who was no mean shot himself, was shocked out of his complacency by the fluency with which Tanaz handled weapons. With every possible weapon, from any possible range, she could effortlessly outshoot him.

'I want you guys to pay special attention to these.' Tiwathia handed them a brace of jet-black .22 pistols each, once they'd finished with the rifles.

'Aren't they tiny?' Iqbal asked, pulling one out of the holster.

'They may appear to be, but don't have any doubts about the damage they can do. In fact, for close-in protection they are matchless, and you can tuck one away just about anywhere.'

'Any special reason why you want us to focus on these?' Tanaz asked, hefting the pair that had been given to her.

'These are what you'll be carrying on the mission,' Tiwathia said, 'so I suggest you zero them in and set your hands to them.'

'Carry them as in...?'

'They'll remain with you as long as this operation lasts. I'll show you how to tuck them away in unobtrusive places all over the house so that they're easily accessible in case of an emergency.'

That got their undivided attention and they spent the next few hours getting acclimatized to their .22s. By the end of the third day, they were wielding them fluently, with practised ease.

'Tanaz is a natural,' Vikram said admiringly to Anbu later that evening. 'And the best part is that she is ambidextrous. You give her a weapon and she can shoot the hell out of the target from just about any position, and that too with either hand. With those .22s she can literally shoot your eye out from across the room.' He grinned. 'In fact, I think she has quite fallen in love with them. Iqbal was cribbing that she insists on having them in or under the bed at night.'

'Good! I'm happy to hear they're shaping up well.' Anbu smiled at him, pleased. 'They need to be better than good if they have to come out of this alive.'

'Don't worry, sir, I'm sure they'll be fine.'

That wasn't exactly how Iqbal felt as he pounded through the early morning chill behind Dhankar the next day.

Why the hell am I calling it early morning? It's late night, that's what it is! Iqbal mentally cursed Dhankar as he staggered up the hill, trying to keep the rapidly receding figure in sight, as they went through what Dhankar had referred to as a light five-mile warm up. *Fucking sadist!*

The fucking sadist was waiting for Iqbal when he finally staggered back into the main playground of the base, possibly the only flat piece of ground in the area that nestled at the centre of the Force 22 base. There was a grim look on his face as he watched Iqbal stumble up to him. Iqbal was about to collapse on the fog-laden grass when Dhankar called out, 'The colonel told me about your injuries. We'll need to pay special attention to those muscles which have suffered damage. Let's begin with some light strengthening exercises.'

There was nothing light about the exercises Dhankar put Iqbal through for the next half hour and the only thing they strengthened was Iqbal's dislike of Dhankar and his training methods. As the minutes slowly and torturously ticked by, Iqbal became more and more convinced that Dhankar had taken an instant dislike to him or that he really was a sadist.

Iqbal would have been quite surprised to hear Dhankar's report to Anbu later that day. 'He is in very decent shape considering he has just recovered from a serious injury. Let me tell you, sir,' Dhankar gave another of his sinister grins, 'I was pretty hard on the kid this morning, but not once did he crib or moan about it.'

'Good!' Anbu was relieved. 'I was worried about his injuries impacting his performance.'

'You can see him favouring the injured side, but I think the guy is basically an outdoor type. He has the right physical frame and the mental conditioning of an athlete.'

Anbu's confidence in his chosen operatives grew with every passing week, as did his affection for the couple who were so willingly and cheerfully putting their lives on the line for the country one loved and the other had adopted. However, it was only after the seventh week of training that he knew for sure that he had chosen wisely and well.

Having laid down the bedrock of physical

conditioning, basic field craft and weapon training, the time had come to start putting the final touches.

'Today,' began Tiwathia as the trainees reported to him that morning, 'we are going to understand everything there is to know about bombs – how they are made, how they function and how they can be defused.'

'I thought we were to pose as fresh terror recruits,' Iqbal said, 'so why get into it at all? No one will expect us to know all that.'

'Yes, you will be new recruits, but you have to know all there is to know about bombs. How else will you sabotage the bombs and make them malfunction?' Tiwathia pointed out.

'But the colonel said you guys would be around to help when the need arises,' Iqbal replied, looking puzzled.

'Sure we will, Iqbal. We'll have a team standing by in your area at all times, but you must understand that you cannot and must not bank on us... at least, not until we reach the end game. Once you turn to us, it's almost certain that your cover will be blown and we'll have to look at closing down the op.' Iqbal was about to respond when Tiwathia raised his hand. 'Please remember that the undercover operative must always be completely self-reliant in every respect. Every contact you make with us once you go undercover is fraught with risk and will simply increase the chances of your cover being blown.'

'So, basically, we are going to be totally on our own.'

'That's the only way to look at it. The simpler you keep this operation, the better your chances of succeeding and coming out of it alive. Just keep in mind the simple fact that if you function with the basic premise that they are onto you and watching you at all times, you will never take them for granted and will always be on guard. That way, you are least likely to make mistakes. Get it?'

Both trainees nodded, the implications of what Tiwathia had said slowly sinking in. Tiwathia noted the change in their mood and quickly added, 'Just keep the basics in mind and function accordingly. Remember that the best operations are those where we rely on ourselves. Hi-tech gadgets and technology are great force multipliers, but that's about all they are. They're also surefire giveaways if they are ever discovered on you. That's why your best bet is to keep things simple and just stay with the basics. Okay?'

Both trainees nodded again, this time a little more cheerfully.

'The best part is that you won't attract any suspicion since both of you will apparently know nothing about bomb making. You see,' Tiwathia explained, 'most terrorist modules have their own dedicated bomb makers. They use new recruits only to plant bombs, not to make them.'

There was a sudden shocked silence as Iqbal

realized for the first time that he would be called upon to plant bombs during the mission.

'Then teach me well, sir,' he said grimly, 'so I can make sure that no bomb planted by me ever goes off.'

'No, Iqbal, that's not the way to go about this mission. If you do that every time, how long do you think you'll last? They will home in on you and take you apart till they get the truth out of you.'

'I will not plant bombs that kill innocent people,' Iqbal replied through clenched teeth.

'Iqbal!' Tiwathia spoke sharply. 'I want you to stop this nonsense and focus on what we're trying to teach you here. There will be enough time later to deliberate on what you want to do and what you have to do.'

Iqbal was quiet after that, but Tiwathia knew he was not paying attention. His eyes mirrored the turmoil within him.

The turmoil festered through the day. It finally found expression a couple of days later when Anbu chanced upon Tanaz and Iqbal strolling through the playground. They were walking silently; the tension that stalked them was palpable.

'Something wrong, you two?' Anbu asked as he began to walk alongside.

'No, sir!' Iqbal's curt tone belied his feelings. Anbu ignored the blunt, almost rude reply.

'You can talk to me, Iqbal,' he said gently. 'In fact, you must talk to me about anything that bothers you. I won't let you out on this mission if there is the slightest doubt or confusion in your mind.' He stopped walking and looked Iqbal in the eye. 'And once you do get going, please remember that Force 22 is your only point of contact, your only lifeline. Nobody will know you are a government-sanctioned infiltrator. So there has to be complete transparency and trust between us.'

Anbu, who had already been given the heads up by Vikram, did not push further. He just kept pace with them as they walked to the end of the playground and then turned back. Nearly two complete circuits went by in stony silence before Iqbal finally began to speak.

'I will not plant any bombs anywhere, sir, not for anything in the world. I will not be responsible for the death of innocent people –'

'Iqbal,' Anbu cut in softly, 'no one can tell you what you should or should not do. In fact, on a mission like this, no one can even tell you which way things will flow and what you will be required to do at any stage. All I can say is,' Anbu stopped and looked squarely at Iqbal, 'you must remember that what you are going to do will save countless lives. You can't do anything that will jeopardize your cover, not until you have uncovered all possible details of the group that you've managed to infiltrate. In fact,' he added firmly, 'you will do whatever it takes to ensure your cover is not blown until the mission is over.'

'But sir...'

'Think it over, Iqbal.' Anbu's tone had the hard finality of a command, it brooked no further discussion. 'It's not too late, even now. If you have any doubts about what you can or cannot do, I suggest you pull out of the mission. Think about it and let me know tomorrow.' He walked away from them into the fog that had begun to blanket the base. *I am glad they feel so strongly about it*, he thought. *Or else, what difference would there be between the terrorists and the rest?*

When Tanaz and Iqbal walked into Anbu's office the next morning, their expressions were strained but the cloud of confusion was missing.

'We are ready, sir.' Iqbal's voice was clear and his gaze firm.

'Sure?' Anbu's tone was soft as always.

'Positive, sir!' Tanaz replied. 'We understand what has to be done and why.'

'Fair enough.'

'I do have a request, sir.'

'Yes, Iqbal?'

'We feel we are ready now.' Iqbal looked at Tanaz. 'As ready as we will ever be. We would like to begin the mission as soon as possible.'

'Okay!' Anbu gave this a moment's thought. 'Let me speak to Tiwathia and the others and get back to you.'

The response he received from the others was unanimous.

'Just give me a few days to get their identity documents and related plastics and brief them about their legends,' Ankita told him. 'After that, they'll be ready to start.'

A week later, Tanaz and Iqbal were back in Anbu's office for their final briefing.

'Remember now, both of you,' were Anbu's final words, 'once you leave this place you are completely on your own. Protect your cover at all costs. The enemy is smart, assume that he is onto you – that way you will make few mistakes. Especially you, Tanaz, please stay as far from the forefront as possible.' He paused briefly before he moved on to the final caution. 'In case you have the slightest doubt that your cover is blown, I want you to activate the emergency response and we'll initiate the extraction procedure immediately. Don't get into any unnecessary heroics... we need you back alive just as much as we need to crack this case.'

'Don't worry, sir.' Iqbal stood tall and determined. 'We will be back and we will succeed.'

'Inshallah!'

'Ameen!' Sami murmured.

Then they were gone, escorted out by Tiwathia who was to drop them off near the Chandigarh airport.

Anbu watched them leave, his heart heavy. When

they had turned the corner and vanished from view, he turned to Sami. 'I hope it goes well.'

'It will, sir,' Sami replied reassuringly. 'For the good guys, it always works out in the end. In any case, these two are really good.'

'It's not their capability that troubles me, MS. In such ops, one can never tell what the blowback will be.'

'Blowback?'

'I mean, one never knows what the unintended consequences of any intelligence operation might be. You can never tell which way things will blow... or who they'll blow away.'

TWELVE

Pune's Asian Institute of Management, or AIM, as it was popularly known, was one of several private institutes that had emerged after the economic liberalization and the expansion of education as an industry in India. Its impressive name notwithstanding, the institute was located in a small, though well-planned building on the old Pune–Mumbai highway, just a short hop from the Khadki railway station.

In the eight years since it had been in existence, AIM had acquired a healthy reputation for being the school of choice for professionals in their late twenties and early thirties who had decided to take a break from work and obtain the much sought after MBA degree. So it was not uncommon to see AIM students strolling around the campus with young spouses and, in some cases, toddlers in tow. The AIM management, on its part, had earmarked a large part of its residential accommodation for students who were accompanied by their families. Even this wasn't adequate, however, so several of these young couples, especially those with children and those desirous of something more than the tiny two-room set which AIM offered, rented apartments in a handful of newly constructed, gated communities that had recently sprouted in the vicinity.

Outside one of these, the Golden Heritage residential complex located almost directly opposite the Khadki railway station entrance, a young woman emerged from a white Toyota Innova with 'CoolCabs' emblazoned on its sides. She was dressed in a smart, conservatively designed salwar kameez. Her head and part of her face were covered with a chunni, which did nothing to hide or diminish her glowing complexion, her large black eyes and her finely chiselled features. A few wayward strands of lustrous black hair swung tantalizingly out from under the chunni. She stood for a moment, taking in her surroundings.

The tall, broad-shouldered young man who followed her out of the vehicle complemented her appearance in that special made-for-each-other way one doesn't often encounter. His body was lean and taut, and his gait was that of an athlete at his peak. His stone-washed jeans and deep-blue Adidas T-shirt gave him the appearance of a typical mid-level executive in one of the many MNCs that were burgeoning in India.

Crossing under a big yellow Blue Dart Couriers billboard that spanned the front of the low-slung, single-storey building to the left of the colony gates, the two of them halted at the guard box. A grumpy looking chowkidar who appeared to be well into his sixties was hunched inside, assiduously unclogging his ears with a matchstick.

'Apartment number C-302, please.'

'Over there.' The chowkidar pointed past the huge red cement gates, to the top floor of a three-storey building at the centre of the housing complex. 'Are you the new people moving in?'

'Yes,' the man replied shortly.

'Haan! I know. Shinde sahib told me to expect you. Here,' the chowkidar extended a hardbound register towards him, 'enter your details. Then I'll show you around and take you to the house.'

In neat, precise handwriting the man carefully wrote their names in the register.

Iqbal and Tanaz Khan.

Apartment C-302 was a two-bedroom apartment with a drawing-cum-dining room. It was newly constructed, like the other buildings in the complex, and the pleasant, tangy aroma of fresh paint lingered. The rooms were not very big but the marble-chip floors contrasted well with the lemon-coloured walls and along with the large windows, lent a bright, cheerful air to the house.

The chowkidar was still showing them around when a truck belonging to Prakash Packers & Movers pulled up outside the complex. There was a flurry of activity as the luggage began to be brought in. The madness lasted two days. By the end of the second day, the house had acquired some shape and was beginning to look more like a home.

Exhausted by the effort, but glowing with the joy of setting up home with the man she loved, Tanaz collapsed on the sofa and called out to Iqbal, who was busy trying to load up the fridge. Half-empty shopping bags from the neighbourhood Reliance Fresh store were strewn all around him.

'I still can't believe we have our own home now.' Tanaz got up and slowly pirouetted, surveying the room lovingly. 'And such a pretty one at that.'

'I know.' He stopped unpacking and went across to her. 'It does seem unreal, doesn't it?'

Tanaz's reply was lost as Iqbal's lips closed on hers. They kissed, long and deep. Before it could go any further, the doorbell rang. The loud, jarring buzz shocked them apart. They exchanged a glance.

'Who could it be at this time of the night?'

'Let me check,' Iqbal whispered as he moved on soft feet to the door and looked through the peephole. Tanaz instinctively inched closer to the .22 pistol she had taped to the underside of the square four-seater dining table just a while ago.

The woman who stood outside, peering expectantly at the door, was in her early thirties. She was holding something in her hands that looked like a tiffin-carrier.

Iqbal looked back at Tanaz with a shrug and whispered, 'Some woman... looks like one of the neighbours.' Then he threw back the bolts and opened the door.

'Hello.' The woman had a soft, shy voice. She pulled the chunni closer around her face when she saw Iqbal in the doorway. 'I'm Zubaida, your neighbour. Is your wife home?'

'Tanaz,' Iqbal called out. 'Why don't you come in, please?' He gestured to Zubaida, stepping away from the door as Tanaz came forward to greet her.

Tanaz's head was pounding. The young RAW agent had never imagined she would have to play the coy housewife with the neighbours and was totally unsure of how to begin and what to do. She decided to fall back on the various family soap operas that she had surfed on television during their stay at Kasauli, while Iqbal was busy with the training that she had been exempt from.

'Hello Zubaida, I am Tanaz. And this is my husband, Iqbal.' They exchanged courteous salaams. 'Come on in. I'm sorry, we are still in a bit of a mess, so...'

'No, no, I understand what it must be like.' Zubaida smiled back at her. 'That's why I brought some dinner for you... I know your kitchen can't be up and running yet.' She held out the tiffin-carrier. 'I only got back today from my parents' home and learned that you had moved in.'

'Oh, that's so kind of you.' Tanaz took the proffered food. 'But you really shouldn't have bothered.'

'Nonsense! That's what neighbours are for. Please don't hesitate to let me know if you need anything else. I am just across there.' Zubaida pointed at the apartment door at the far end of the corridor. 'In fact, we are the only two occupants in this block so far.'

There was a slight, somewhat awkward pause. 'Now I'll leave you two alone. I'm sure you have tons to do,' Zubaida said. Then she was off with a wave and a smile.

'Phew!' Tanaz closed the door and leaned back against it with a smile. 'I've never done that before.'

'Get used to it… it's what normal life is all about.' Iqbal took the tiffin from her and putting it down, took her in his arms again. They resumed where they had left off when Zubaida had rung the bell, the unpacking forgotten.

The following Monday saw the start of the new diploma course in business management at AIM. The course had fifty-nine students; thirty-eight male and twenty-one female. One of the thirty-eight males was the young man named Iqbal Khan, originally from Aligarh who, according to his resume, had worked briefly with a couple of small BPOs in Lucknow and Delhi, before he decided to upgrade his skills and enhance his career prospects. Had anyone decided to investigate his credentials, they would have run into a dead-end since the first

BPO had been swallowed up by an MNC and the second had shut shop not long ago.

'The best legends are those that stick as close to reality as possible,' Ankita had said in her briefing to them. 'That way, you are not forced to learn any extraneous data and are less likely to make mistakes. You've lived in Lucknow and Delhi, so you must be familiar with those little details that you would be expected to know. And in case someone decides to go checking on you, they won't find anything out of sync.' There had been a tiny hesitation before she resumed, 'Even the deaths of your mother and sister will bear out.'

Iqbal winced when she said that.

'I don't want to capitalize on your loss, Iqbal, but even the manner of their deaths will strengthen your cover. The fact that they were martyred...'

'They were not martyred!' Iqbal almost shouted. 'They were murdered by those bastards...'

Ankita had patiently explained to him that once he left the base at Kasauli, he must live his cover down to the smallest detail, at every moment, in every possible way. That, and only that, would get Iqbal past their suspicions and deliver him into their midst.

Iqbal understood her logic. He didn't like it, but he accepted it.

'Walk away from all the liberal thoughts that you've grown up with,' Ankita had said, 'and internalize the fact that you are, in every which way, a moral and religious hardliner. Adopt the most narrow-minded, Taliban mindset and learn to live it. It will act like a beacon and draw them to you.'

'How can I pretend to be something I'm not?'

'That's what I'm trying to tell you, Iqbal. You don't have to pretend to be anything that you are not. You have to become it... in here...' Ankita had tapped her forehead.

'That sounds impossible.'

'Impossible? No. It will certainly be hard in the beginning, but not impossible. Start with the things around you.'

'For example?'

'For example, the way you treat Tanaz.'

'What's wrong with the way I treat Tanaz?'

'Nothing, Iqbal. That's the point. Don't you get it? Haven't you seen and heard the way these hardliners treat women?'

Iqbal remembered the disdain and contempt with which the doctor and the others at the camp in Pakistan had treated Tanaz, and he bristled at the very thought.

'But that's not me! How can I force myself to...'

'You see the point I am trying to make, Iqbal? That is not you... exactly! You have to think like one to become one. Get it?'

Iqbal had nodded. Yes, he got it, but he didn't like it.

'I understand the dilemma, Iqbal,' Ankita had said

sympathetically, 'but you must realize that your act has to be word perfect. Your lives depend on it. And the only way it can happen is if you stop playing the role and start living it.'

Iqbal remained silent.

'Why do you think it's so hard to find someone to successfully execute an infiltration?' Ankita said softly. 'The person who is ready to go undercover for a prolonged period of time must be exceptionally strong in the head. He has to retain his essence and his values even as he becomes someone else and starts living the life of a totally different person. Which is even tougher than it appears because the persona he has to adopt is invariably that of an enemy, of a person with a radically different mindset.'

This disturbing medley of thoughts reverberated through Iqbal's mind as he surveyed the classroom. Somewhere in this lot was the person who would lead him to his goal...

For the first few days Iqbal, like everyone else attending the course, was immersed in the process of settling down, getting to know people and sorting out the day to day administrative hassles that are part of the territory when one moves to a new city. It was only by the end of the week that life began to take on the normalcy of a fixed routine. And it was only then that Iqbal began to take stock of the other students at the institute.

He began to assess each one of them. The intelligence inputs had been unequivocal, though not precise. Pune had become one of the major hubs from which YPS recruited gullible youngsters. Everything seemed to point to this and the profile of the students who attended AIM's courses was almost perfectly in line with what the terror groups were looking for. That was why Anbu had chosen this particular institute.

Which one will it be? Iqbal asked himself often as he discreetly studied the others. How can I attract their attention without appearing to do so? How and when will someone approach me – if they do. Until then, I just have to live the lie...

They were coming out of the institute after classes. Tanaz was waiting near the gate for Iqbal so they could go straight to the doctor's for her monthly checkup. She was already in the fifth month of her pregnancy, and luckily things were going well. She looked beautiful now, in a pale pink salwar kameez, her head partly uncovered.

'Wow!' one of the men walking past Iqbal whispered to his companion. 'Check out that chick near the gate.'

'What a knockout!' His companion gave a low whistle. 'Wonder who she is waiting for.'

'Lucky bugger, whoever he is. Man, that's what they call visual Viagra.' They both sniggered.

Iqbal felt a violent surge of anger. 'Shut your

dirty mouths, you morons.' Balling his fists, he hissed at them with such ferocity that they both backed off immediately. The other students walking past looked towards them, surprised by the rage in Iqbal's voice. Breaking free from the crowd of students, Iqbal walked out to Tanaz.

'What is wrong with you, you stupid woman? Where is your shame? Cover your damn face!' His tone was low but bursting with anger and it was loud enough to be heard by the other students in the vicinity. Several of them, especially the female students, stared at him in shock before they hastily looked away, unwilling to embarrass the woman who had just been so rudely admonished in public. The two men who had made the lewd comments made themselves scarce.

'I am sorry.' Tanaz's face went beetroot red as she quickly used the chunni to cover her head and face. She knew Iqbal was only living his role, but that did nothing to reduce the angry pain of humiliation. She could feel the pitying glances thrown her way by the other students as they passed by.

'You should be! Come!' Iqbal kept walking, allowing Tanaz to fall in behind him. They got into the autorickshaw that Tanaz had come in and drove off. 'I'm so sorry, jaan,' Iqbal whispered to Tanaz, holding her hand tight as they drove away. Her fingers returned the pressure; she knew how much the whole scene must have hurt Iqbal.

Two young men on the fringes of the crowd exchanged glances when they heard Iqbal's heated outburst. They didn't say anything to each other then, but over the next few days they kept a sharp eye on Iqbal, observing him carefully.

Their attempts to befriend him began with a casual sharing of the cafeteria table, and a few days later, a request for some class notes they had missed out on. The first direct approach only happened a fortnight later, when Iqbal sat down for lunch in the campus cafeteria. Having got there first, he was sitting alone at a corner table near the window overlooking the open fields.

'Mind if we join you?' The young men came up, their food trays in hand.

'Sure, go ahead.'

'Hi! I am Abid,' said the shorter of the two. He gestured at his companion. 'And this is Imtiaz.'

Iqbal responded to the introduction with a polite smile.

'You're not from Pune, are you?' Abid asked as they sat down.

'No. Aligarh, originally, though I grew up in Lucknow.'

'Really? We're not that far from each other then.' Abid smiled at him. 'I am from Azampur. In fact, we're both from Azampur.' He nodded at Imtiaz.

'That's good. I've never been there, but I've heard a lot about it.'

'You have? Good things, I hope?' Imtiaz chipped in with a broad, somewhat flaky smile.

'Of course!' Iqbal smiled back. 'My father was a staunch follower of the Deo –' He broke off abruptly.

'You were saying.'

'My father had many fond memories of the place.'

'Had?'

'Both my parents have passed away.'

'Oh! Sorry to hear that.'

Iqbal merely shrugged in response.

The two men exchanged glances. Abid couldn't help the tiny smile that crossed his lips. Imtiaz frowned at him. From the corner of his eye, Iqbal watched the expression on their faces.

'So, Iqbal,' Imtiaz asked after a while, 'which mosque do you go to for your prayers?'

'I have yet to find one,' Iqbal replied hesitantly, with the slightly embarrassed air of someone who doesn't go at all, but is ashamed to admit it. From his training, Iqbal knew that most terror groups preferred to recruit the religious newbie because his views would be unformed, and he would lack a vocabulary to respond to religious debates. Also, there was no danger of such a person having been brought to the anxious attention of the local police for any overtly zealous religious activities.

'That's bad.' Imtiaz clucked reprovingly. 'Why

don't you come with us? We go to the mosque in the market just behind Khadki station.'

'That would be great. Where do you stay?'

'We're at the AIM hostel. You?'

'I'm just down the road... at the residential complex opposite the railway station.'

'Perfect! That's an easy stroll from here and it's on our way to the mosque in any case. So we can go together from now on.' Once again, the two of them exchanged a brief glance and Iqbal felt a leap of anticipation. *This has to be it!*

On their third trip to the mosque, Abid introduced Iqbal to a man they happened to run into as they emerged after evening prayers. It appeared to be a chance encounter, but Iqbal's instincts told him otherwise.

'Trust your instincts, Iqbal. They seldom let you down,' Tiwathia had often reminded him. Iqbal decided to do so now.

'Iqbal, meet Asif, a very good friend of ours,' said Imtiaz.

There was something about the man called Asif that made Iqbal certain. Perhaps it was the assessing look he gave Iqbal. Perhaps it was the acute interest with which he eyed him. Either way, Iqbal instinctively knew that this was the enemy. Apprehension and excitement pulsed through him as he reached out and took Asif's proffered hand.

It was at that precise moment that he was sure… *contact had been made.*

Blinded as he was by his so far successful run and still unaware of how devastatingly fast failure could strike, Asif eyed his latest find with quiet anticipation.

THIRTEEN

Asif only sent in the first probe after Iqbal and he had met over a dozen times. That day, classes had finished early and Asif, Imtiaz and Iqbal were sitting together in an empty coffee shop across the road from the German Bakery in Koregaon Park.

'Isn't it amazing how easily we Muslims bear the brunt of every single problem?' Asif remarked to no one in particular as he tossed down the newspaper in his hand.

'Why? What's happened?' Imtiaz looked at him curiously.

'Some bloody fool calling the Palestinians terrorists just because they are fighting for a homeland.'

Break the ice by talking about Palestine, that's what Asif had been told by Mujib. He was quoting from the jihadi recruitment manual. 'Don't scare away a potential recruit by talking about the concerns of Muslims right at the beginning; doing that will make it obvious you're trying to recruit him. And don't get into arguments about religion or even criticize him. As the conversation progresses, you can talk about the mujahideen and the jihad, but always in a general, casual way. Avoid mentioning any particular group since your potential recruit may be negatively affected by the calumny spread by the media about that particular group.'

While Asif was talking, Iqbal leaned forward and rapidly scanned the article Asif had been reading. 'Obviously, Asif!' he said when he had finished. 'A suicide bomber killed twelve people in a shopping mall; almost all of them were kids or women buying groceries. What else should they call the guy?'

Don't make it too easy for them. Let them work at recruiting you; don't just roll over and fall into their laps. The harder they work at recruiting you, the more they will tend to trust you when you finally agree to join them.

'So you think it's fine, all that the Palestinians are going through because of these Jews?' Asif countered.

'I never said that, but is this the right way to fight back?'

'What option do the Palestinians have? The Jews are well armed and have powerful countries like America backing them. They are crushing the Palestinians and forcing them to fight back with whatever little they have.'

'Come on, Asif, let's at least get our facts straight.'

'What do you mean?'

'How come nobody is ready to acknowledge that the first major terror bombing took place on 24 February 1948, a good ten days before the Jewish state even came into existence? It was a massive triple truck bomb that killed about fifty-four people on Jerusalem's Ben Yehuda street.'

'You seem very well informed.'

'Why shouldn't I be?' Iqbal countered defiantly.

'All right, all right, but what's the relevance?'

'The relevance is this, Asif – the Arabs have a problem with the mere thought of a Jewish state, so let's not say the suicide bombings and terror attacks are only because of the occupation, because I don't think that's true.'

'You sound like a Jewish sympathizer,' Imtiaz spat out angrily.

After a pause Asif asked, 'So you don't think what's happening to the Palestinians, our fellow Muslims, is wrong?'

'No!' Iqbal shook his head vehemently. 'I think it's very wrong and extremely unfair. It makes my blood boil, but...' He shrugged helplessly and let his voice trail away. 'What can I do about it?'

'I know what you mean.' Asif smiled. He had his man where he wanted him. 'The very thought makes me sick with anger.'

Imtiaz spoke up on cue. 'Well, if we don't do something quickly, they'll continue to walk all over us.'

'That's easier said than done,' Asif remarked,

almost too casually. 'Iqbal is right, what can we do? The Indian government should...'

'The Indian government? It's run by kafirs!' Imtiaz exclaimed, his voice low, but the vehemence in it unmistakable. 'Why should they do anything for us? When have they done anything to protect us?'

'I don't think that's entirely true,' said Asif, playing devil's advocate.

'You don't, do you?' Asif sat back as Iqbal snatched at the bait angrily. 'Tell me what happened in Gujarat. Did they punish those who literally massacred dozens of Muslims? Our women were raped, our children burnt alive... did anyone pay for it? No, everything came down to mindless legalities; witnesses were bribed, judges were bought off or prevailed upon to look the other way. The same thing happened in Mumbai.'

'You could say the same thing about all those times when Hindus got killed, or Christians, or Sikhs,' Asif goaded him on.

'So you think it's all right for us to sit back and allow our religion to be driven into the ground?' Imtiaz asked.

'No! I never said that,' Iqbal retorted, allowing his anger to show.

'Then what do you think we should do?'

'I don't know.' Iqbal slouched back in his chair with a helpless shrug. 'I just don't know.'

Before the conversation could go any further, a group of students walked into the coffee shop. Soon a lot of the tables were taken, including the one next to them. The conversation returned to more mundane topics till Asif threw a glance at his watch and muttered, 'Man! Is that how late it is? I must be going. Let's meet again tomorrow.'

As Asif smiled at him and got up to go, Iqbal was suddenly reminded of the old maulavi at the Savita Nagar mosque who had recruited him for the Lashkar-e-Toiba. He had that same calculating smile, the quietly persuasive tone, the outwardly peaceful demeanour. Iqbal had to fight to keep the revulsion off his face as he shook hands with the man.

Imtiaz flashed Asif an ingratiating smile. 'Sure! Let's catch up again tomorrow evening.'

And they did, the following evening and several evenings after that. Each time they met, Asif the recruiter wove his relentless web of words and deceit. And every day, Iqbal the undercover operative watched Iqbal the reluctant recruit being hemmed in by lies and slowly falling deeper and deeper into the web. Iqbal allowed Asif and Imtiaz to go home every day feeling satisfied that they had hooked the fish and were now, slowly but surely, reeling it in.

As the days went by, what began to eat into Iqbal, more than the playacting, was the resemblance between Asif and his old nemesis, the maulavi. With each passing day, the similarities became more and more marked. And there were times when Iqbal the man rebelled against Iqbal the operative. He felt compelled to snatch up a weapon – anything, even a knife or a fork lying on the table – and put an end to the hateful man sitting in front of him, lying to him about religion, misquoting both the Quran-e-pak and the Holy Prophet. But each time, Iqbal the operative stepped in and took charge, remembering the words of his patient trainers back in Kasauli.

Live the lie, Iqbal. You have to live the lie. Only then will you succeed.

And so he did.

'Can you imagine?' Asif's voice intruded on his thoughts, forcing him back to the present. They were in one of the numerous coffee shops that marked out Pune as a student town. 'The fucking Americans have started to call this so-called war of terror a clash of civilizations. I tell you, Iqbal, it's going to be a repeat of the Crusades. They've already decimated Afghanistan and Iraq. It's just a matter of time before they seize control of the entire Middle East.'

'You're right, Asif,' Imtiaz said, 'they've already started forcing the Pakistan Army to conduct operations against our brothers in the NWFP and Baluchistan.'

'I wouldn't worry too much about that,' Asif remarked with a knowing smile. 'The Pakistan Army is too smart to actually do anything. Sooner or later, they will do something to instigate the Indians and force them to deploy the Indian Army on the border. The minute that happens, Pakistan will have a legitimate excuse to pull out their forces from the NWFP and move them to the Indian border. That will put paid to any efforts to suppress the jihad.'

'What do you mean, Asif?' Iqbal asked innocently.

'It's simple, really. You think the Americans can do anything on their own in these areas? The minute the Pakistan Army moves out of NWFP or FATA (Federally Administered Tribal Areas), Afghanistan will fall back under the Taliban's control. So, for that matter,' he added after a moment's pause, 'will Pakistan.'

'What are you saying?' Iqbal could not control the shock that pulsed through him. Luckily for him, the others were so caught up in the conversation that they misread his horror as excitement.

'Exactly what you are hearing, my friend.' Asif smiled, a pleased, almost affectionate smile. 'America cannot and will not retain troops in Afghanistan forever. They are always ready to deliver their famous shock and awe from the skies, but seldom put their troops in the line of fire. They just don't have the balls for a fight when their own people start dying.' He laughed derisively. 'And when that happens, it's just a matter of time before the Taliban takes over Afghanistan and Pakistan. They will restore Islam to its pure, original state.' His voice rose as he declaimed, 'Nothing can stop our march then. We'll see that the Islamic crescent rules the world.'

They fell silent after that, each man immersed in his thoughts. Then Asif turned to Iqbal again. There was something in his manner that altered the atmosphere instantly. All three of them knew that the moment of reckoning was at hand. The recruiter had decided the time was ripe to make the final pitch.

'That is why, my friend, I ask you again, as our good old friend George Bush put it so eloquently, are you with us or against us?' He levelled a hard, unwavering look at Iqbal.

Live the lie, Iqbal.

'With you, obviously!' Iqbal retorted, his eyes steady as they met Asif's.

'Are you sure?' Asif's voice throbbed with barely controlled energy.

'Of course!'

'It could well mean your life one day.'

'One must have a reason to die, rather than nothing to live for.'

'Well said, Iqbal. That's very well put,' said Imtiaz admiringly, repeating the words softly. Iqbal ignored him, his eyes still fixed on Asif.

'It's a one-way street, Iqbal.' Asif held his gaze, and now there was a hint of menace in his eyes. 'Once you join us, there's no going back.' Iqbal didn't reply. He just nodded, letting his eyes do the talking for him.

'Good!' Asif leaned closer to Iqbal until their faces almost touched. 'If you ever betray our cause... if you ever let us down... you will not live. Neither will those close to you.'

Iqbal started up angrily. 'Are you threatening me? What gives you the bloody right to question my faith?'

'I'm not doing either.' Asif was unfazed by his outburst. 'I just want you to know the way things are in this world you want to enter.'

'Just tell me what I have to do to prove myself,' Iqbal retorted, glaring back at him.

'I will.' Asif pulled away abruptly and leaned back in his chair. 'When the time is right, I will. For now, just prepare yourself and be ready to move quickly. The time is not far when we will strike at the kafir again.'

'Again? You mean...' Iqbal left the question hanging between them.

'All in good time, my friend.' A cold smile settled on Asif's face. 'Just be ready.'

'I am,' Iqbal said firmly.

He pushed back his chair and took his leave of the other two, barely able to conceal his excitement.

FOURTEEN

A week later, Asif was waiting for Iqbal outside the Golden Heritage complex when he returned from the institute.

'Hi!' Iqbal did his best to conceal his shock. 'What a surprise! Just passing by, or did you come to look us up?'

'I need to park this with you.' Asif pointed at a battered, dirty grey VIP suitcase near his feet.

'Is that your luggage? Are you going somewhere?'

'No!' Asif lowered his voice. 'It's the stuff we need for our next operation. Let's go in.' He picked up the suitcase, which was obviously a lot heavier than it looked. 'I'll tell you about it inside.'

As they entered and Iqbal switched on the lights, Asif asked him, 'No one at home? Where's your wife?'

'She must have stepped out for some household stuff. She should be back by six or so… that's when I normally get back.'

'Great, we have time then.' Asif looked at his

watch. 'Here, let me show you.' He placed the suitcase carefully on the dining table and unlocked it. On top was a layer of clothes. When he removed them, the actual contents came to light. Iqbal suppressed the shock he felt when he saw the array of detonators and slabs of RDX inside. Forcing an expression of innocent curiosity on his face, he asked, 'What's all that? Are they...'

'The materials we need to make the bombs.' Noting his surprised expression, Asif gave a pleased laugh. 'I thought it best to leave it here. After all, with your wife staying with you and this being a nice, quiet residential colony, it's the last place anyone would think of looking for such things.'

'Is it safe?' Iqbal leaned forward and touched them gingerly.

'Of course it is.' Asif grinned wickedly. 'Unless you decide to plug in the detonator, wire up the timer and start it.' Moving with practised ease, he pushed one of the detonators carefully into a slab of RDX and then pointed at the wires of the timer that needed to be attached to the detonator. 'We plug that into a power source, start the timer, and boom!' He threw up his free hand, his fingers opening out like a flower.

'Wow!' Iqbal whistled appreciatively.

'Anyway.' Asif unhooked the items, covered them with the clothes again and shut the suitcase. 'Let's get this out of sight before your wife gets in. She'll freak.'

'That's true. She may support me in my cause, but doing that and actually seeing bombs in the house are two different things.' Picking up the suitcase, Iqbal carried it into the spare bedroom and slid it under the bed. 'There! That should be good enough.'

The two men returned to the living room.

'So when do we move out?' Iqbal tried to keep his tone casual.

'Probably the day after tomorrow.' Asif saw the flush on Iqbal's face. 'Excited?' he asked.

'Of course!' Iqbal laughed. 'Where are we going?'

'You'll come to know in due course,' Asif replied, 'when the time is right.'

'Oh, I see!' Iqbal looked offended. 'You don't trust me, Asif?'

'I do! Why else would I leave that stuff with you?' He gestured towards the bedroom in which the suitcase was kept. 'But there are some basic security rules that we all have to follow. You see, what you don't know, you won't be able to give away even by mistake.'

'Right! I understand.'

'Anyway, I guess I'll move on now.' Asif made to leave. 'We'll get together tomorrow afternoon.'

Asif had been gone just a few minutes when the door opened again and Tanaz let herself in. She was carrying a bag full of vegetables. Iqbal was onto her before she could even put the bags down. He quickly briefed her about Asif's visit.

'Fantastic! What a break!' Tanaz said. 'You must call Captain Sami right away.'

'That's exactly what I was going to do.' Iqbal retrieved the tiny Sony mobile handset from his pocket and dialled a number.

Just two miles away as the crow flies, Sami answered his phone. He, along with Tiwathia, Dhankar, Khare and Ankita were parked at the Officers' Mess behind the military hospital at Khadki. Anbu had given them carte blanche for this operation.

'Hi, Iqbal, what's up?'

Iqbal quickly filled him in on all that had happened. 'What do we do now? You guys want to move in and take them down?'

'It's way too early for that, Iqbal. You know only these three or four guys. The group is much bigger, we already know that from the strikes they've carried out till now. Secondly, we need to know much more – their sympathizers and supporters and most importantly, their planners, financers and suppliers.'

'Why? If we take these guys in, we can get the truth out of them.'

'Maybe we can, but by that time the others will have vanished. We'll never get our hands on them, especially if they decide to cross the border like they normally do.'

'I understand,' said Iqbal, some of his initial excitement abating. 'So, what do you want me to do?'

'First, I want you to open the suitcase and photograph it. Take careful note of the way everything is packed.'

'I don't see why,' Iqbal said impatiently.

'You'll have to make sure that when you finish doing what needs to be done, everything is repacked exactly the way you found it,' Sami explained. 'You see, we don't know what kind of person Asif is. Maybe he packs things in a particular way, whether by habit or by design. He may realize that the stuff has been tampered with if he finds it packed differently. That's why the photos are necessary. You can refer to them as you repack. Got it?'

'Right!' Iqbal was impressed by Sami's thoroughness. For a moment it occurred to him that he was lucky Sami and he were on the same side. He felt his confidence begin to rise as he hauled out the suitcase, placed it on the dining table, opened it and began to take photos using the 8-megapixel camera in the deceptively tiny Sony handset that he had been given in Kasauli. 'I'm done,' he told Sami when he called him again.

'Good! Is your phone linked to your laptop?'

'It is now.' Iqbal clicked the Bluetooth icon on the laptop, mating it with the phone.

'Perfect! Now take out all the bomb related items and start clicking them. Meanwhile, tell Tanaz to retrieve the photos from your phone and email them to me.'

They went to work rapidly. Tanaz retrieved the photos from the camera's memory and emailed them to Ankita almost as soon as Iqbal clicked them.

At the other end, Dhankar began to analyse each photo as it came in. It took him only a few moments to break down the components and understand the type and construct of the bombs that they would be used to make.

'It's a fairly simple device, Iqbal,' Dhankar said, taking the phone from Sami. 'The Integrated Circuit is the key we can use to get the bombs to malfunction. Have a look at the seventh photo you sent.' He tapped the picture of the tiny IC chip that glowed on the laptop screen in front of him. 'That's what is going to trigger the bombs. Just take all of them out and then rejig them as I tell you.'

'Hang on then. Let me get the goody bag out,' Iqbal replied. Dhankar grinned, because that was what he called his own toolkit. They waited as Iqbal retrieved the toolkit from the false base of Tanaz's vanity case.

Using the computer link between them, Dhankar talked Iqbal through the process, ensuring that none of the ICs could send out the required current to trigger the detonators. He also got Iqbal to embed a GPS locator in every IC.

'Use the smallest ones from the set I gave you,' he said. 'The microdot ones.'

'Will they have the power we need?'

'They will, once the bombs are hooked up,' Dhankar clarified. 'The way we've rejigged the ICs, it will be the GPS locators that use the bomb's power source instead of the impulse being passed on to the detonators.'

'Right! Got it! Give me a minute.'

'Take it slow and easy, Iqbal,' Dhankar cautioned. 'You have to be careful you leave no trace of your work.'

It took them nearly three hours to take care of all the ICs.

'That's the lot.' Iqbal finally leaned back in the dining chair, rotating his shoulders to relieve them of stress.

'Good! Now pull the first picture back on your laptop screen and use it to repack everything exactly the way you found it. While you're doing that, ask Tanaz to delete all the photos and emails from the laptop and the phone memory. Clean it out fully. Nothing pertaining to this should remain in the memory.'

'Don't worry, we'll take care of it.'

'And call me back as soon as you're done.'

'I will,' said Iqbal. He remembered what Ankita had told him: 'We're not going to call you because we wouldn't know who else is with you at that time, so it's always you who must call us.'

'What if there is an emergency? How will you reach me?' Iqbal had asked worriedly.

'We will. Trust me,' she had said with a confident smile. 'When the time comes, you'll see how.'

The memory comforted him now as they went to work. Thirty minutes later, the suitcase was back under the bed. The laptop and camera had been cleaned up.

'It's all done,' Iqbal finally reported in, giving a detailed account to Sami, who clicked through a mental checklist to ensure they had not missed anything.

'Well done, guys.' The appreciation in Sami's voice came across clearly. 'Delete the call history from your phone and get some sleep. Now we just have to wait for the operation to blow up in their faces.'

'As long as the bombs don't explode, I'm fine,' Iqbal said with a laugh.

'Don't worry, Iqbal. Dhankar here knows all there is to know about bombs. Why do you think we call him the ultimate blowjob?' They all laughed.

It was a satisfied set of people who finally took to their beds that night. So far, things had gone without a hitch.

Inshallah, they will continue to do so. That was the last thought in Iqbal's mind before he fell asleep, with Tanaz snuggled up against him. He sighed with contentment as he rested his palm against the tight swell of her stomach. It was good to feel the life within.

Once again, Asif was waiting outside the apartment complex when Iqbal returned home.

'Come on,' he said impatiently as Iqbal came closer, 'we need to move fast.'

'What's the matter?' Iqbal was unable to mask his anxiety. 'Some problem?'

'Our train leaves in exactly one hour and forty minutes,' Asif replied, 'and you know how lousy Pune traffic is. Come on, grab the suitcase and let's move.'

'Train?' Iqbal was taken by surprise. 'Where are we going?'

'I'll tell you on the way, let's get the stuff and move now.'

'What do I tell my wife?' Iqbal protested.

'Why do you have to tell her anything?'

'Come on, yaar,' Iqbal protested, 'she is due to deliver in just a few weeks. She'll want to know why I'm leaving her at this critical time.'

'Tell her we have to go to Mumbai for an institute project and we'll be back the day after tomorrow.'

'Are we going to Mumbai?' Iqbal was trying to keep the desperation out of his voice.

'No,' Asif replied, 'but how will she know?'

'Okay, give me a moment to tell her,' Iqbal said with a resigned expression on his face.

Tanaz was not pleased to hear that Iqbal would be gone for two days. Aware that Asif was listening to their conversation, she complained bitterly and at some length about being left alone at such a difficult time. The performance seemed to go down well with Asif: he turned away to hide the smirk on his face when Iqbal emerged from the bedroom with the suitcase and his own carry bag.

'Do you have a mobile?' Asif asked when they were at the door.

'Yes. Don't we all?'

'Not on these missions, we don't,' Asif replied shortly. 'Leave it behind.'

Iqbal was about to protest but decided against it. Pulling his mobile out of his pocket, he meekly left it on the dining table.

Fifty minutes later, they were at the Pune Junction railway station, rushing along the noisy, crowded platform. By the time they had run up the metal overbridge and pushed their way down the crowded staircase onto the platform from which their train would depart, both were drenched in sweat and breathing heavily. The suitcase seemed to be wearing Asif down. He was nearly diagonal, one hand flung out to balance the weight.

'Surat? Are we going to Surat?' Iqbal panted, trying to catch his breath as they boarded the 1096 Ahimsa Express.

'That's right!' Asif nodded.

'So what was the big secret?' Iqbal protested. 'You could have told me. Unless you trust people, how can...'

'I've already told you, Iqbal, there are some things you just don't question... operational security is one of them,' Asif retorted curtly. 'You like it, fine; you don't like it, that's also fine.'

Iqbal bit back an angry retort as he grabbed his bag and boarded the train.

At the other end of the platform, alerted by Tanaz's call as soon as Asif and Iqbal left the apartment, Tiwathia watched the two men board the train. He waited till the train was ready to move before he boarded the same compartment. Luckily, it wasn't too crowded and he managed to find a vacant berth from where he could keep an eye on his subjects. By now Asif and Iqbal had been joined by Abid and Imtiaz.

What a jolly crowd. Tiwathia watched the silent, almost sullen quartet settle down for the night. Then he reached for his mobile phone and shot off a text message to Sami.

Within minutes, a helicopter took off from the Indian Air Force base in Lohegaon with the remaining members of the Force 22 team from Pune on board. It gained height, then steadied on the flight path for Surat.

FIFTEEN

Making sure he maintained a discreet distance, Tiwathia followed the terror team as they ploughed through the busy railway station at Surat. He made sure there were a few people between them as he watched the four men exit the station. Then he reached for his mobile and called Sami.

'We are here,' he said.

'Yes, I can see you,' Sami replied. Tiwathia did not look around to try and spot him. 'We've been waiting for you guys to clock in.'

'Good. So I'm letting them go now.'

'Do that. We have people in place to take over.'

Tiwathia allowed the distance between him and his quarry to increase before he spoke again. 'You got them? The two guys behind Iqbal and the one in front.'

'Got them.' There was a pause as Sami spoke to someone. 'Come out now, turn left, and then wait for me.'

Tiwathia did so. From the corner of his eye, he watched as the four men he had tailed climbed into autorickshaws and vanished into the crowded city in pairs. He knew the tails would be on them, he could now relax.

About two minutes later, Sami pulled up next to him. He was behind the wheel of an umarked police Maruti Gypsy. 'Hop in, dude.'

'Where are we operating from?' Tiwathia asked, jumping in beside him and throwing his duffel bag in the rear, where two cops in plainclothes sat.

'The local ATTF headquarters,' Sami replied. 'The Old Man coordinated it.'

'Cool.' There was a pause. 'I wonder where they've gone.'

'Why wonder? We have people on them. In any case, we'll know the minute they assemble and power up the bombs because the GPS locators will come on.'

'Yeah! If Dhankar and Iqbal haven't screwed up.'

'They can't have.' Sami was as confident as he was optimistic.

Dhankar and Iqbal had not screwed up. The first GPS locator embedded in the tiny ICs came alive just as the clock struck four. By 1645 hours, one by one, all sixteen locators were glowing red dots on the screen of Ankita's laptop.

'That's a guesthouse.' The local ATTF officer tapped on the map spread out on the table. 'It's in a rather shady part of town – the red light area.' He added, 'We have fourteen people in place around it. Should I tell them to move in now?'

'No!' Sami's tone was sharp. 'You guys will function precisely as we direct you to.' Then, softening a little, he explained, 'This op is just a part of the bigger picture, so we have to be very careful we don't screw up – okay?'

'Sure.' The ATTF man nodded. His orders had come from very high up, and were very clear – they were to cooperate fully with these guys. *Whoever the hell they are, they seem to know what they are doing. That's good enough for me.*

He listened as Sami explained the plan in detail before he nodded. 'Fine, I get it. So where do you want me to position my people now?'

'Explain this area to me first.' Sami gestured at the map. 'Considering where these guys are right now, what would be the main markets, important buildings… you know what I mean? Show me the places that are most likely to be targeted.'

'Here, here and here.' Unhesitatingly, the ATTF officer tapped the map, indicating the areas immediately to the north, east and west of the guesthouse. 'That's where they would head if they're looking for crowded, soft and high value targets.'

'Fair enough.' Sami gave it a moment's thought as he studied the target area, and then made up his mind. 'Okay, so five teams each in these three areas and put the last one here... to the south.' Noticing the query on the man's face, he explained, 'Just as a backup... in case they decide to go that way for some reason that we haven't factored in.'

'That makes sense.' The ATTF man nodded approvingly. 'It's always best to err on the side of caution.'

'Tell all our teams to be in or close to the major markets, places of worship, important government buildings and hospitals.' Sami's tone was brisk and business-like. 'But they will all maintain a low profile.' The ATTF man nodded again and began to reach for his phone. 'And please make it very clear to everyone – nobody will be in uniform and all weapons will be kept out of sight. The camera guys should be careful to only go for long shots. Tell them to record everything they can. I want the chain of evidence to be as perfect as possible. Okay?'

They all watched and waited as the ATTF officer spent the next ten minutes shooting off instructions to a host of people. When he was finally done, Sami took over again.

'Let's split the Bomb Disposal Squad into three teams. Tell them to take up positions at the most convenient police stations in the north, east and west and wait for our orders. I want them ready to move the moment we call them.'

'They'll all be in place within fifteen minutes,' the ATTF officer assured him as he got back on his phone. Sami took the opportunity to call Anbu and bring him up to par.

By the time Sami, Tiwathia and Dhankar left the

room and headed out in three separate vehicles, the local ATTF and BDS teams were firmly in position. Everything was going as planned. They all knew that as long as the GPS locators were lit up, it meant that the faulty ICs had not been detected and the bombs would not go off. Even so, the stress of completing the mission was inevitable and unavoidable.

'Dear god, please keep Mr Murphy far away from us today,' Sami murmured as the three vehicles headed out. The ATTF officer remained in Sami's vehicle. It made sense for the command elements to remain together, to cater to the unforeseen eventualities that always arise as a battle ebbs and flows.

The three Force 22 commandos were still some distance away from their destinations when, at the temporary command post at the ATTF headquarters, Ankita saw the first of the glowing dots on her laptop screen separate from the others and begin to move away. It moved very slowly, as though the man carrying the bomb with the GPS locator was on foot. A moment later, another electronic dot began to move; this one too, advanced slowly. And so it continued until, within a matter of thirty minutes, the sixteen glowing dots had spread away from the point of origin and were variously heading north, east and west.

Like evil aliens in a Friday night horror movie. Ankita could imagine the havoc the bombs would have caused had they not got to them. She suppressed a shiver as she reached for the phone and began to update the three Force 22 commandos and the ATTF teams out in the field.

The strike on Surat had begun.

Iqbal's head was throbbing as he watched the fifteen men who had assembled in the guesthouse leave one by one. The large, almost airtight room they were in was as dingy as the rest of the guesthouse. It was the kind of place that didn't ask too many questions of those who checked in and rented rooms by the hour, which was not surprising considering its location in the town's red light area.

Under normal circumstances, Iqbal would not have even registered the names of the fifteen others, just as most people seldom catch the names of those they are introduced to at parties. This time, however, his newly trained mind captured every name and embedded every face indelibly in his memory. He knew he would be able to put together almost perfect Identikit photos of each of the twelve men who had joined the original team of four that had travelled in from Pune. He was also confident that he would be able to link up the snippets of information that he had systematically collated during the casual conversations that took place while they waited for the bombs to be assembled.

Imtiaz – who, Iqbal had learnt by now, was the designated bomb maker – had wrapped each bomb in a dull blue-green piece of polythene after it had been assembled.

'The polythene will keep the bomb dry and also hold together the ball bearings and nails that are being used as shrapnel, till the bomb explodes,' he explained to them as he finished wrapping the first one. 'Now all you have to do to activate the bomb is push this lever to the right.' Holding up the wrapped bomb, he showed it to them. 'Now place it in the target area and move out. Don't worry, you'll have at least thirty minutes to get away. Any questions?'

'Good!' he said as they shook their heads.

'As soon as you're done, I want you to head home,' Asif told them. 'Make damn sure none of you starts getting adventurous and goes back to have a look at what you've achieved. Okay?' He looked around at them with narrowed eyes. 'Remember that just one arsehole can get all of us screwed. Okay?' He waited till each one of them had acknowledged the order. 'Right! Similarly, the outstation people will head straight for the railway station or the bus stop.'

'Grab that and let's get going.' Asif's voice intruded on Iqbal's troubled reverie. Asif was pointing at the last remaining bomb on the table. 'Come on, Iqbal, where are you lost?' His voice tugged Iqbal back to the present. 'Let's go, we're getting late, miyan.'

Picking up the bomb, Iqbal carefully put it in his

duffel bag and began to follow him to the door. 'We're both going to place this one?' he asked.

'Of course! I'll show you how it's done. New recruits never operate alone.'

'You don't trust anyone, do you?'

'Like I told you,' Asif said with a shrug, 'security is security. Nothing changes. Anyway, how would a newcomer know the correct way to do the job unless we show him?'

'Right!' Iqbal didn't try very hard to keep the sarcasm out of his voice.

'Why are you always so touchy?' Asif asked, lowering his voice as they hit the road and began walking east.

'I don't like not being trusted,' Iqbal retorted. 'After all, why would I be here if I didn't want to, if I didn't believe in the cause?'

'I don't fucking care!' Asif snarled back, taking care to keep his voice low. 'Rules are rules and they are the same for everyone. If you want to play with the big boys, you behave like one, otherwise...' His voice trailed away, leaving the threat hanging in the air.

Realizing he had pushed it as far as he could, Iqbal held his tongue and followed him.

Ten minutes later, they went up to the newly opened Pizza Express outlet in the market in Loktej. Straddled between an electronics showroom on the left and a music store on the right, the glass-fronted, brightly coloured store had a large red plastic dustbin just outside, to the right of the huge swinging glass doors. To the other side were a couple of blue, red and white scooters with large blue food carriers strapped to the rear, the kind used by pizza delivery boys all over the country. A continuous stream of people, mostly youngsters, moved in and out of the three stores, all of them in animated conversation with their companions. Two huge speakers placed outside the music store pounded out the latest Bollywood numbers, adding to the cacophony of the marketplace.

Asif stood on the other side of the road for a long time, observing the target carefully. Satisfied that there was no suspicious activity in progress, he murmured softly, 'Now watch me,' and casually crossed the road. Pausing briefly near the dustbin, he threw a quick look around and then leaned down and planted the bomb just behind, making sure it was well out of sight.

Turning away equally casually, he crossed the road again and the two men began to make their way back to the railway station. They had almost reached the autorickshaw stand on the street corner when Asif stopped so suddenly that Iqbal, a few steps behind, almost ran into him.

'Shit! Did I arm the b – the device?' Asif whispered, mindful of the people passing by.

'I don't know! I couldn't see,' Iqbal whispered back. 'You must have.'

'I'm not sure.' Asif looked at his watch. 'Four

minutes gone already.' He thought for a moment. 'I think I need to go back and check.'

'You want me to do that?' Iqbal asked.

'Will you? You know what has to be done?'

'Of course. Imtiaz showed us. The lever has to be to the right, correct?'

'That's right,' Asif said with a nod. 'Okay, then will you recheck it while I get hold of an autorickshaw? You'll have to be quick, though... we just have twenty-six minutes left.'

'Don't worry.' Iqbal turned and began to stride back.

The press of people was just a little lighter than it had been earlier and Iqbal was able to reach the dustbin without drawing attention to himself. *In any case*, he thought, *everyone is so caught up with themselves that they seldom stop to notice what others are doing*.

Despite that, his breathing was as uneven as his heartbeat as he reached down behind the dustbin to check the lever. It was pushed all the way to the right. Knowing the bomb would malfunction, he resisted the urge to push the lever to the other side, and got up. Only to stumble into Asif, who was standing right behind him. The shock of finding him there rendered Iqbal motionless for a moment.

'Shit! You scared me,' Iqbal exclaimed. 'What are you doing here? You were supposed to...'

'I wasn't sure if you'd know how to do it correctly,' Asif muttered as he leaned forward and rechecked the lever before leading the way out of the market.

'You weren't sure, or you were testing me?' Iqbal blurted out without thinking.

'Come on, Iqbal.' Asif's smile was unreadable. 'I just wanted to reconfirm. It has nothing to do with not trusting you.'

'Yeah, right!' Iqbal allowed his anger to show this time.

'And even if I was testing you, do you blame me?' Asif shrugged. 'Either way, you passed with flying colours.' Iqbal looked away, still trying to control the churning within him. It had been a close call. *I wonder what would have happened if I had disarmed it,* he thought with a shudder. *Bloody hell! Tiwathia was so right. You can't let your guard down even for a moment. You just have to live the lie. There is no other way.*

'Come on, Iqbal! We have only nineteen minutes left.'

The two men rapidly made their way out and were soon inside a rickety autorickshaw they had managed to flag down.

I just hope we've done our job well, Iqbal prayed as he watched the crowds fade away in the distance. *If that bomb goes off...* He shivered.

'What happened?' Asif asked, catching the sudden shiver.

'Nothing.'

'Don't worry.' Asif smiled condescendingly at

him. 'That always happens the first time. You'll get used to it soon.' He laughed. 'By the third or fourth time, you'll actually start enjoying it.'

As usual, the railway station was teeming with a sense of chaotic urgency when the two men alighted from the autorickshaw and made their way inside. The medley of sounds ebbed and flowed as a train thundered in or whistled its way out, the sounds magnified as they ricocheted off the corrugated roofing over the platforms. Cries of 'Taxi? Hotel? Coolie!' added to the pandemonium. The railway platform smell, a strange blend of sweat, tea, food, cold drinks and cigarettes, hung heavy in the air.

Asif halted on the fringes of the crowd and pulling out his mobile, made a short call. Iqbal heard him mutter softly into the phone, 'Send it now...Yes.' There was a pause. 'Good! I'll be seeing you.' Asif returned the phone to his pocket and rejoined the crowd of people flowing into the station, with Iqbal in tow.

Two hundred and fifty miles away, in Mumbai, the same slim, well-dressed man in his late twenties accompanied by the same short, dark man driving the same maroon Ford Endeavour put away the mobile phone on which he had just answered Asif's call and turned his attention back to his laptop. This time he was already connected to the unsecured wireless network he had caught a few moments ago.

With light, precise taps on the keyboard he sent out the email that was waiting in the drafts folder. The list of recipients was almost the same as the last time. So was the reaction. Moments later, security forces in Surat and Mumbai jolted into action. This time, however, the action was destined to be differently choreographed.

Due to the heavy crowd, it took Asif and Iqbal nearly ten minutes to reach the platform from which their train was to depart. But it was still early and the train had not yet been marshalled onto the platform.

Asif made his way towards a raised television on the platform, the screen aglow with the logo of the local news channel. The sound had been muted; not that it mattered, because even if it had been on full volume, the hullabaloo around would have ensured nothing was audible. And it made no difference to the two men who came to a halt in front of it, one watching the screen eagerly, the other with anxiety.

They had been there for a couple of minutes when Iqbal saw Imtiaz and Abid making their way towards them. None of them acknowledged or spoke to the others.

The news anchor was conducting an animated discussion with a vaguely familiar sports expert, probably an ex-vice captain of the Indian cricket team. They could not hear what either of them was saying, but the focus of the discussion was clear from the news ticker scrolling continuously across the prominent blue bar at the bottom of the screen. Apparently there was some fresh controversy between the selectors and the current captain of the team.

Every few seconds, Asif anxiously checked the time on his wristwatch. *It should have started by now! The first bomb was timed for... what...* Asif checked the time again... *eight... almost nine minutes back. By now they should have got the news on air.*

Asif was about to look at his watch again when it happened. The long blue bar at the base of the television screen turned red and a large, bright yellow BREAKING NEWS icon began to flash.

Two unexploded bombs have been discovered at... the headlines screamed. Simultaneously the news anchor's demeanour changed and he began to talk even more animatedly. Almost immediately, the shell-shocked sports commentator was banished to the sidelines.

Unexploded? Asif's face changed hues when the contents of the news ticker hit him. He turned to glare at Imtiaz, who was also watching the screen, confusion and bewilderment written all over his face.

Just then the train arrived on the platform and people began to scramble on board.

Another unexploded bomb has been discovered at... Just moments earlier, an email was received by various government officers and media channels, warning of a strike. The email was sent by the same group that had...

By now Asif's face was tight with anger. Turning away with a final, disgusted look at the television, he strode into the crowd that was still fighting to board the train and began to push his way through, unmindful of the dirty looks and curses that were flung his way. Iqbal followed suit, relief fluttering inside him.

Even though their berths were in the compartment closest to where they had been standing on the platform, it took them a good five minutes to fight their way through. From their seats inside, they could still see the television screen. By the time the train pulled out of the station, all but three of the bombs had been discovered by the police. The news of this latest terror attempt had spread fast and heated discussions had broken out all around them. By now dozens of security personnel could be seen scouring the platform.

Unaware that the exercise was cosmetic and orchestrated solely for their benefit, Asif immediately moved to the upper berth that had been reserved for him. Stretching out, he covered his face with his arms, as though warding off the light, and pretended to be asleep. Iqbal happily did the same, thankful for the opportunity to be alone with his thoughts. He was, in any case, having a hard time controlling the exhilaration that filled him.

Poor Imtiaz! Iqbal almost laughed out loud. *Asif is going to give him hell!*

SIXTEEN

By the time they reached Pune, Asif's simmering anger was waiting to explode. He turned on Imtiaz the moment they entered the hostel room.

'What the fuck happened? Why didn't they go off?'

'I have no idea, Asif bhai.' Imtiaz quailed before his fury. 'I just...'

'Are you sure you assembled them correctly?'

'Of course!' Imtiaz said indignantly. 'I could have made a mistake with one or two of them, but not all of them. That's not possible. It must have been some fault in the...'

'What?' Asif was almost shouting now. 'What could have been faulty?'

'Well, either the detonators or the ICs must have been faulty. There was nothing else that could have... I mean, it could hardly have been the explosives, right?'

'You're an arsehole!' Asif would have continued with his rant but his phone rang just then. He stalked off to one corner and took the call.

'Haan, Mujib bhai,' Iqbal heard him murmur. 'No! No! I'm sure! We did everything by the book. What? No, I'm very sure… yes, he's reliable. There must have been some problem with either the ICs or the detonators.'

The man at the other end had clearly launched into a tirade; Iqbal could see Asif shake his head vigorously from time to time.

'Could you at least speak with the guy in Kochi?' Asif pleaded. 'He could check the remaining ICs and detonators and see if there's anything wrong… Yes, I promise I'll investigate thoroughly at my end.' Then Asif turned his back to the others and Iqbal couldn't hear any more.

As soon as Asif had hung up, he began a detailed investigation of the fiasco. Everyone, including Iqbal, was questioned in great detail, then Asif pilloried the men in the other cities over the phone.

A couple of hours passed in Asif's aggressive questioning, but the investigation was going nowhere. Asif was on the verge of putting an end to it when his phone rang again. He snatched it out of his pocket and glared at the screen. At once his demeanour changed. He scurried to a corner again as he answered.

'Haan ji, bhai?' The silence in the room ensured that his part of the conversation at least was audible to the others, though they all pretended not to hear. 'Did he find out what was wrong? *What?* That's not possible, Mujib bhai, something had to be…'

Whatever it was that the caller at the other end was telling him, it made Asif turn slowly and scrutinize each of the men in the room. His gaze finally came to rest on Iqbal and lingered there.

'Only two, Mujib bhai, one from Pune and one from Delhi… the rest are all old-timers. They were all there in the previous operations.' Iqbal felt a cold finger of fear crawl up his spine at Asif's words. 'Of course I'm sure. Yes, yes, don't worry. I'll do that.'

He listened in silence for another minute before he ended the call. All the while, his unflinching gaze was fixed on Iqbal.

Iqbal waited until Asif had hung up and then stepped forward. 'May I borrow your phone to call my wife?' he asked, his tone nonchalant.

'Where's yours?'

'You made me leave it at home.'

'Okay. Here.' Asif handed it to him. It was a black Motorola phone with a full-fledged QWERTY keyboard, similar to the one Iqbal had seen Sami using. Pretending unfamiliarity with its functioning, Iqbal pressed the green dial button and looked at the last few calls that were displayed on the large rectangular screen. He committed the last incoming number to memory before he dialled Tanaz's number.

Iqbal could feel Asif's gaze on him, so he kept the call short. 'Take care of yourself,' he said loudly. 'I should be home soon.'

Then he handed the phone back to Asif with a murmured thank you. He was about to turn away when Asif reached out and touched his arm – lightly, but still it felt like a threat.

'When I left the stuff at your place that evening, did anyone come home?'

'My place? No! In fact, I took my wife to the doctor just after you left and we went for a movie later that night. Why?'

'Did you open the case and fool around with the things inside?'

'No, Asif, why should I? That stuff scares the hell out of me.'

'Does it now?' His gaze was still fixed intently on Iqbal's face.

'You know that.' Iqbal gave an embarrassed laugh.

'No, I don't.' Asif was unrelenting. '*You* say it does.' He looked him in the eye. 'Are you sure, Iqbal?'

'Of course I am,' Iqbal said emphatically. 'Why are you asking me all these questions, Asif bhai?'

'Someone tampered with the material, that's why.'

'Well, it wasn't me. Why don't you do what Imtiaz suggested – check with the guy who supplied them; maybe he screwed up.'

'I've already done that. The Mallu has checked all the other items from the same set and they're perfectly fine.'

'The Mallu?'

'The guy in Kochi. He has been supplying us right from… never mind,' Asif broke off suddenly, realizing he had said more than was necessary. 'Only this lot malfunctioned. That's why I'm sure that whatever was done to it was done after I got the delivery. In that case, there are only two possibilities – you, or Imtiaz. No one else could have done it.'

'Well, then, I suggest you ask Imtiaz,' Iqbal said with a shrug. 'I know nothing about bombs and I never touched them. The suitcase was put under the bed in my house in front of you and taken out by you. Nobody touched it while it was there.'

Asif continued to hold Iqbal's gaze, his hand on his arm. Then his phone rang and he walked over to a corner again.

Iqbal could tell from Asif's deferential manner that it was Mujib bhai's call. Asif seemed afraid of him, or at the very least, watchful.

This time Asif kept his voice really low and Iqbal couldn't hear a word. As soon as the call ended, Asif turned to them.

'Right guys, we have a new target!' he announced.

'Already?' Imtiaz asked, his question mirroring the surprise they all felt. 'So soon?'

'Yes, we have to make up for this fucked up operation, so we leave in a couple of days. I suggest you all go home now and make your presence felt in town.' He called after them as Abid, Imtiaz and

Iqbal trooped out, 'And be ready to move soon, maybe even the day after tomorrow.'

They went out onto the main road together, where they flagged down three autorickshaws and went their separate ways.

Iqbal thought about what he had just heard as his autorickshaw accelerated into the traffic. *The explosives come from some guy in Kochi and the person who called Asif from that outstation number, someone called Mujib, designates the targets.*

He recited to himself the number he had memorized.

I must pass on all this information to Captain Sami as soon as possible. They need to get working on it immediately. Another city was on the hit list. He wondered which one it was.

Iqbal fought the mounting anxiety he felt as he began to mentally format the report he would send out to the Force 22 officers as soon as he got home. Things were moving too quickly for comfort.

I must warn them to be very careful, he thought. *Asif is suspicious as hell. I wonder what he'll do. Perhaps he'll put me under observation.*

The questions plagued Iqbal as the autorickshaw trundled towards his house, finally coming to a halt outside the now familiar gates. As usual, he couldn't be bothered to wait for the lift and ran up the stairs, two at a time. Seconds later, Tanaz was in his arms. And for a while, all the worries and questions faded away as her warm fragrance filled his senses.

What Asif did next caught Iqbal totally by surprise.

Two days later, Iqbal returned from the institute to find Asif waiting for him at the Golden Heritage gates. He had a suitcase with him, just like the one he had been carrying the previous time, perhaps even the same one. This time he also had a small bag slung over his shoulder.

'Oh, hi, Asif!' Iqbal's greeting was rather tentative, as the apprehension built within him. *What did Asif want now?*

Asif simply nodded. 'Come on, let's go up to your place.' Nothing more was said until they were inside the apartment.

I hope Tanaz is not home, Iqbal prayed as he let himself in; he loathed the thought of exposing her to Asif. Unfortunately, she was.

Tanaz emerged from the kitchen when she heard the door open. The warm smile on her face faded abruptly when she saw Asif. Quickly covering her face with the chunni around her neck, she murmured a subdued salaam and retreated into the kitchen, unnerved by the long, appraising stare that Asif directed at her.

'Please sit down, Asif.' Iqbal gestured at the sofa. 'Would you like to have some tea?'

'I would like that.' Asif gave a sly smile. 'In fact, if it's okay with you, I'll spend the night here.'

'You want to stay over for the night?' Iqbal couldn't contain his surprise.

'Is there a problem if I do? You have a spare bedroom, don't you?'

'No, there's no problem. Of course we have a spare bedroom. It's just that...'

'Yes?' Asif was watching him keenly.

'No, nothing. You can stay over.'

'Good!' Asif gave a smile of grim satisfaction. 'It's only for one night. We all leave tomorrow in any case.'

'We do?'

'Yes. We have to make up for the fiasco at Surat and this time I want to make sure I don't let the materials out of my sight even for a moment.'

'Oh! Okay!' Iqbal shrugged, trying to keep the dismay off his face. 'Sure! Why not?' His head whirled as he tried to work out a solution to this unexpected twist.

With Asif in our face the whole night, how do I get word out to Force 22? Which city are we going to hit? How the hell am I going to prevent the bombs from going off this time?

'You seem preoccupied.' Asif was watching him closely. 'Any problem?'

'No, no. None at all.' Iqbal pulled his mind back to the present, aware that Asif's attention was entirely focused on him.

Despite Iqbal's best efforts, dinner was a silent, morose affair. Mercifully, the television offered some respite as Asif spent almost two hours completely absorbed in some song-and-dance reality show that was being telecast. Tanaz kept out of the way, mostly confining herself to the kitchen while Iqbal kept Asif company in the living room. Both Tanaz and Iqbal were plagued by a single thought – how to get information of the forthcoming strike out to Force 22. Asif's presence in the tiny apartment made it impossible for either of them to use the phone or the laptop.

They were about to retire for the night when Asif threw the next googly.

'May I have your laptop for the night, Iqbal? I need to use the internet.'

'Sure, there it is.' Iqbal pointed at it. 'The data card is plugged in.'

'Great!' Asif walked across and picked it up.

Crap! Iqbal cursed wordlessly. *There goes my chance...*

'And listen, may I borrow your mobile phone too? I've forgotten my charger and I need to make some calls.'

'Oh! Okay!' Iqbal handed it over. 'Just give it back when you're done.'

'You need it at night?' Asif raised a questioning eyebrow.

'Not really, but sometimes we get calls.'

'That's okay.' Asif grinned. 'I'll let you know if any calls come in. Are you expecting anything important?'

'No no, it's not that, but you know how it is

when the wife is pregnant... all kinds of relatives call in all the time.'

'Not a problem, Iqbal. I'll give it to you if there are any important calls. It's just that I need to coordinate stuff for tomorrow and I'd like to keep my battery going as long as I can.' Asif's tone was bland, but Iqbal sensed the unsaid.

The bastard is making sure we are totally incommunicado. How much does he know?

From their bedroom Tanaz and Iqbal could hear Asif moving around in his room. Every once in a while they could hear him talking on the phone. They were both aware that the tiny apartment did not afford real privacy, either to them or to him. Only much later at night could they have any meaningful conversation.

'What should we do now?' Tanaz whispered as they lay huddled in each other's arms later that night. 'How are we going to get word out to the colonel?' Her unease was palpable. Before getting into bed, she had pulled out the .22 pistol that they kept hidden inside a shoe under the bed and placed it under her pillow.

'I think we should activate the emergency contact procedure,' Iqbal said.

'Do we have any other option?'

'None that I can think of.'

'Then let's do it.'

'There is nothing else we can do,' Iqbal whispered. 'I'm sure Asif is not going to leave us alone until we move out for the strike tomorrow. By then it might be too late...'

'Let's activate it right away then. We're running out of time.'

'True. It's almost morning.'

Iqbal got up silently and went across to the cupboard where he kept his clothes. He was careful not to make any noise as he slid open the well-oiled door and reaching inside, pulled out a slim black and brown leather belt from the back of the top shelf. The belt had one of those rotating buckles that are fixed on reversible two-colour belts. Iqbal rotated the buckle twice in a clockwise direction and then thrice counter-clockwise, activating the GPS locator embedded in it.

'Activate this at the last possible moment, Iqbal,' Tiwathia had warned when he gave him the belt. 'The battery backup is minimal.'

'What happens when I do that?'

'Well, if you leave the signal on, then we know the emergency response has been activated, and we come in and get both of you out. However, if you move to intermittent mode, which you can do simply by waiting for a minute or so and then turning the buckle back counter-clockwise three times,' Tiwathia demonstrated on the belt he was holding, 'then we get the message that there is a problem and we need to initiate contact with you right away, but your cover is intact and the operation is still alive.'

'And how do I shut it down?'

'That takes time since you need to open it first. It has to be reset and the battery changed. And be careful, okay? It's a delicate piece of equipment and needs to be handled with care. You go twisting it all over the place and it's liable to break.'

'Don't worry, I'll be very careful.' And he was. Iqbal held the belt gingerly in his hand, unsure what he should do next. How long do I need to wait before I turn it again and move to the intermittent mode, he wondered silently. He decided to give it a couple of minutes.

Unseen and unheard by Iqbal, the minute the GPS locator in the belt came alive, a small red beep began to pulse rapidly on the electronic map that glowed on the wall of the Force 22 Ops Room at Kasauli. Simultaneously, a text message alert beeped on the mobile phones of Anbu, Sami, Tiwathia, Khare and Ankita. Despite the unearthly hour, all five of them moved into action instantly.

At Kasauli, Anbu and Khare reached the Ops Room at the same time, both breathless. Khare's fingers slid rapidly over the keyboard as he manoeuvered the map and homed in on Iqbal's location.

'They're at the apartment,' he confirmed to Anbu.

'Get eyes on it,' Anbu ordered as he turned to the phone. He was reaching for it when it rang.

'Iqbal has activated emergency response, MS,'

said Anbu, his steady voice betraying none of the tension he felt.

'We're on it, sir. Dhankar is moving out with the extraction team in a moment.'

'What was the last report from him? Any idea what's happening there?'

'We spoke this morning,' Sami replied. 'Iqbal said things were quiet since they got back from Surat. Asif had dropped out of sight, presumably to prepare for the next strike he told them about.'

'That's right! The ATTF tracked him to Kochi.'

'Great! Did they manage to identify the Mallu?'

'Yes, they did. He's their main equipment supplier. They have him under 24x7 surveillance now. They're clocking everyone who meets him. Hopefully, we'll uncover that end of the network pretty soon. We need to know where he gets the stuff from.'

'Fantastic, sir! And Asif?'

'Unfortunately, they lost him in the city not long after he left the Mallu's house.'

'Crap!'

'I agree, but these things happen.'

'Maybe he's back in Pune and that's why Iqbal activated...'

'No guesswork, MS, not after emergency response has been activated. We do this strictly by the book. I want you to...'

Just then, the light on the screen began to blink

intermittently and the urgent red colour changed to a more sedate orange.

'The signal has moved to the intermittent mode now, sir,' Khare called out, sounding relieved.

'Yes, I see that too,' Sami said when Anbu told him.

'Excellent.' Anbu felt some of the stress recede. 'Place the extraction team on standby and activate the milk run.'

'Good idea, sir!' Putting down the phone, Sami swung into action at once.

The irritating buzz of the doorbell shattered the early morning calm in the apartment. Even though he had been expecting someone to arrive, by the time Iqbal opened his bedroom door Asif was already out of his room and halfway across the living room. He was either a light sleeper or had already been awake. Though it was slack by his side and almost out of sight, the pistol in Asif's hand gave Iqbal a cold shock.

Why am I surprised? Of course he would be armed!

Peering through the peephole, Asif carefully surveyed the area outside the door. Then he turned to Iqbal and whispered, 'Seems like the milkman. Doesn't he just leave the milk outside and go away?'

'That's what he normally does,' Iqbal replied, matching his decibel level.

'Then why is he...?'

The doorbell buzzed again.

'Open the damn door before he wakes up the whole world!' With an exasperated glare Asif motioned to the door with his pistol and took position to one side, from where he could cover the door if required.

Although Iqbal had expected one of the Force 22 officers, he had to fight to contain his surprise when he opened the door and saw the man who waited outside. 'Yes? What is it? Why are you ringing the doorbell at this time?'

'Sorry, sahib, but I need the month's payment. Memsahib told me to collect it today.' The accent was typical of the bhaiyya from the cow belt, but the careful observer would have noticed that this particular milkman was well-built and well-fed, almost as though he consumed more milk than he delivered. Luckily, from where he was positioned, Asif couldn't see beyond the doorway.

'How much is it?' Iqbal allowed his exasperation to show, the normal reaction of any person woken up so early for such a tiresome task.

'Four hundred and eighty-two rupees, sahib. I had given the details with the bill to memsahib and...'

'Okay, okay! Let me get it for you. Wait.' He closed the door and turned back to Asif with a shrug. Asif had heard the exchange and returned the pistol to his ankle holster. 'Pay the idiot and get rid of him,' he muttered as he returned to the spare bedroom.

Iqbal went to his bedroom and quickly pulled out his wallet and extracted five hundred-rupee notes from it. He used the special pen Ankita had given him to scribble a short message on the currency note in the middle. Returning the pen to his cupboard, he went out again.

This is the best way for you to pass on messages even in the face of the enemy. The writing will only be visible under a special lamp.

'Here, this is five hundred.' Iqbal opened the door and held out the money. 'Put the balance in our account.' He kept his tone normal, keenly aware that Asif was listening to every word.

'Thank you, sahib. Here is the milk.'

Iqbal took the milk and was closing the door again when he stopped and said, 'Oh, why don't you give me one more litre? We have a guest today.'

'No problem, sahib.' Iqbal took the second packet held out by the milkman and closed the door. He went into the kitchen and put the milk in the refrigerator. He was heading back to his room when Asif called out, 'I don't drink that much milk, you know.'

'That's fine, Asif, but you know how it is with tea and all.'

'Thanks, but there isn't much time for tea and all, Iqbal,' Asif said with a mysterious smile. 'We leave in two hours.'

'Oh.' Iqbal contained his dismay. 'Then I guess I'd better get my stuff ready and tell Tanaz to give us some breakfast.'

'Do that.' Asif stepped back inside and closed the door to his bedroom.

Iqbal had just begun to throw his things into his backpack and Tanaz was in the kitchen getting breakfast ready when the incongruous milkman returned to his destination. He held out the five notes to Ankita, who began to scan them under the special lamp kept beside her laptop. She found the note with the message immediately.

Asif here. Another strike today. We have no comm.

She was reading it aloud when the door reopened and Dhankar, who had gone out with the extrication team, entered. Sami was with him. The two of them read the note as well.

'So that's where Asif is!' Sami exclaimed. 'I guessed as much. Let me get the Old Man up to speed.' He turned and headed for the phone.

'You're looking good, Vikram,' Dhankar said with a chuckle as he watched Tiwathia climb out of his milkman's attire. 'You may like to consider this as a career option once we retire you.'

'Right!' Tiwathia grinned back at him. 'Good to know I won't starve when the time comes to hang up my boots.'

The two men laughed again, but their hearts were

not in it. They were both thinking about the woman and the man who were at that moment carrying the bombs, literally.

They didn't know which city would be targeted, where and how the operation would go, and how they would stop the terrorists. This time they wouldn't be able to sabotage the bombs to stop them from going off. They would have to find and defuse them, and do it in time.

SEVENTEEN

It was almost six in the morning when the 1033 Darbhanga Express from Pune pulled into Varanasi railway station the next day. As usual, Asif was first off the train and he led the way into the city. Despite the early hour, there were enough rickshaw-wallahs hanging around and they didn't have any problem reaching their destination near the Banaras Hindu University.

It was yet another ubiquitous, tiny two-room apartment, the kind often rented by students. Both rooms were bustling with an assortment of young men when the quartet from Pune entered. Iqbal was cursorily introduced to the four men who had not been with them during the Surat strike. Instinctively, Iqbal committed their faces, names and whatever else he could glean from them to memory. By now he was confident that a few moments were enough for him to churn out an Identikit picture and a reasonably accurate personal profile even several days later.

'Come on, Imtiaz,' Asif called out as the others settled down. 'Let's get this stuff together.'

'You're going to help me assemble them?' Imtiaz asked, sounding surprised and not too pleased.

'Sure! Any problem?' Asif held his gaze in a clear challenge.

'So!' Imtiaz could not contain his anger. 'You think what happened in Surat was my fault?'

'I didn't say that, Imtiaz,' Asif said brusquely, 'I just need to be sure that we get it right this time.'

'Fine! Suit yourself.' Throwing down his duffel bag, Imtiaz stalked across to the table where they would be assembling the bombs. The two of them began to work in uncomfortable silence.

From across the room, Iqbal watched the interplay between Asif and Imtiaz with interest. He was glad to see that the mistrust was no longer directed at him alone. *The fiasco at Surat must have really messed things up for Asif,* he thought, feeling pleased. *That Mujib bhai, whoever he is, must have really taken his trip... I wonder where the Force 22 team is.*

Iqbal, and because of him Asif, had been under surveillance from the time Iqbal had initiated emergency contact. Dhankar had followed them all the way from Iqbal's apartment to the railway station and onto the train. When the train pulled out of the platform, Dhankar was seated just two compartments away in the same bogie. The GPS locator in his mobile phone was powered by the phone battery and would keep working even if the phone failed for some reason.

Ankita was squashed between Sami and Tiwathia in a chopper flying a dozen miles to the right of the train. The chopper was too far to be seen or heard by anyone on the train, yet close enough to sweep in and deliver them to the desired destination, wherever and whenever Dhankar disembarked.

'It looks like they're heading for Varanasi,' Ankita said as the train swept past Allahabad, the last major city on that route. 'There's no other big stop en route.'

Sami leaned forward and studied the map. 'You're right. That sounds logical.'

Tapping out a fresh string of commands on her laptop, Ankita pulled up a detailed city map of Varanasi on the screen and began to study it intently.

'Is there anything special happening in Varanasi that we need to know about?' Tiwathia mused.

'Let me find out.' Sami reached for the horn and began to communicate with Khare at Kasauli. Finally he turned to the others in the chopper. 'In addition to the usual pilgrimage rush, the CBSE and ICSE board examinations are going on. Otherwise, it's just business as usual.'

'Fine! In that case, let's focus on the major temples,' Ankita replied. She studied the map quietly for a few minutes and then looked up. 'Damn! There are so many of them here.'

'Of course, didn't you know that? Why do you think they call it the temple city?' Tiwathia laughed grimly. 'Let's wait and see where these guys go to ground. That should give us a pretty decent idea of what they're planning to target.'

'Right! Meanwhile, let me activate the local ATTF and have them standing by with the BDS.'

'And with plenty of bomb blankets. This time we don't have GPS locators to help us find the bombs, so it's going to be touch and go. We need to be prepared for the worst case scenario.'

'True!' Ankita added sombrely. 'Let's just hope we're able to find the damn things in time.'

Silence fell upon the inmates of the chopper. Professionals that they all were, each one knew that in live operations things seldom went the way they should.

In such ops one can never tell what the blowback will be. Anbu's words as they had bid farewell to Iqbal at the start of the operation echoed in Sami's mind. *One can never tell which way things will blow... and who they will blow away.* Sami suppressed a shiver.

'Why not move in and take them all out?' Tiwathia wondered aloud.

'You know why, Vikram,' Sami said impatiently. 'Not until we identify the real brains behind the YPS and their conduit to the Pakis. Otherwise, this whole operation is meaningless.'

'I know,' Tiwthia said resignedly, but his eyes reflected his deep unease.

If they made a mistake the cost would be paid in blood – the blood of innocents.

Most of the others had dozed off by the time Asif and Imtiaz finished assembling the bombs. They used the same method as the previous time and the bombs were wrapped in similar blue-green pieces of polythene. The amount of explosive and shrapnel used in each was also the same; that was the only way Imtiaz and Asif had been trained to assemble bombs.

'Right, guys,' Asif called out as he stepped back from the table. 'Gather around.' One by one the bombers roused themselves and began to cluster around the table. 'This is what we're going to do.' Giving precise commands, he paired them off into teams and began to brief them over the large city map that had been pulled out of a tourist brochure and spread across the table. The briefing this time took much longer since they had not carried out a dry run or a reconnaissance earlier. 'As soon as you're done, I want all of you to head straight to the railway station and take the train to Delhi.'

'Delhi? Aren't we going back to Pune?' Imtiaz voiced the question before Iqbal could.

'No, we'll take the first train out and that happens to be the one going to Delhi. We need to clear out of the city immediately,' Asif explained. 'From Delhi, arrangements have been made for us to move back to our own cities.'

'Where do we stay in Delhi?' one of the others asked.

'Just head straight for Bardhan House.'

'The one near Jamia?'

'That's the one.' Asif nodded. 'You lot stay with Zia, he knows the way... it's his place.' Asif indicated five of them. 'You three,' he said, pointing at three others, 'will move with Nissar. The others – Imtiaz, Abid and Iqbal – will be with me. And if anyone gets separated, you know my number, get to a PCO and call me.'

'How about some money, Asif bhai?' Ashraf, the youngest of the lot, asked sheepishly.

'That's all you ever think about.' Asif gave him an almost playful grin. Ashraf was about to protest when Asif cut him off. 'Don't worry, I was just kidding. Here.' He reached into his bag and pulled out some bundles of five-hundred-rupee notes and began to dole out one half of each bundle to every man in the room. Iqbal hid his revulsion as he took the twenty-five thousand rupees that Asif gave him.

These guys are well funded for sure. I wonder who is doling out such huge chunks of money to them? Is it Mujib bhai? Colonel Anbu was right, we need to get to the root of it if we want to eliminate this group.

One by one the strike teams began to move out. Once again Iqbal found himself paired with Asif, so they were the last to leave the room. Asif subjected the apartment to a thorough scrutiny, to make sure that nothing incriminating had been left behind. Then, carefully placing the last bomb in his backpack, he led the way out of the apartment, locking it behind him. He hid the key in the flowerpot near the door and then they headed out. They hailed the first empty cycle rickshaw that went past and Asif told the driver, 'Railway station chalo.'

'Railway station?' Iqbal asked as he got in behind him. 'Aren't we going to first...' Iqbal stopped when Asif glared at him. Putting his mouth close to Iqbal's ear, Asif hissed, 'Just shut up and do what I tell you to.'

Iqbal subsided as the rickshaw creaked its way through the chaotic city traffic but his mind worked furiously around the possibilities of where they were headed and what might await them there. He suppressed a shudder as he remembered the destruction after the Sarojini Nagar bombings and he thought of Tanaz, by herself at home. Then he forced himself to focus on the present. Looking around at the city trundling past, he tried to spot any of the Force 22 officers. *Where are they?* he thought worriedly.

Try as he might, Iqbal was unable to shake off the dark sense of foreboding that nagged at him.

Dhankar had followed the terror cell moving with Asif from the railway station to the apartment without any problem. None of them was trained and all were complacent enough not to watch for a tail or any surveillance. Holed up in a tea shack across the road, from where he could keep an eye on the entrance to the apartment block that the terrorists had entered, Dhankar reported in to Sami.

The Force 22 chopper had already landed in Varanasi and the team had hit the ground running. Ankita had set up base at the nearest police station, where the local ATTF and BDS teams had also converged.

Sami and Tiwathia left immediately and linked up with Dhankar at the tea stall. Dhankar quickly brought them up to speed.

'There are fourteen of them, including Iqbal.'

'That means a minimum of seven targets or a maximum of fourteen,' Tiwathia surmised.

'I would say seven,' Sami said thoughtfully. 'From what Iqbal has told us, after what happened in Surat, Asif is not going to trust anyone to operate alone.'

They thought about that for a moment.

'I tend to agree with you,' Tiwathia finally concurred.

'Anyway, you two keep an eye on things here while I coordinate with the local cops. How long do you reckon we have?'

'The last team just got in twenty minutes ago, so I would say we have at least a couple of hours before these bastards go live. No! Wait! I don't think they'll execute in the afternoon. That's the lean time at most temples and wouldn't make much sense.'

'I think they'll target the evening aarti, that's when the temples are most crowded.'

'Makes sense.' Sami checked his watch. 'So that gives us at least four hours... three at the very least. That should be enough.' He got up and headed back to their temporary base. Despite the confidence he had displayed to the others, Sami was sweating; he knew that three hours were barely enough. There was too much to be done.

All likely targets had to be identified and covered with adequate troops. And all this had to be done discreetly. Neither the terrorists, nor the media or the public could get even a whiff of it. If it leaked, there would be total panic and the operation would blow. Sami arched his back, trying to rid himself of the stress he could feel starting to build. The surveillance teams would have to be in position to follow the terrorist strike teams whenever they moved out. Sami surveyed the area around the tea stall. It occurred to him that it wasn't the best place to plant surveillance teams. They would stand out like priests in a brothel. *We'll need a ton of luck to pull this one off.*

Luckily, they had a fair share of luck coming their way that day. The first lucky break was Shashank Pandey, the local ATTF boss. Pandey was a completely hands-on guy and one of the first city cops to receive specialized training in anti-terror operations. He was also a local Varanasi lad and knew every narrow lane that meandered through the temple city. The second stroke of luck was that the Varanasi BDS was up to speed and geared for such threats. When Sami walked into the police station, Ankita was busy plotting likely targets with them on the large city map that spanned the wall.

'What have we got so far?' Sami asked, taking charge of the situation.

'We have firmed up on eighteen likely targets,' Ankita said, pointing at the red thumbtacks plotted on the map all around the apartment where the bombers were holed up. 'There are fourteen more if we include the ones that are farther away and of course, the most obvious ones like the bus stations, the railway station, the court house, etc.' She indicated a second set of orange thumbtacks that were spread out farther away, around the red ones in the inner ring. 'As for when; we are guessing they will strike around –'

'– evening aarti time,' Pandey finished. 'That's when the crowd is at its densest and they can hope for maximum casualties.'

'That's exactly what we thought,' Sami replied. 'So what do you suggest?' he asked Pandey, deferring to the local man's knowledge of the terrain they were operating on.

'I suggest we deploy the BDS here, here and

here.' Pandey unhesitatingly pointed out a series of positions on the map. 'We should deploy the ATTF to cover the routes in and out of the safehouse they're using; that way we'll pick up the jokers when they move out and follow them to their destinations.'

'Fair enough. How good are your guys?'

'Good enough!' Pandey met his gaze calmly, understanding why the question had been asked and not taking umbrage at it. 'They'll get the job done.' There was a short silence before he added, still speaking in his quiet tone, 'I understand your concern, sir, but this is our town and we won't let any stupid bastards take it apart.'

'Good!' Sami felt a surge of confidence. 'Then let's do it. And remember, we have to be very careful that no one gets wind of this, especially the media.'

'Don't worry, they won't.'

The meeting broke up and a stream of orders began to flow out. Within minutes boots began to hit the ground. Quietly, without any fanfare, a cordon of security personnel spread out and began to take position, covering the potential targets. By the time the first terror bomber team had moved out of the apartment, the security cordon was in place.

The bombers left the apartment in pairs at intermittent intervals. No one spotted the surveillance teams that had carefully taken position behind them. As they moved out with their lethal cargo, a host of quietly whispered instructions went back and forth between the hunters, adjusting and realigning the security cordon as the destinations and targets of the bombers became increasingly apparent. Cameras equipped with long-distance lenses began to whir into action, recording every possible nuance of the strike, gathering the evidence that would one day help deliver these death merchants to the gallows.

Dhankar and Tiwathia were already in position at the railway station when the first of the bomber teams arrived after delivering the bombs. By the time the sixth team arrived at the station, the first three bombs had already been found and defused. The fourth and fifth bombs were defused just as Asif and Iqbal reached the station. Tiwathia was just a few feet away when Asif halted to make the phone call which, yet again, triggered the dispatch of the email threat by the wardriver in Mumbai.

However, as in any battle, things didn't go exactly as planned. The men following the sixth team lost sight of them when they were a hundred metres away from the Sankat Mochan Hanuman temple. By the time the surveillance team located the bomb, the timer was close to running out. With swift presence of mind, the BDS man threw a bomb-suppression safety blanket over the bomb and placed a bomb blanket around it. Then he quickly began to hustle people away from the site.

A bomb blanket is made of multiple layers of treated Kevlar ballistic fibre sewn into a fire retardant and water resistant cover. Depending on the type of material used, it offers varying degrees of protection by containing the shrapnel and fragments generated by the bomb blast.

The BDS man had just started shepherding people away when the timer on the bomb completed its stipulated run and unleashed the explosion. The bomb blanket minimized the impact of the explosion by reducing the shrapnel that shot out with the blast. Even so, the four people closest to it were cut down. One of them was the BDS man. In other circumstances he would have been shielded by the Kevlar jacket BDS personnel wear on operational duty, but today they had been ordered to dress in normal civilian clothing.

Asif and Iqbal were halfway across the platform when news of the blast came through. Asif paused briefly in front of the television before he ran towards their train which had just begun to move.

Dhankar and Tiwathia also saw the newsflash and it distracted them momentarily.

Shit! How did that happen?

They were distracted long enough not to notice that Asif had halted near a bench placed opposite the television. Barely stopping for a second, Asif lowered the bag he was carrying and shoved it under the bench before he resumed his race towards the train that had now started to pick up speed. Following a few steps behind him, Iqbal only realized that Asif no longer had the bomb bag slung over his shoulder when they were boarding the train. He looked back and saw Tiwathia and Dhankar jump into the bogey behind them. For a moment their eyes met. Tiwathia noted the desperate look in Iqbal's eyes, but it didn't register that Iqbal could be trying to tell him something. Their eye contact broke as both men were pushed inside as the last minute press of people tried to board the train and a shoal of red-shirted porters scrambled to get off.

Iqbal grew frantic as panic drove out all cohesive thought from his mind. He could see the bodies of his mother and sister in the carnage that would ensue when the bomb went off on the crowded platform. His mind was a blank. *How do I let them know? Should I just jump off and get to the bomb myself?*

But even that option ceased to exist as the train pulled away from the platform and gathered speed.

Should I pull the chain and bring the train to a halt? Should I tell Asif that I have to go to the bathroom and run across to inform Tiwathia?

He was still trying to figure out a solution when Asif tugged at his arm. 'Those are our berths. You sit. I need to go to the toilet.' He headed towards the end of the bogey, moving in the direction opposite from where Tiwathia and Dhankar had boarded the train.

The minute he was out of sight, Iqbal turned and began to push his way through the crowd of people trying to settle their luggage and themselves for the night ahead. Harried looks, frayed nerves, bawling kids, scattered bags and the unadulterated stench of people packed together like sardines made his progress maddeningly slow. It took all his willpower to stop himself from screaming at those who blocked the narrow aisle. Finally he reached the end of the bogey and lunged through the inter-connecting doors and yet another set of people. By now he was almost light-headed with anxiety. Then he suddenly spied Tiwathia on the lower berth, facing away from him.

Tiwathia was shocked when he felt someone grab his shoulder and looked up to see Iqbal.

'What are you doing here?' he hissed, quickly looking around to see if anyone was watching them.

Ignoring the question, Iqbal bent low and whispered in his ear, 'Asif planted a bomb somewhere near the television on the platform.' The shock on Tiwathia's face told Iqbal that his message had been received and understood.

Iqbal felt some of his panic recede. Turning away abruptly, he made his way back to his berth. The return journey was almost as painful, although some people seemed to have settled themselves down for the night, leaving the aisle clearer than it had been. However, Asif was already there by the time Iqbal finally managed to get back to their berths.

'Where did you go?'

'To take a leak,' Iqbal said casually.

'Fine.' Asif didn't seem perturbed. 'I'm going up to get some rest.' He climbed into the upper berth and appeared to fall asleep.

Iqbal collapsed into his berth, nearly paralysed with worry. *Would they get to the bomb in time?*

As soon as Tiwathia registered Iqbal's warning, he took action. Yanking out his phone, he called Sami.

'What? Are you sure?' Sami was stunned but he recovered quickly and asked, 'Which platform is it on?'

'Number two. To the right as you enter. There's only one television on that side of the platform.'

'Okay!' Sami cut the call and began to dial the BDS chief. *I only hope the nearest BDS team gets to it in time*, he thought.

It didn't. The BDS men were running towards the television set installed on platform two when the bomb detonated.

The mind-numbing explosion sent shrapnel slashing into the crowd, dropping dozens of people in their tracks. The corrugated sheet roof above the bench where the bomb had been placed blew several metres into the air before it hurtled down on the screaming crowd.

Even in the train, which was now almost six or seven hundred metres clear of the platform, the sound of the explosion boomed like a roll of distant thunder, jolting Iqbal. Clambering to the edge of his berth, he peered out the window. The glow of a dozen fires triggered by the explosion smouldered angrily in the distance.

That bastard! He must have set the timer for a really short time.

Iqbal's knuckles grew white as his grip on the window rail tightened. He could feel the rage gather within him. He looked down at his hands and imagined them clenched around Asif's throat. He knew they were more than adequate for the task. He nearly reached out, then stopped when he remembered that the mission was not yet over. They had to get to the people behind this murderous spree. They were the real killers, the people who funded, supported and used men like Asif, who were and would always be expendable.

Iqbal forced himself to take a deep breath and sank back into his berth.

EIGHTEEN

The sun was a big red ball of fire by the time Asif, Abid, Imtiaz and Iqbal crossed the city and reached Bardhan House from New Delhi railway station. Traffic was still light and they covered the distance in good time. The aging, badly maintained one-room set on the top floor of Bardhan House was yet another typical student accommodation. Zia and Nissar, who were enrolled at the nearby university, had rented it. The lower floors were occupied by three or four large families.

The solemn mood in the apartment deepened when Asif strode angrily into the room. The full details of the fiasco in Varanasi were on the front page of the newspaper that Asif had picked up at the first stop they had hit that morning. His frustration had begun to simmer with every word that he read about the failed strike. By the time the train reached Delhi, he was fuming.

'How the hell did it happen again?' Asif exploded as soon as he entered, tossing the newspaper down in front of the men seated in the room. 'What on earth have you guys been doing?'

'It wasn't our fault, Asif bhai,' the tempestuous Ashraf began to protest heatedly.

'Then whose fault was it?'

'You helped to assemble the bombs yourself, so...'

'Are you blind? There can be no doubt about it any longer; we have an informer in our midst.' Asif glared at the men gathered around him. Every one of them looked away, unable to meet his gaze. 'One of us has turned traitor. There can be no doubt at all. How else could the police have found every single bomb?'

'That's not entirely true, bhai. Two of them exploded.'

'Bullshit! Didn't you hear the news?' Asif shouted. 'The one in the temple was found and had been covered by a bomb blanket before it went off. That means they knew about it, but reached too late.'

'Well, the one at the railway station exploded.'

'That was the only one, you idiot,' Asif snapped at him. 'And possibly because no one knew about it except Iqbal and me.'

'Come on, bhaijaan, how...'

'Tell me, how else could it have happened?' Asif turned savagely on the man who had spoken. 'There is a traitor here and I intend to find out who it is.'

'Bhai, we have been with you for each and every

strike. How can you suspect us?' Ashraf and Imtiaz spoke simultaneously.

'So have I,' Abid joined in.

'I know. In fact, barring these three,' Asif glowered at Iqbal and the two men from Delhi, Zia and Nissar, 'all of you have been with me right from the beginning.' Automatically, the rest of the group moved away from the tainted three. 'You,' Asif pointed at Nissar, 'this is your first time with us so I don't know how involved you can be, but Zia and Iqbal, you two are the only common links between Surat and Varanasi.'

'Come on, Asif,' Iqbal said angrily, 'you can say what you want but you know for a fact that I was with you every minute during both missions. How can you blame me for anything? We have been together every minute of the day, right from the time you planned Varanasi.'

'Hmm!' Asif eyed him narrowly. 'And you?' He turned to Zia. 'What do you have to say?'

Guilty or not, the youngster cringed back in horror at the accusation. 'Come on, bhaijaan, why would I betray us?'

'You tell me,' Asif cut him off impatiently. By now everyone in the room was staring accusingly at Zia, who was whimpering as he pleaded with Asif, trying desperately to prove his innocence. Ashraf suddenly rushed at him and grabbed his collar. 'Tell us, you bastard,' he hissed. 'Why the hell did you...'

'Keep it down, you fool,' Asif hissed at him angrily. 'You want the neighbours to hear everything?' Just then Asif's phone buzzed. He snatched it out of his pocket and looked at the screen. It appeared to be a task reminder. 'Okay, listen guys, I need to go and make an urgent call. Meanwhile, you all lie low.' He glared at Zia. 'And I'll talk to you in detail when I return.' He turned to the others. 'Make damn sure he stays put until I get back.'

He was heading for the door when Iqbal called out, 'Can I also come with you? I need to call home urgently. Today was my wife's eighth month checkup. I need to know if all is well with the baby and her.'

Asif looked at him for a moment before he replied, 'Okay, come on.'

Imtiaz also piped up bravely, 'Can I come too, bhaijaan? I just need some fresh air.'

'Yes, yes! Anyone else?' he asked sarcastically. He stalked out with Iqbal and Imitaz behind him.

The noise level in the room began to rise the minute Asif left. Halfway down the narrow stone staircase, he looked up and grimaced. 'When will these fools learn? Bloody idiots!' He started to go back up, then changed his mind and continued on his way out.

They emerged onto the road from the alley and turned right, heading towards New Friends Colony instead of the university. It was a brisk ten-minute walk to the community centre market.

'Is this the closest PCO?' Iqbal asked, hurrying along behind him. 'I'm sure there's one in the market that we left behind.'

'There is, but I don't want to call from close to where we are staying. Why take a chance?'

'Okay, you two go ahead with your calls. I'll just take a walk in the market and then head back.' Imtiaz peeled away from them as they came to the market. Asif grinned as he watched him head straight for the Bikanerwala sweet shop in one corner of the market. 'Walk, my ass!' he grinned wickedly. 'That bugger just has to feed his face every hour. But that's not such a bad idea... maybe we'll join him for a bite after the calls.' He turned to Iqbal. 'What do you say?'

'Why not?' Iqbal shrugged. 'We have to eat some time.'

By now they had reached the PCO-cum-cybercafé at the opposite end of the market square. Asif dived into the telephone booth. It was a good fifteen minutes before he emerged and he didn't look happy. 'Go ahead,' he mumbled absentmindedly at Iqbal. 'I'll wait for you.'

Iqbal's call lasted five minutes. Speaking in an undertone, one eye on Asif who stood outside brooding, Iqbal gave Tanaz an update so she could pass on the information to Colonel Anbu. When he emerged, Asif was still standing near the booth looking distracted. Iqbal paid for both the calls and pocketed the bill. The details of the numbers called by Asif and Iqbal were on that bill.

Asif began to walk towards Bikanerwala when he saw Iqbal come out of the telephone booth and pay the PCO owner. 'Did you pay for both of us?'

'Yes.'

'Thanks. I'll settle with you.'

'No big deal, Asif. You can pay for the chhola batura and lassi I'm going to have now.'

They crossed the quadrangle in silence. Imtiaz smiled sheepishly when he saw the two of them enter.

'Come, join me. I was getting hungry so I popped in for a bite.'

Neither man bothered to reply as they joined him. In fact, the meal that followed was a silent affair with each one wrapped in his own thoughts.

About an hour had elapsed by the time they finished eating and began to walk back to Bardhan House.

They had just turned onto the road leading to Bardhan House when a crash of gunfire froze them in their tracks. There was a sudden surge of activity and the street ahead filled with policemen. Some were in uniform, some in plain clothes, but most of them wore body armour and they all had guns in their hands.

The people on the street scattered and ran for shelter as guns roared to life. Most of them raced for the safety of the shops that lined the road.

The three of them joined the crowd that had begun to gather.

'What's going on?' Asif asked one of the bystanders, who appeared to be the owner of the shop they were standing outside.

'Apparently the police have cornered some terrorists or gangsters there.' The man had to shout to be heard over another, louder burst of gunfire.

'Where?'

'There... Bardhan House.' He pointed down the alley radiating away from the road. 'That one... the greenish-yellow building in the corner.'

'Really!' Asif gave a low whistle. 'What happened? How did the cops find out about them?'

'Apparently there was some fight between the terrorists or criminals, or whoever they are. The neighbours heard them and alerted the cops.'

Asif glanced at Imtiaz and Iqbal. 'Must have been that idiot, Ashraf,' he murmured as the man left them to join the crowd.

By now the thunder of gunfire was almost continuous. It lasted a good nine or ten minutes and was immediately followed by the ululating wail of a dozen sirens. They watched as several red and white ambulances raced down the street heading for Bardhan House, their flashing lights dancing on the road.

'I think we'd better get out of here,' Asif whispered softly to the others as the ambulances turned the corner. Both men nodded in agreement and they began to move as unobtrusively as possible, retracing their way to the market they had just come from.

'How much money do you have?' Asif asked. 'Everything I had is in the bag back there.'

'I have everything you gave me in Varanasi.' Iqbal patted his pocket.

'Me too,' Imtiaz added, 'barring whatever little I spent on food.'

'Good. Then let's go straight to the airport and get the hell out of Delhi.' Asif began to walk faster as they approached the market. 'I knew those idiots would get into trouble one day, especially that fucker Ashraf, he has no control over himself... jumpy fucking bastard!' They walked in silence for a while and Iqbal heard Asif mutter to himself, 'I just hope the cops don't manage to take any of them alive, otherwise we are all screwed for sure.' *Cold-blooded bastard,* Iqbal thought viciously. *Human life has no value for him!*

With great difficulty, Asif managed to hail a cab going past and the three men began the long drive to the Delhi airport through the rush-hour traffic. Except for the sounds of the cars around them, the journey was silent and tedious, as was the late evening flight that they finally managed to catch.

It was almost midnight when the flight touched

down at Pune airport. They had just exited the aircraft and Asif had barely switched on his mobile phone when it began to ring. He grimaced and took the call almost reluctantly. Iqbal was unable to hear what the caller said, but the look of discomfort on Asif's face heightened at once.

'Mujib bhai, I have no idea how it happened.' Mindful of the crowd around him, Asif spoke in hushed tones after the caller's initial outburst subsided. 'We did everything...' Another explosion at the other end silenced him. 'Yes, bhai. I understand... really! You are? Okay, I'll meet you there at noon.' The call ended and Asif lapsed into a thoughtful silence.

The three men parted at the airport, after Asif had given them instructions for the next day. 'Let's meet tomorrow evening – we may have to go into action again pretty soon. Mujib bhai is very angry.'

'Who is Mujib?' Iqbal seized his chance.

Asif replied without thinking, 'He is the one who is helping us. He is...' He broke off suddenly. 'We'll meet tomorrow.' Then he turned and walked away. Imtiaz followed suit a moment later, leaving Iqbal to find another autorickshaw.

So, finally, the elusive Mujib is surfacing... we've really shaken them up. This is the best chance we'll have to round up the entire group – or whatever is left of it after today's shootout. I must get word to the colonel immediately.

Iqbal was soon racing up the steps to his

apartment. He told Tanaz what had transpired. Then they flicked on the television and caught the Bardhan House Shootout, as the media had named it. No one had been taken alive.

'So that is one wish of Asif's that has been fulfilled,' Iqbal said grimly.

Two cops had also died in the shootout. Iqbal was pondering this as he saw file-shots of bodies being carried out to the ambulances, when the realization suddenly hit him.

If we had not stopped to eat with Imtiaz, that could have been me they were carrying out of Bardhan House. Iqbal shivered. *I don't want to die. Not now, when I have Tanaz. Not when we are going to have our baby in just a few weeks. Not yet. A few more years with Tanaz and life will be complete.* He shivered again. *No! I don't want to die.*

Tanaz wrapped her arms around him, holding him tight.

'Don't you think you should call Colonel Anbu now?' she whispered, when she felt some of his stress lift.

Iqbal got up reluctantly and telephoned Colonel Anbu. He gave him a detailed account of all that had happened, from the time they left Pune.

'Good thing you were not in the house,' Anbu said sombrely when Iqbal had finished.

'I know, sir.'

For a moment both were quiet.

'Any idea where Asif has gone tonight?'

'No sir, he doesn't have any fixed place as far as I know.'

'Damn!' Anbu said. 'If we could latch onto him, we could take Mujib down as well and shut down this damn network once and for all.'

'I never thought of that, sir.' Iqbal racked his brains, trying to work out where Asif might be, but he could come up with nothing concrete. 'Now what?'

'Now nothing, Iqbal, you two just stay the course for a few days more, but be very careful now. I don't want either of you taking any unnecessary risks. I think we are very close to cracking this network wide open. In any case, we managed to get most of them in the shootout.' Anbu sounded satisfied. 'So don't worry, we'll lay our hands on the rest very soon now.'

'Right, sir.'

In his excitement Iqbal forgot all about the piece of paper lying in the pocket of his coat – the bill with the telephone number that Asif had called from the PCO in New Friends Colony. Had he remembered to pass on the number, it is possible that many lives would have been saved and the course of many others altered, for the number belonged to a mobile that sat inside Mujib's pocket, and Mujib was at that moment lying dormant in a guesthouse a few miles away. The mobile phone company would have led the cops to him within minutes.

But that was not to be.

NINETEEN

The next evening Asif looked agitated when he arrived at the coffee shop in Koregaon Park where they usually met. Iqbal and Imtiaz were already at their favourite corner table.

'We have to execute another job soon,' Asif murmured as he pulled up a chair and sat between them.

'So soon?' Imtiaz was unable to hide his surprise or his dismay. 'And how? We've lost almost everyone.'

'I'm activating some of the other guys who were recently recruited.'

'But those guys are absolutely fresh,' Imitaz protested. 'Is it safe to go in only with newcomers? What's the tearing hurry, Asif? Why don't we take some time out to consolidate and then start afresh?' Imitaz didn't realize it, but he was making tremendous tactical sense.

However, Asif looked too distraught to argue with him; perhaps he too, was unconvinced about the urgency, but unable to resist the pressure Mujib was mounting on him. This may have been why, at least for that moment, Asif spoke more freely than he normally did. 'I agree with you, Imtiaz, but it's not in my hands. Mujib bhai has made it very clear that we have to do it right away.'

'Who the hell is Mujib bhai to order us around like this?' Iqbal needled him. 'He's not the one putting his head on the line here.'

'Let me put it this way, Iqbal – he's the one who calls the shots. Even if he's not putting his head on the line, trust me, arguing with him or defying him will only mean that we're left without our heads.' For the first time, Iqbal heard a note of despair, or was it fear, in Asif's voice. 'And don't think he has nothing to lose. Mujib bhai is coming down for this strike.'

Imtiaz sat up straighter at this. 'Are you trying to tell us...'

'I'm not trying anything, Imtiaz, just understand that we have to carry out one more... task... and soon.' Suddenly becoming aware of the other people in the coffee shop, Asif checked his words.

'But why the hurry?'

'The papers are screaming that the Indian Mujahideen has been eliminated and there will be no more strikes.' Asif leaned forward and kept his voice very low. 'That's why Mujib bhai wants us to execute one right away; to let the world know that the Indian Mujahideen is a widespread national movement, it will not die just because some of our fighters have been killed. More importantly, Mujib says that if another strike takes place, our brothers can go to town yelling that the people who died at Bardhan House were innocent, that the police faked the encounter and shot down innocent students who had nothing to do with it.'

'That doesn't make sense to me.'

'It actually does, Imtiaz,' Iqbal cut in. *What a devious bastard this Mujib is,* he said to himself. 'Already some people and newspapers have begun to question the Bardhan House encounter. Another strike right now would strengthen their hands and allow them to claim that the real bombers are still at large.'

'Precisely!' Asif said, looking a little surprised that Iqbal was actually endorsing his stand. 'And this time we'll do things very differently, with a far greater aim in mind.'

'What do you mean?'

'Well, this time we'll be using low-grade bombs and the targets are going to be a real shocker.'

'Don't talk in riddles, Asif.' Imitaz was unable to hide his irritation. 'What's the point of using low-grade bombs?'

'Just to vary the modus operandi and confuse the police. They won't be sure how many groups are at work and which one is doing what.'

'Okay! And what targets are you talking about now?'

'I'll tell you about that later. Right now I need

to mobilize the others and coordinate our move to Delhi.' He stopped abruptly.

'Delhi?' Imtiaz repeated in shock. 'Are you crazy? Delhi will be in the highest state of alert after what happened yesterday. Have you gone...'

'No! On the contrary, they'll be fucking complacent after taking out what they believe is the complete cell. It's possibly the best time for us to hit Delhi again.'

'I think you've fucking lost it!'

'Anyway,' Asif snarled, 'this is not your decision, Imtiaz. If you want to back out, just say so.' He glared at Imtiaz, almost daring him to pull out. Momentarily subdued, Imtiaz backed off with a muttered 'whatever'. Asif waited a long moment, till he was sure that the mutiny had been nipped in the bud, before he leaned back in his chair. 'You two had better be ready to move out the day after.'

Imtiaz and Iqbal sat in complete silence for a long time after Asif left.

'I think they've gone crazy,' Imtiaz finally muttered, staring gloomily at his empty coffee cup. 'Delhi will be...' He broke off with a helpless shrug.

'What is a low-grade bomb?' Iqbal asked, more to flatter Imtiaz's sense of expertise and keep the conversation going than out of any real curiosity.

'Come on, let's get out of here. I need to take a walk and clear my head.' They walked out of the coffee shop and began to stroll down the street.

Imtiaz resumed, 'Basically, you just bung together some potassium nitrate and charcoal in a plastic or cardboard container. You can also add ball bearings or any other metallic scrap to act as shrapnel. The damn thing can be set off with a simple fire-lit fuse or with a detonator fitted to a timer.'

'So what's the big deal if they want to use them this time?'

'It's hardly worth the effort, man,' Imtiaz whined. 'You go through all the stress and danger and it doesn't do half the damage that RDX does.'

Thank god for that! Iqbal felt better for the first time that day.

'Where do you think we'll stay in Delhi this time?' he asked.

'I have no clue.' He mused for a while. 'Not at Bardhan House, for sure.' He giggled uncertainly, catching Iqbal by surprise.

The bugger is scared! But then, so am I.

They walked on in silence for some more time before Iqbal made his excuses and returned home. He was itching to get back and report to Colonel Anbu.

'Are you sure it's Delhi again?' Anbu asked when Iqbal had finished briefing him. 'Is there any chance that he is misleading you?'

'I think it's Delhi, sir, because it just slipped out of his mouth. But with Asif one can never be too sure. He is one devious bastard.'

'Okay, Iqbal,' Anbu replied after a moment's

thought. 'I think we've taken this as far as we want to. I am going to...'

'Sir,' Iqbal interrupted, 'please let's proceed with this just a little longer. We've got them on the run and I'm confident that this time, we can take Mujib down too. He's the key. If not the main supplier and financer, he is certainly the main conduit and the one who is allocating the targets and planning the strikes.'

'Hmm. What you're saying may be true, but I think we're playing it too close to the edge now. The additional risk isn't justified.'

'Please sir, just this last one,' Iqbal pleaded. 'We've gone so far and are so close to wrapping it up. Landing someone as important as Mujib is going to be a big blow to them.'

'That's true, Iqbal, but we may not be as lucky a third time. What if they manage to detonate the bombs?'

'Sir, right now we have a very fair chance of bringing them down without having any bombs go off, but if Mujib gets away he'll simply find more Asifs and then there'll be many more bombs exploding all over the place.'

'Hmm... yes, you're right.' Anbu rapidly evaluated the situation and made up his mind. 'Okay, listen, this is what we're going to do. Instead of trying to second guess Mujib and Asif, I want you to ensure at least one GPS locator is on you all the time from now on. Make sure it's a part of your clothing. I suggest you use the GPS belt, it's the most innocuous.'

'Right, sir.'

'Have you reset it since you last used it?'

'Yes, sir. Changed the battery too.'

'Excellent! Activate it only when you're sure you've identified Mujib and know where the bombs are.'

'Yes, sir. Unless, of course, the bombs are about to be deployed and I don't have an option.'

'That's right. Remember, Iqbal, the belt locator battery doesn't last very long.'

'I'll keep that in mind, sir.'

'Excellent! Delhi works well for us since we can have the whole team on standby and move in as soon as you activate the GPS signal. Since you say Mujib is going to be there, we can get the whole network and shut down the op... but I'm warning you again, Iqbal, it's becoming increasingly dangerous.'

'I'm aware of that, sir. Asif is now extremely wary. He's literally jumping at shadows. In any case, sir, Imtiaz and I are the only remaining links to the previous failed strikes, so we have no choice but to take them all down this time; they'll know it's me as soon as this operation fails.'

'I'm glad you realize that, Iqbal. We're very close to the endgame on this one. You have to be very careful now. Don't take unnecessary risks.'

'I won't, sir, please don't worry.'

'Good!'

Anbu didn't put down the phone when the call ended. He waited for the dial tone and made a series of other calls. One by one, the cogs began to move. Soon the various components of Force 22 began to converge in Delhi.

Anbu's second set of calls activated the ATTF and BDS teams. Slowly but surely, Delhi began to move to a heightened though silent state of alert.

In Pune, a frown marred Iqbal's forehead as he put down the phone and turned to Tanaz. Anbu's final words lingered in his mind and he was suddenly besieged by a sharp sense of unease. Tanaz caught the feeling instantly.

'What's the matter, Iqbal? Is something worrying you?'

'No, nothing really.' He tried to shrug off the feeling, not wanting to worry Tanaz.

'Tell me about it, Iqbal.' She touched his cheek in a gentle caress. 'What's bothering you?'

'I don't know, Tanaz, it's nothing specific... I just don't have a good feeling about this trip.' He shrugged again. 'I can't explain it... just one of those things, I guess.'

'Don't worry, Iqbal, things will work out.' She forced a bright, cheerful smile. 'They always do in the end.'

'I know. I know they will.' He smiled at her,

trying to embrace her optimism. 'But I don't feel good about leaving you alone this time.'

'I'm never alone, Iqbal.' Pulling him into the warmth of her embrace, she buried her face in his chest and whispered softly, 'Do you know, whenever you are away and I start to feel lonely or scared or upset, I just close my eyes and lean back in my mind and immediately, I can feel your arms around me, holding me close.'

Her words drove a hard, painful spike of love through him and his arms tightened around her. He was keenly aware of the anguish she suffered every time he left her alone and moved out on one of these trips. He knew that though she always put up a brave front, she worried herself to death as she waited for him to return.

Words eluded him as he tried to will away their fears and comfort her.

'Don't worry about me, Iqbal… just come back to me safe and sound,' she whispered as he tried to reassure her. 'And if you ever start feeling alone or low, just do what I do: close your eyes and lean back in your mind. I'll always be there to catch you, just as you catch me.'

'Promise me that!' He pushed back the tears and hugged her tighter. 'Promise me you'll always be there to catch me, and I'll be fine. As long as you are by my side, I can take on the world.'

'I promise. I'll always be there to...' Just then

the tiny life nestled in Tanaz's womb came awake and kicked. Iqbal felt the surge of life reach out and touch him. 'See!' Tanaz murmured, 'even our baby is telling us that everything will be fine.'

All at once, the need and time for words was past. But try as he might, sleep eluded Iqbal that night. Something told him they would all be caught by surprise with what lay ahead.

TWENTY

The first surprise was that they flew to Delhi, instead of taking the train.

'What's the deal, Asif bhai?' Imtiaz asked when he realized they were heading for Pune airport. 'How come we're flying?'

'Time is at a premium, miyan. Nothing else to it,' Asif said with a shrug. 'In any case, this time we are not carrying anything... problematic.'

'Who is getting it there then? Someone coming in from Kochi?'

'No! Not this time.'

'Then?' Imtiaz persisted.

'What's your problem, Imtiaz? Why are you suddenly so damn inquisitive?' Asif eyed him suspiciously. It was obvious that he was still upset about the recent failed strikes and trying to fathom the reason behind them. 'I told you it will be there, so it will be there. Why bother about who is bringing it and where it's coming from?'

'What the hell!' Imtiaz muttered angrily before lapsing into a sulky silence. And that was all the conversation they had for the remainder of the journey.

None of the three noticed Ankita watching them as they checked in, collected their boarding passes, cleared security and headed to the departure area.

Ankita waited for them to board the aircraft before she hurried out of the terminal. She was already dialling a number.

'Pankaj,' she told the BCAS (Bureau of Civil Aviation Security) Liaison Officer when he answered, 'the Indigo flight to Delhi is scheduled to leave soon. I want you to have it stalled for at least twenty minutes, if not more.'

'Consider it done.' Pankaj had already received orders to cooperate.

'But only do so when they've closed the doors and are about to taxi. I don't want anyone getting off,' she explained.

'No problem,' he assured her and then he rang off and called the Air Traffic Controller.

Meanwhile, Ankita made another call.

'Hey, beautiful!' Manoj answered at the first ring. 'How are you doing?'

'I'm good,' she answered, unable to stop the smile that lit up her face as soon as she heard Manoj's voice. 'They've moved out. We're also on the way now.' They chatted until she reached the vehicle waiting outside. Then she was speeding towards the Indian Air Force section of Lohegaon airport.

Sami, Tiwathia and Dhankar were already on board when she walked up to the waiting Force 22 jet. The smaller, slower aircraft lifted off immediately while the plane in which the terror team was travelling cooled its heels on the runway. So the hunters and the hunted landed at Delhi airport within minutes of each other.

The hunters made their way straight to the ATTF Ops Room in Delhi Cantonment and sat down to wait. Their eyes were glued to the screen as they waited for Iqbal to activate the GPS locator.

The end game had begun.

The second surprise was the man waiting for Asif and company at Delhi airport when their flight landed. Of medium height, with unremarkable features, the clean-shaven, thirty-something man was dressed in a decent, though inexpensive business suit. He looked so ordinary that nobody would give him a second glance.

'This is Khalid.' Asif introduced him to the others as they left the arrival hall and headed to the parking lot across the road. Because of the airport reconstruction work, the entire area outside the terminal was a mess of vehicles and people threading their way past worksites lined with steel-sheet barricades. Khalid led them straight to a maroon Maruti van in the middle of the parking lot.

'Has he reached?' Iqbal heard Asif ask Khalid

softly as he got into the front passenger seat and Khalid took the wheel.

'Yes.' Khalid kept his voice low too. 'We got in yesterday with the stuff.' Then he started the van and asked, louder this time, 'Where to first?'

'Have you checked out your site?'

'No.' Khalid shook his head. 'We had no time. You have no idea how crazy it has been. Mujib has been...'

'Then let's go there first,' Asif interrupted hastily.

'Okay, Punjabi Bagh it is then.' Khalid took several frustrating minutes to navigate out of the parking lot. Finally he got clear and turned left, heading towards Dhaula Kuan. Steering clear of the cantonment roads, where surprise security checks are always more probable, he finally got onto Ring Road and continued towards Punjabi Bagh.

Iqbal was still wondering where they were going when they got off Ring Road and slowed down on a crowded narrow street lined with cars parked on either side. Khalid nosed the car along slowly until he spotted a space and carefully eased the van into it. Just across the road from where they had stopped was a large metal gate with a blue and white signboard letting the world know that the said premises belonged to the Punjabi Bagh Club.

'You guys wait here,' Asif told the others as Khalid and he alighted from the van. 'We'll only take a few minutes.'

Imtiaz and Iqbal watched them walk away till they were lost in the swirling crowd.

'What a secretive bastard!' Imtiaz muttered, obviously still smarting from Asif's rudeness earlier that morning. Wanting to be alone with his thoughts and sensing that Imtiaz was bursting to start a conversation, Iqbal did not respond. He looked away, staring aimlessly at the signboard.

Ten minutes later, the two men returned. They were in animated discussion as they approached the car, but both clammed up as they climbed in. Khalid started the van and entered the traffic again. Asif had obviously told him where to go next since they drove in silence. An hour later, Khalid pulled over to the side of the road. They were on Sansad Marg.

'I can't park here, bhaijaan. The traffic cops will be on us in minutes.'

'Go and take a circuit then. Meet us back here in fifteen minutes.' Then Asif turned to Iqbal. 'Come on, let me show you your target.'

Filled with dread even as he itched with curiosity, Iqbal got out of the car and followed Asif down the road till they came to the Free Church.

The large, red and white brick church building was surrounded by a small, lush green lawn and exuded serenity. At this time of the day it was almost deserted, but with Christmas coming up there were a few youngsters, probably student volunteers, laying out decorations and cleaning up the area around.

'Don't go in yet, Iqbal. Take a walk around and get a feel of the place,' Asif said quietly when they were still on the other side of the road.

'What for? Is this where I have to...?' Iqbal asked, struggling to keep the horror out of his voice.

'Obviously! We're not here for a Delhi darshan, you know.' Asif was still surveying the church carefully. They took a slow, complete circuit of the church. Several bright, colourful canopies had been set up for the Christmas fete that would be held after morning service on the following Sunday. Also clearly visible were the large metal detectors at both entrances to the church. It was not hard to imagine the boisterous, bustling crowd that would gather there for the church service and fete.

'Why a church, Asif?' Iqbal asked softly as they walked away.

'Why not?' Asif stopped and looked at him searchingly. 'Any problem with that? You're not getting squeamish, are you?'

Iqbal couldn't think of a suitable reply so he shook his head and fell silent. Asif glared at him a moment longer before he resumed his march to the waiting van. Iqbal followed gloomily, a few feet behind, a conflicting herd of emotions stampeding through him.

An hour later, they pulled up outside the Free Church at the junction of Green Park, facing Aurobindo Market. From inside the van, Iqbal could see Asif and Imtiaz slowly circle the church. Barring the size of the building and the church compound – this one was almost one-and-a-half times larger – there didn't seem to be any difference between the two targets.

Here too, a number of bright canopy-covered stalls were being set up in the lawns around the church. Perhaps because the church campus wasn't large enough to house all the stalls, some of them were being put up in the area just outside the gates. The same kind of doorframe metal detectors stood sentinel over these gates too. Iqbal imagined the crowds that would mill around the stalls after the Sunday service and felt a renewed surge of anger. He watched the two terrorists walk back, engaged in conversation.

How can anyone be so damn casual about killing people, innocent people who have done nothing to harm them? For a second, Iqbal felt he couldn't control himself any longer. In the rearview mirror, Khalid noticed the flush on his face and misunderstood it. 'Relax, man. This is only a reconnaissance. There's no danger.'

'I know,' Iqbal muttered bleakly, still struggling to control the anger simmering within him.

'Yes, but tell me,' Imtiaz was asking Asif as they got back into the van, 'how do I get the... er... item past that metal detector?'

'I'll tell you in the evening. When you see the items, you'll understand.' After that vague explanation, Asif nodded at Khalid. 'Let's go to the base now. We have to get the items ready.'

All at once, the strike appeared more real and tangible. Suddenly death seemed so close that Iqbal felt he could reach out and touch it. He shivered as Khalid started the vehicle and drove into the traffic, heading through and then past the Green Park market.

Seated literally on the edge of the backseat, Iqbal began to fret about how he would get word out to Force 22. Without meaning to, he began to scan the crowd, hoping against hope that he would be able to spot one of them tailing the van. Sharp as ever, Asif noticed his scrutiny at once. 'Take it easy, miyan.' He nudged Iqbal casually in the ribs. 'No one is watching us.' The other two sniggered. Iqbal gave him a subdued smile and lapsed back into his thoughts. He was still worrying about where the Force 22 team was when they reached Bhikaji Cama Place. Just short of it, Khalid left the main road and turned left into Mohammedpur.

For one crazy moment Iqbal couldn't believe his eyes. He felt everything around him go still and an eerie sense of déjà vu overwhelmed him. From the depths of memory, the face of Omar floated into his mind.

Omar! The young man who had trained with Iqbal at the Lashkar camp at Muzzaffarabad, the only other terror recruit who had survived the ambush when they had infiltrated back to India after their training in POK, the man whom Iqbal had later tricked to his death at the Chakoti Pakistan army post.

Thoughts of the dead man and his home in Mohammedpur where Iqbal had spent a night flooded back to his mind, causing him to hyperventilate. He forced himself to breathe deeply but he only managed to relax when he realized they had entered the lane before the one that led to Omar's house.

Khalid dropped them off as the lane narrowed, then drove away while Asif led Imtiaz and Iqbal down the lane. They stopped outside the second last house on the lane, and Asif unlocked the door. Like Omar's house, this one also opened into a tiny, dingy courtyard with a grilled skylight on top. Several doors led out from the courtyard to rooms on either side. The paint on the walls was peeling and the accumulated dust spoke clearly of the fact that the house had not been occupied for quite some time.

'Wait here for a bit while I...' Asif broke off as he opened one of the doors and ushered Imtiaz and Iqbal into the room. 'I'll join you in a minute.' There was something surreptitious about the way he closed the door on them and walked away.

'Wonder what's with him,' Imtiaz remarked as he threw himself on one of the two dirty unmade beds that filled most of the cramped room. Puffs of dust billowed out as he hit the bed, making him cough and grimace. He sat up and began to brush the dust off the bed, causing it to rise up like a small cloud that quickly filled the entire room. Ignoring it as best as he could, Iqbal gingerly seated himself on the edge of the other bed, as close to the door as possible. He focused on trying to work out what was happening outside.

Asif seemed to have crossed the courtyard and entered the room opposite. Iqbal could hear muted voices but try as he might, he was unable to hear what was being said. Silently crossing over to the door, he eased it open a crack and peered out.

'What the hell are you doing?' Imtiaz stopped dusting his bed and exclaimed in surprise.

'Nothing. I just want to see what the hell he is up to.'

'Asif will kill you if he thinks you're spying on him. The bugger is crazy.'

'Hush!' Iqbal whispered. 'I'm just looking. What's wrong with that?'

Imtiaz collapsed back on his bed with a shrug as Iqbal turned his attention back to the narrow crack in the doorway and peered out.

Asif was standing in the courtyard talking to another man whose back was turned to Iqbal. He was taller than Asif, but that was all Iqbal could make out. As they talked, the man turned slightly and Iqbal finally caught a glimpse of his face.

The tall, dark man with saturnine features was similar to Asif in build and had the same nondescript air about him. The two men were engrossed in a muted but intense discussion that lasted for a long time. Suddenly the stranger's mobile phone began to chirrup; it seemed like either an alarm or a reminder, Iqbal wasn't sure. The man glanced at it briefly and clicked it off before he said something to Asif and then patting him on the shoulder, started for the main door. At the door, he paused and called over his shoulder, 'Remember, Asif, no fuckups this time. Okay?' Asif nodded grimly. 'Good!'

'Are you going back to Pune right away?' Asif asked, raising his voice slightly.

'No way! I'm staying right here till this is over. You guys go ahead and get the bombs ready while I take care of the vehicles with Khalid. I should be back in,' he checked his watch, 'about four hours.'

'You're coming with us?' Asif sounded genuinely startled.

'No, no, of course not, but I'll come back to check on the stuff, as well as go over the final details with you once again. I need to be very sure that this one goes down smoothly; otherwise my ass is grass... so, for that matter, is yours.'

'Fine, Mujib bhai.' For the first time Asif showed a trace of annoyance; perhaps he didn't like his capabilities being doubted. 'If that's what you want.'

So this is Mujib! Iqbal's mind captured the image of the man instantly, embedding it in his memory. *And he is going to be back in a few hours. Excellent!*

That gives the colonel enough time to move in and take him down along with the others. Iqbal felt a surge of satisfaction. *We've got you now, you bastard! Thank god! Soon this whole thing will be over and we can all look forward to...*

'All right then,' Mujib said, ignoring Asif's outburst. 'I'll see you around midnight.' He let himself out and was gone.

Iqbal quickly shut the door and had just sat down on the bed when Asif entered the room.

'Come on, guys, we need to get moving. There's a lot to be done.' He led them across the courtyard to the room outside which he had stood talking to Mujib. Throwing open the door, Asif gestured grandly. 'This is what we have to finish.'

The room was bigger than the one they had been allotted. Barring a large wooden dining table and six matching, though rather battered chairs lined up against the far wall, it was devoid of furniture.

The minute Iqbal laid his eyes on the items that had been arranged neatly on the table, he knew without doubt what Asif had in mind for the church bombings. And he was filled with a sudden dread that the plan was more than likely to succeed. With a sinking heart he stepped forward, taking care to retain a curious expression on his face.

'What's all this, Asif bhai?' he asked innocently.

There was a touch of pride in Asif's tone as he explained. By the time he finished, Iqbal's dread had hardened into an awful, gut-wrenching certainty. He realized that Mujib had indeed thought things through. The plan was so simple that it would almost certainly succeed.

'But why do we need so many of them?' Imtiaz interrupted Iqbal's chain of thought. 'I thought we were just placing three bombs...'

'Four!' Asif corrected him. 'You're forgetting that I'm here too.'

Crap! I wonder what the fourth target is. Not that it matters. Colonel Anbu's team will be here as soon as I activate the GPS locator. After that it will be of theoretical interest only. Iqbal tried to still his fears as he began to plot his next move.

'But we only checked out three targets today,' Imitaz persisted.

'Arre, miyan, forget all that and understand what we need to do now.'

Pulling his thoughts back to the present, Iqbal tried to focus as Asif began to explain, but his mind was in a whirl as he tried to figure out his own course of action.

'We are going to assemble the bombs,' Asif said to Imtiaz as he led them to the table. 'You,' he pointed at Iqbal, 'are going to decorate them. Make sure they all look the same.' He waited till both men had nodded in acknowledgement. 'Come on, let's get cracking. We only have till midnight to finish getting all the bombs ready.'

Imtiaz and Iqbal checked their wristwatches

automatically. It was just a few minutes after eight. Iqbal rapidly did the math; by the time Mujib returned, the bombs would be ready. He began to work out when he should activate the GPS.

'Do we have time to grab a bite before we start?' Imtiaz's legendary appetite intruded on his thoughts.

'Do you ever think of anything but food?' Asif snorted with laughter. Imtiaz started to protest when Asif raised his hand, cutting him off. 'Don't worry, I knew you'd need food. Come!' He led the way to another small room at the far end of the courtyard. It was the kitchen and not a very clean one at that; a graying 165-litre refrigerator leaned awkwardly against a black granite kitchen counter on which rested an old-style two-burner LPG stove. Asif opened the refrigerator and pulled out some food packets. 'Khalid has arranged for kebabs and roti… and knowing him, they're bound to be excellent.'

By the time they got down to work after heating up and eating the food, it was well past eight-thirty. Iqbal watched as Asif and Imtiaz began to assemble the bombs. Both men worked with trained precision. As Iqbal watched them, the sequence of events began to fall into place, his training at Kasauli coming back to aid him.

'Asif, where are the ball bearings and nails?' Imtiaz asked suddenly.

'Not required this time,' Asif replied.

Imtiaz looked at him in disbelief. 'What damage can we hope to do without any shrapnel?'

'Trust me, Imtiaz,' Asif said without looking up from the bomb he was working on. 'Just finish the damn things and leave the rest to me. The plan is good and in any case, without metal shrapnel it will be that much easier to get them past the metal detectors.'

Imtiaz returned to the bomb with an exasperated shrug, obviously dissatisfied with the incomplete explanation. Twenty-five minutes later, Asif pushed the first completed bomb towards Iqbal. 'Do your bit now.'

Iqbal used the assortment of items that Asif had purchased and began to decorate the miniature Christmas tree. Twenty minutes later, the three-foot high plastic tree had been fully decorated and looked exactly like the trees that most showrooms and hotels have on display during Christmas.

'Is that good enough?' he asked Asif, standing back and pretending to admire his handiwork.

'Add some more of those mini Santas and stuff,' Asif said after examining the finished product minutely. 'There! That's much better,' he added a few minutes later, when Iqbal had complied.

'How are we going to trigger them?'

'I'll be doing that with my mobile. Just one text message or call to that phone buried in there,' he pointed at the pot in which the Christmas tree was planted, 'and boom...' He unclenched his palms and threw his hands upwards.

'What a caller tune that will be!' Imtiaz gave a neighing laugh.

Asif laughed and clapped Imtiaz on the back. 'Good one, that!' With an effort Iqbal joined in the laughter, controlling his horror and disgust.

They were midway into the fourth bomb when Iqbal looked at his watch. It was nearly half past eleven. He knew it was time to activate the GPS locator. That way Mujib would be with them when the Force 22 team moved in.

'I'm just going around the corner.' Iqbal made for the door.

'Too many kebabs, eh!' Imtiaz said with a crude laugh.

'It's the last door at the end of the courtyard.' Asif pointed after he had finished laughing. 'The light switch is just outside, to the left of the door... oh, and the door doesn't lock.'

'The door doesn't lock?'

'What difference does it make? It's only us here. What have you got that we don't?' There was another burst of laughter.

Laugh all you want, you morons. Just one hour more and you will be singing to a different tune. Iqbal cursed them as he made his way to the bathroom at the end of the courtyard. Not only did the rickety metal door of the bathroom not lock, the stink in the tiny, filthy cubicle was unbearable. Blocking his nose with one hand, Iqbal pulled the door shut and held it closed with his foot as he removed his belt.

'You have to turn the buckle clockwise once, then counter-clockwise thrice and then clockwise one last time. That will activate the GPS locator in the buckle.' Iqbal kept Dhankar's instructions in mind as he carefully removed the belt from the loops in his trousers.

'Why all these twists and turns?' he had asked Dhankar.

'To ensure it's not activated by mistake.'

'And how will I know it has come on?'

'You won't.'

'Actually, you will,' Tiwathia had said with a laugh. 'When we beat down the door and kick the bad guys' asses, you'll know all right.'

They had all laughed at that. Now Iqbal caught hold of the buckle and began the activation sequence. He was starting to make the final clockwise turn when there was a sudden pounding on the door.

'Hey! If you're done, I'd like to go too.' Imtiaz's yell and the bang on the door startled Iqbal. The door almost flew open and he had to lunge forward to keep it closed. As he did so, his hand twisted and he looked down in horror to find that the buckle had snapped free from the belt.

'Hang on, miyan.' Iqbal struggled to keep his voice even. 'I'm almost done... another couple of minutes.'

'Okay, but hurry up, yaar,' Imtiaz grumbled and

began to pace the stretch of courtyard outside the toilet.

Iqbal couldn't believe his eyes as he examined the broken buckle in his hand. His heart was thudding. *Damn! Damn! Damn! How on earth did this happen?* Then he spied the tiny wire running out from the broken buckle. *Shit! If these buggers see it, I'm dead.*

Hurriedly, he removed the tiny GPS locator inside the buckle and the cell that powered it. Dropping them in the Indian style commode, he flushed the toilet. He waited for the water to settle and checked that nothing was visible.

Okay, so that's one problem solved. But how the hell do I get word out to Colonel Anbu?

'Are you done?' Imtiaz called out again.

'Coming, coming,' Iqbal replied irritably. He was about to step out when he realized he was still holding the belt and broken buckle in his hands.

Asif might notice something... he is so suspicious about everything.

The tiny ventilation hole in the rear wall came to his rescue. In better days, it had probably housed an exhaust fan to keep the air fresh inside the toilet. Right now it was just a gaping circular hole, eyeing the silent darkness outside. Iqbal knew it would open onto the alley at the rear of the house.

He chucked out the belt and buckle and finally emerged from the bathroom, making a show of tucking his shirt into his trousers. 'Go!' he told

Imtiaz, who was pacing outside impatiently, and made his way back to the room with the Christmas trees, his mind in a tailspin. Luckily, Asif was so preoccupied with putting together the last bomb that he didn't notice anything untoward.

'Come on,' he said cheerfully, clearly very pleased with their progress, 'we're almost done. Just dress that up while I finish this last one.'

Iqbal put his hands to work, mechanically tagging on the required decorative items as his mind went over the options available to him. He knew Asif wouldn't allow him out of the house. Suddenly realizing that he was completely on his own, he felt his heart sink and a sense of helplessness swept through him. Tiwathia's words of caution came back to him.

'Remember that the undercover operative must always be fully self-reliant in every respect.'

'So basically we are going to be totally on our own.'

'That's the only way to look at it.'

Iqbal cursed to himself. He knew he had to somehow disable the bombs himself. He had begun to apply his mind to this new thought when Asif stood up and stretched. 'That's it then. You finish this and we're done for the night.'

'Okay.'

Just then Imtiaz returned. 'We're done here; now Iqbal just has to complete the camouflage,' Asif told him proudly. 'Tell you what, why don't you get some tea and snacks ready while I go and lighten the load too.' He patted his belly, a satisfied expression plastered over his face. 'Then we can all get some rest.'

'Excellent idea!' As always, the thought of food enthused Imtiaz. 'There are still some kebabs left.' He headed for the kitchen and Asif went to the bathroom, leaving Iqbal alone with the bombs. He knew this was his best chance.

Iqbal thought back frantically to what Dhankar had told him about disabling bombs.

'When a mobile phone is used to trigger a bomb, it's switched on only at the time the bomb is actually being deployed.'

'Why? Why not do it earlier when there are no prying eyes around?'

'Right!' Dhankar had given a short laugh. 'Can you imagine what would happen if some pesky telemarketer decided to call that number to make some asinine sale?' He laughed again. 'That would be pretty funny, wouldn't it?'

Without further thought Iqbal pushed his fingers into the flowerpot in front of him, and gently pulled out the mobile phone buried in it. Sliding open the back cover of the phone, he withdrew the tiny white SIM card, inverted it and re-inserted it. Then he replaced the phone cover and pushed it back into the pot. With the contact broken, Iqbal knew that no calls or messages to the phone would go through; the bomb was as good as dead.

Groping inside the pot of the second tree, he repeated the same procedure. He had just buried the fourth phone back inside the pot when he realized that he could have used one of those phones to get word out to Colonel Anbu. For a moment his hands paused as he thought it over quickly; talking was no good, they would hear him, but he did have the option of sending out a text message. It seemed doable. He was just reaching back into the pot when he heard Asif returning from the bathroom. He quickly pulled out his hand and headed for the door, emerging just as Asif came up to it.

'You done?'

'All done.' Iqbal's heart was pounding wildly, as much at the close call as at the missed opportunity.

'Okay, then let's go and grab a bite.'

'You go ahead. I'll just wash up first.' Iqbal needed to be alone for a minute. His heart was pounding so hard he was sure Asif could hear it. He headed for the washbasin in the corner of the courtyard. The cold water delivered him to the present with a snap, bringing some semblance of normalcy.

When he went back to the kitchen, Asif was saying something to Imtiaz. The minute Iqbal walked in, he broke off and moved away. It was the way he did it that raised Iqbal's antenna immediately. He knew they had been talking about him and Imtiaz's shifty demeanour only confirmed his suspicion.

Iqbal wondered what they had been talking

about. *Did they see me when I was working on the mobiles? Are they onto me?* he thought wildly.

'Come on, Iqbal, grab a bite.' Asif gestured at the food on the kitchen counter. 'Imtiaz has heated it up for us.'

Pushing away the nagging worry and pretending he had not noticed anything, Iqbal forced himself to eat. But the hot, succulent kebabs tasted like cold ash in his mouth.

They had just finished eating when Asif's phone rang. As usual, he moved away from them and answered.

'Haan bhai,' Iqbal heard him mutter. 'Yes, they're all done... okay... sure. No problem, I'll wait for you.' He ended the call and turned to them. 'Right, guys, let's get some rest.' He threw a quick look at his wristwatch. It was just a shade after midnight. 'We hit the road sharp at seven-thirty tomorrow.'

'You mind explaining the programme to us?'

'Sure I will, Imtiaz, but tomorrow morning. Right now, I have other stuff to catch up on.' With that he hustled them away to their room.

Imtiaz didn't take long to fall asleep. Iqbal lay in the bed next to his, trying to prevent himself from tossing and turning. The fact that he had managed to defuse the bombs didn't bring the sense of relief that he had hoped for. Instead, something kept nagging at his mind. He was unable to put a finger on it, but he couldn't push away the feeling that something was seriously amiss, that he had missed something critical.

Damn! Had it not been for this idiot, he glared at the man sleeping on the other bed, *Colonel Anbu and his team would have been here by now and this operation would be over. Now, even if I manage to alert him in the morning, we won't be able to take down that bugger, Mujib. All this effort will go to waste.* Suddenly, another thought struck him. *What if they stick someone else onto me tomorrow morning? Then how will I get word out at all?*

This new worry was beginning to gnaw at him when he heard the main door open. He could hear three or four people moving in the courtyard and in the room where they had been making the bombs. Though he tried hard to make out what they were saying, the unseen men kept their voices very low. Iqbal fought the temptation to stand at the door and eavesdrop again. He knew that if they caught him, they would take him apart mercilessly.

The muted commotion lasted a good half hour before he heard them exit, and silence returned to the house once more. A moment later, he heard footsteps coming up to the door. He closed his eyes and pretended to be asleep as the door opened and Asif looked in.

Asif examined the two sleeping men for a moment before he shut the door again and moved to the adjacent room. And Iqbal returned to his relentless fretting.

'Rest is a weapon,' Dhankar had told him more than once. 'The body needs rest far more than it needs food. Make sure you give it that rest whenever you get the chance.'

Knowing that there was nothing else he could do right now, Iqbal closed his eyes and willed sleep to take over.

Tomorrow is another day, another battle. It will all be over tomorrow, Inshallah.

TWENTY-ONE

The loud, incessant knocking on the door woke Iqbal with a start. He opened his eyes to see that shards of daylight had crept into the room through the curtained window.

'Come on guys, rise and shine. Time to get cracking.' Asif's voice was loud as he sauntered in. He was already dressed and looked all set to go. 'You two have half an hour to get ready... and make sure you shave and put on your Sunday best. Remember, we're going to church today.'

Twenty-five minutes later, when Iqbal and Imtiaz entered the kitchen, Asif was there with Khalid. He started off without any preamble.

'Right! This is what we're going to do. We'll load one Christmas tree, a few dozen plum cakes and some chocolate fudge packets in each of the four Maruti vans parked outside. Also, one Santa Claus outfit each – make sure you carry one that fits you properly.'

'You never said we would have to wear fancy dress!' Imtiaz exclaimed.

'Can you think of a better disguise?' Asif shot back. 'Just close your eyes and think of what you would say if you were asked to describe a man dressed as Santa Claus. And give some thought to how people react when they see a man dressed as Santa.'

'I see what you mean.' There was grudging admiration in Imtiaz's voice. There was no doubt about it, all Santa Clauses looked pretty much the same and any attempt to describe one was not likely to go beyond red clothes, a red cap and a big white beard. And most people would view them with amusement rather than suspicion. 'It's perfect.'

'I know it is!' Asif said cockily. 'Imtiaz, you'll take the first van and drive to the Green Park church. Stop en route at a suitable place and put your Santa outfit on over your clothes.'

'Why not do it right now?'

'Just a precaution. I don't want anyone associating the clothes with this house.'

'I see.'

'Park the van in the area I showed you yesterday. You must try to keep it as close to the church gate as possible. Get the plum cakes and chocolates out and head for stall number seven – that's the second one to the left as you enter from the main gate. It has already been booked and paid for by one of our people.'

'What if the security guards want to check the packets?'

'Don't wait for them to ask you. Instead, I want you to start opening the boxes and showing them to the security on your own... in fact, you could even offer one of the cakes or a box of chocolates to them... spreading Christmas cheer, as it were. Okay?' He waited till Imtiaz nodded.

'Once you've got all your cakes and chocolates on the table in your stall, come back and take the Christmas tree from the van. With the tree already assembled, it's going to be just a little too wide to go through the doorframe metal detector. Make a show of trying to push it through and then, with the right apologies, walk it around the detector.'

'What if the cops don't allow me to take it in, or want to check it properly?'

'That's the only thing you have to avoid. If they start insisting, then grumble about not wanting to spoil it and just cart it back to the van and leave it there.'

'What happens to the plan in that...?'

'Nothing,' Asif cut him off. 'Just allow me to finish.'

'Okay.'

'If you manage to get the Christmas tree inside, place it just behind the desk so that the top of the tree is visible, but you are able to dig out the phone from inside the pot and switch it on without being seen. Got it?' Imtiaz nodded. 'Good. Now, between 0900 and 0915 hours, activate the mobile phone in the pot, head for the bathroom, get rid of the Santa outfit and leave the church quietly. As soon as you're out, head for the nearest taxi stand and get out of there. You got that?'

'What if I haven't been able to get the tree in and it's still in the van?'

'Even then, by 0915 hours you must get rid of the Santa dress, get back to the van and switch on the phone. But in this case, I want you to stop at the nearest phone booth and let me know.'

'Okay! That sounds simple enough. Where do I go then? Come back here?'

'No! You head back to Pune immediately. Your return ticket is in this.' Asif tossed him a sealed envelope. Imtiaz was starting to open it when Asif stopped him. 'No. You do that when you're alone. I don't want anyone to know anyone else's escape route. That way, all of us don't get compromised...'

'...in case any one of us is taken,' Imtiaz completed the sentence for him. 'Yeah, yeah, we know that.'

'Fine. Now you,' he turned to Iqbal, 'will follow the same procedure as Imtiaz here except that you will head for the stall on the extreme right, the one closest to the main door of the church. It has a yellow canopy and a signboard with "Cakes and Chocolates" tagged on the front. Any doubts?'

Iqbal shook his head after a moment's thought, trying to visualize the position of the stall on the mental map he had of the church. 'None,' he said.

'Fine. The rest of your drill is exactly the same.

Now, are you both sure of your route from here to the target?' Both Imtiaz and Iqbal nodded. 'Even so, just to prevent any hassles, keep these.' He tossed two Garmin GPS navigators at them, one for each man. 'Both have been preset and your routes plotted on them. All you have to do is switch it on and follow the instructions.' He leaned out and switched on the one in Iqbal's hands. 'Okay?'

'Boy! You're really well prepared this time, Asif,' Imitaz said with a chuckle as he fondled the sleek navigation device in his hand. 'Do I get to keep this after the mission?'

'Keep it,' Asif said with an exasperated sigh. 'You guys have enough money on you?' The two men nodded.

'Fine.' Asif handed over another envelope to Iqbal. 'That's your return ticket.' He turned to Khalid. 'And you already have yours.'

Khalid responded with a smug smile; obviously, he was the one who had booked the tickets.

'Now guys, remember the key points; first, you have to get in early so that the parking lot is not full and you can park as close to the church gate as possible; second, make sure you put on your Santa outfit before you reach the church; third, be very polite and helpful, not just to the security staff but to everyone you meet there. Remember that you are supposed to be full of Christmas cheer and you're selling this stuff to raise money for charity. Fourth, do *not* activate the phone in the tree till you are entirely ready to move out. And finally, the minute you get clear of the church, take the first available transport and get the hell out of Delhi.'

'What happens once we've done our bit? Who does the final activation?' Imtiaz was not one to stop till all his doubts were cleared.

'Oh, it's really very simple. At 0945 hours sharp, I'll send a group text message to all four mobile phones. That will trigger off the explosions.'

'But what good will that do?' Imtiaz protested. 'We're using low-grade bombs and there's no shrapnel in them. There will be hardly any casualties.'

'Patience, miyan,' Asif said with a broad smile. 'They are not meant to cause casualties. The explosions will simply drive people in a rush towards the church gates. In the ensuing panic, there will be a stampede and not only will some more people get hurt, but the gates will get blocked. While they're trying to get people moving away from the church, just a few minutes after the first explosion, I'll send out the second text message and the bombs planted in the vans will go off. These are RDX-based and there's enough masala in them to take out half the parking lot.'

Iqbal felt himself go very still as he realized he had been outwitted. Screwing up the tree bombs would minimize casualties but not by much.

Through the haze enveloping him, Iqbal heard Imtiaz ask, 'What if the tree is still in the van? Won't that...'

'That's why you must let me know if you haven't been able to get the tree into the church. In that case, I'll simply activate the bomb in the van directly. Even that will be more than enough...'

The rest of the conversation was lost on Iqbal as he tried frantically to think ahead.

Khalid's target is obviously a church in Punjabi Bagh since he is carrying a Christmas tree bomb too, so that shouldn't be too hard to find. How many churches can there be in Punjabi Bagh? And it can't be far from where we parked yesterday, since they were only gone a few minutes.

Iqbal visualized the route they had taken and the place where they had parked the van. The Punjabi Bagh Club signboard was sharp in his memory. He was confident he could guide people there easily. But Asif's target remained a mystery to him.

'Come on, Iqbal! Where are you?' He came to with a start as Imtiaz thumped him on the back. 'Let's go.'

'I was... I was just trying to figure out if there's some other way to get the tree into the church,' he said, trying desperately to deflect the attention from himself.

'And?' Asif was watching him closely.

'No! Nothing!' Iqbal shook his head lamely. 'I think you've pretty much covered all the possibilities.'

'Fine.' Asif gave a satisfied smirk. 'Let's get moving then.' A flurry of activity ensued as the four men selected their costumes, divided up and loaded their materials into the four vans parked outside. At precisely 0732 hours, the first man, Khalid, kicked off since he had the farthest to go. Iqbal went next, a few minutes later.

Accelerating out of the narrow Mohammedpur lane, Iqbal turned left on the main road and headed straight down Africa Avenue. After crossing Ring Road he would go past the old Chanakya theatre till he hit the T-junction at Ashoka Hotel. There he would swing right and continue straight ahead to Sansad Marg after crossing Race Course Road. As it was a holiday, the traffic was reasonably light and Iqbal made it in very good time. Even the traffic light at the Ring Road intersection was green, saving him a precious couple of minutes.

As soon as he had crossed the red light, he moved over to the kerb and brought the van to a halt. He climbed into the back and hauled out the mobile phone from the base of the tree. His fingers were trembling as he removed the cover, reversed the SIM card and powered up the phone again. He began to dial Anbu's number.

You do not have sufficient balance to make this call, an impersonal voice informed him. Cursing, he threw down the phone on the co-passenger's seat and drove off again. He would have to find a phone somehow.

He was driving past the Chanakya complex when he spotted the familiar colours of a black and yellow ISD-STD signboard; it stood out prominently amidst the bilingual signboards on which Russian and English showed up with equal prominence. Taking a hard left, he pulled into the Yeshwant Place parking lot. Throwing a ten-rupee note at the parking attendant, Iqbal ran towards the telephone booth.

It was not open.

Iqbal raced back towards the parking lot like a madman.

'You have a mobile?' he asked the attendant. The man nodded; these days, everyone had one.

'Can I borrow it for one minute? Please! It's an emergency. I can pay you.' Iqbal reached for his wallet with shaking fingers, his chest heaving not so much from the exertion as from the rapidly escalating stress.

'You can, but I don't have any balance on my phone.' The man pulled out his phone and held it up. 'But maybe he has.' He pointed at his assistant, who was hovering at the other end of the parking lot. 'Oye, you have balance on your mobile? He has an emergency.' He jerked his thumb at Iqbal.

'Haan, I do, but very little.' The man strolled up towards them casually and pulled out a mobile phone from his pocket.

'It will do. I just need it for one second.' Iqbal's hands were shaking as he stuffed some money into the man's hands, grabbed the mobile from him and dialled Anbu's number.

Ring! Ring! Come on, damn it! Hurry up!

It was precisely 0803 hours when the phone began to ring and Anbu, who had been restlessly pacing the floor of the ATTF Ops Room, answered.

'Iqbal! Where are you? We've been trying to...'

'Sir, there's no time. I want you to call me back on this number immediately. This phone has no balance left.'

'Okay.' Anbu grasped the situation immediately. 'End the call.'

The phone in Iqbal's hand began to ring almost as soon as he had disconnected.

'Sir, they've already moved out and...' In a rush, Iqbal brought the colonel up to speed, giving details of the church that Imtiaz was targeting and the directions to Khalid's target. 'It can't be more than a couple of minutes away from the Punjabi Bagh Club.'

'Okay! Got that! And you have no idea where Asif is headed?' Anbu asked as he rapidly made notes and assimilated the details.

'No, sir, not the faintest.'

'And Mujib?'

'No clue, sir.'

'Fine, now listen.' Anbu had already weighed the options available to them. 'First, we need to focus on preventing the strikes. We can have the Green Park church and the one at Punjabi Bagh covered well in time. You stay where you are till I send someone there to defuse the bomb in the van.'

'And what about Asif, sir?'

'We'll simply have to cover the major churches and hope for the best, Iqbal.'

'But what if...'

'There's no time for that now, son,' Anbu cut him off urgently. Then, realizing the state of Iqbal's mind, he added more gently, 'You've done a fine job, Iqbal. Now stand by till Dhankar reaches you.' Disconnecting the call, Anbu started the counter-attack immediately.

Within minutes the Force 22 officers had swung into action. The ATTF and BDS teams were not far behind. Ever since they had assembled in Delhi, they had been on tenterhooks, waiting eagerly for that tiny blinking light that would guide them to Iqbal and their unsuspecting quarries.

The wait was finally over, though not in the manner they had hoped for.

Dhankar and Tiwathia were lucky to get a clear run from the ATTF base in Delhi Cantonment and reached the Yeshwant Place complex at precisely 0828 hours. They found Iqbal in the parking lot, pacing around the van feverishly.

'Let's get this damn thing out of here.' Tiwathia got into the van with Iqbal and they headed out of the parking lot, Dhankar following closely behind. 'Head for Nehru Park, that should be isolated enough.'

A mile or so along the road, Tiwathia pointed at

a narrow service lane running along one side of the park. 'There, that should be okay. Pull up.'

Six more minutes had elapsed by the time Iqbal brought the van to a stop in the almost deserted service lane. Dhankar halted behind him and ran forward with his tool kit. Popping open the hood of the van, he first disconnected the battery terminals and then began to scour the van, starting from the front. Almost instantly, he spotted the additional wiring that had been jury-rigged for the bomb. Finding the bomb did not take more than a minute. Disarming it took five.

'Now let's get back to the base,' said Dhankar as he emerged from the van, wiping his hands on his jeans and beating the dust off his clothes.

'Any idea if they've located Asif yet?' Iqbal couldn't help asking. 'And what about the others...'

'Don't worry about it, Iqbal. We're doing everything we can.' Tiwathia pushed him into the van. 'Let's go.'

There was no point in explaining the obvious to Iqbal – that finding Asif in the short time available could be close to impossible. Delhi had an abundance of churches; almost all of them had Christmas carnivals and fetes on today. Finding Asif was going to be a real challenge and would require more than luck.

Taking down Imtiaz and Khalid, of course, was going to be easier.

Imtiaz was about to head for the bathroom to get rid of his Santa outfit when Khare and Katoch came up from behind and pinned him down, much to the consternation of the people milling around the colourful stalls. Imtiaz saw the cold, pitiless look in the eyes of the men holding him and realized the game was over. He went without a fight.

'Which van is it?' Khare prodded him with his handgun.

'What van?' Imtiaz tried to keep his face expressionless.

The handgun slammed into his collarbone with a thud, driving him down to his knees. Though no sound escaped him, tears of pain swam into his eyes. 'Don't fuck around, shithead,' Khare snarled. 'We don't have time for these games. Which one is it?'

'That white one over there,' Imtiaz croaked, pointing with a shaky finger, trying to press down the pain in his almost certainly fractured collarbone with the other hand.

There were still four minutes left for nine o'clock when the bomb in the van was defused and the vehicle driven away to the safe confines of the nearest BDS compound.

Khalid did not go down without a fight. He tried to break free and run when Deopa and Vashisht closed in on him. His brief flight for freedom lasted until the butt of Deopa's pistol slammed down on his head. Knowing they needed him alive and awake until the bomb was found, Deopa had aimed the blow at his upper body, but in the struggle, it landed bang on his head. In the heat of the moment, Deopa struck much harder than he had intended to and Khalid went down as though he had been poleaxed. There was only one minute left for nine when he fell unconscious to the ground.

'Shit! What did you have to do that for, dumbass? We needed him awake to tell us which van the bomb in is.'

'Sorry! I didn't mean to, but the fucker moved...'

'Bugger it. Let's get to the parking lot. How many vans can there be?'

There were sixteen; after all, the moderately priced Maruti van is a cost-effective option for the large Indian family. It took almost as many minutes for the BDS people to sweep through them. Even then, it was just 0914 hours by the time they located the bomb and rendered it harmless.

'Luckily the morons had not booby-trapped the bombs,' the sweaty BDS man remarked as he finally emerged from the van, throwing off the heavy protective gear he was clad in.

Three of the four strikes had been neutralized. That left only one unaccounted for.

Where the hell can he be? The thought gnawed at Anbu as he paced the floor relentlessly, listening to the stream of reports pouring in on the ATTF Ops Room radio set. He knew they had to find Asif. The alternative was too terrible to contemplate. But the hardened combat veteran also knew that it was a mammoth, if not impossible task. *There are just too many churches... and with Christmas round the corner, all of them will be packed to the brim.*

Deopa was raising his gun hand to strike Khalid down when, a dozen miles away, Asif noticed a knot of tense-looking men stride into the Vasant Kunj church which stands on the tri-junction of D Block. They were scanning the crowd intently as they slowly made their way through the fete.

Cops? His instincts kicked in instantly. *Either they know, or...*

Realizing that he didn't have time to arm the tree bomb, he decided to give it a miss. Slowly backing away from the stall he was manning, Asif used the happy, boisterous crowd of people milling around as cover to move towards the toilets at the rear of the church. He moved slowly, careful not to do anything to draw attention to himself.

Other than two young boys, the men's toilet was empty when Asif entered. Neither boy paid any heed to Asif as he got into one of the cubicles. It took him a couple of minutes to get rid of the Santa outfit, two more to clean up and smoothen out the suit he had been wearing underneath, straighten his hair and leave.

'It's almost 0915 hours, sir,' Ankita reminded Anbu softly in the ATTF Ops Room. 'Should I tell them to activate the jammers?'

Jamming all the mobile networks functional in Delhi was the final option available to Anbu. Ever since Iqbal had told them that Asif would be using his mobile to activate the bombs, he had known that it was the one feasible option they had. It would give them some more time to find the remaining bomb. He was loath to do it only because he knew the furore it was bound to create later.

'Iqbal said they were planning to activate only at 0945 hours, right?'

'That's right, sir.' Ankita nodded, her eyes drawn towards the clock again.

They watched as the long black hands raced on inexorably, with unbelievable rapidity, towards the designated time.

'Give them another couple of minutes... if we don't find the bastard by then, we'll activate the jammers.' Anbu made up his mind as the fragile second hand swept around the clock face once more like a racehorse out of control.

Blending effortlessly into the noisy crowd, Asif exited the church along with a large group of people who were also leaving. Almost immediately, he saw a second set of men with a sniffer dog scanning the vehicles in the car park. They seemed to be concentrating on the Maruti vans, of which there were plenty.

Asif felt a flash of rage as he realized they had been betrayed. It was only a matter of time before the police found the van with the bomb. He continued walking slowly and separated from the group of people he had been walking with only when they were well clear of the gates.

Asif was crossing the road when an ATTF man spotted the crumpled Santa costume in the toilet cubicle.

'I have the costume. He is out here somewhere.'

Radio sets began to hiss urgently.

'Look for a guy in a suit.'

Trained eyes began to scan the crowd. In the frenzy, the detachment commander forgot to report the sighting to the ATTF Ops Room.

There were dozens of young men in Sunday suits strolling all over the place. Several of them were accosted, most of them not too gently, and none with any positive result.

It was 0919 hours when Asif got into the cab parked at the taxi stand, just ahead of the T-Junction, about two hundred metres away from the church.

'Sir.' Ankita's voice nudged Anbu's attention back towards the clock on the ATTF Ops Room wall. 'It's 0920 hours now.'

'Go ahead, Ankita, we still have twenty, twenty-five minutes, but I think you're right, they may not be able to find the right church in time... we can't take a chance.' Anbu nodded. 'Activate the jammers.'

Ankita picked up the phone and began to order activation of the jammers. Each of the cellular service providers operating in the National Capital Region of Delhi had already been warned and all of them were ready to go into action. Just one call from her was enough to render every mobile phone in the National Capital Region useless, and no calls, text or multimedia messages would get through.

One by one, Ankita began to shut down the cellular phone networks.

Ankita was speaking to the second cellular phone network when Asif told the cab driver, 'Domestic airport. Let's make it fast. I have a flight to catch.'

The rather ancient, black and yellow Tata Indica cab had just pulled onto the road and begun to gather speed when Asif extracted his mobile phone and began to key in a short text message to the phones embedded in the bombs in the vans.

The message was short and ironically appropriate: *BOOM!*

It took Asif virtually no time to key it in. Adding the numbers of the four recipient phones from his phonebook took a little more time. Out of sheer habit or some deep-seated instinct, the first recipient phone was the one embedded in the bomb of the van he had left parked near the Vasant Kunj church.

Having added the other three numbers, a moment later Asif thumbed the green SEND button on his phone and the deadly text message swirled away in the ether even as Ankita started dialling the third cellular servicer provider.

Nine hundred metres away, the sniffer dog gave his first warning growl as he closed in on the sky-blue Maruti van parked in the middle of the parking lot outside the church. That was when the phone in the bomb received the incoming text message alert and activated the detonator. The phone was in silent-vibration mode but then, it wasn't required to ring or vibrate; all it had to do was pass on an impulse. It did so, silently and efficiently. A second later, with a deafening roar, the forty kilograms of RDX planted in the van exploded. The van buckled briefly before it blew apart. The dog and his handler were thrown into the air as hot fiery metal enveloped the parking lot.

Like a series of thunderclaps, one by one, the fuel tanks of several other cars parked around the van followed suit, spewing lethal metal fragments and fire all around. Terrified screams and shattered bodies mingled in the bloody maelstrom that engulfed the area around the church.

'Stop here for a minute,' Asif told the taxi driver as they went past the Vasant Kunj Central Market. He had heard the dull boom in the distance, over the screech of the Punjabi song erupting tinnily out of the cab's ancient music system. It brought a smile of satisfaction to his face. 'I just need to pick up a couple of things.'

He returned fifteen minutes and three shops later with a full duffel bag and they set off again. Apart from the expected traffic jam at the Mahipalpur bottleneck, the ride to the airport was uneventful.

At 1017 hours Asif entered the domestic flight departure terminal of Delhi airport. The e-ticket and Income Tax PAN card he handed over to the CISF (Central Industrial Security Force) man guarding the airport entry gate introduced him as Ian Smith. Heading straight for the toilet, he locked himself in the cubicle at the far end. About twenty minutes later, he exited the toilet and went across to the bank of Jet Airways check-in counters. The check-in for the 1150 flight to Pune had just started.

The clean-shaven man with rimless spectacles, clad in jeans and a matching jacket, bore little resemblance to the moustached, suited Asif who had entered the airport. Twenty minutes later, Ian Smith had cleared security and was sitting in the waiting area, reading a newspaper as he awaited the departure call for his flight. Right in front of him was a large plasma television silently displaying the news. He had been there for less than five minutes when scenes from the blast at the Vasant Kunj church flooded the television screen, spreading waves of consternation and anger in the waiting lounge. Almost all activity came to a halt as more and more people began to cluster around the television. People reached into their pockets and began to frantically check on their families and friends. Not many of them got through, since the cellular companies had only just started reactivating their networks.

A short while later, the camera cut to the Hauz Khas police station, where a dejected Imtiaz was being taken out of a police jeep and into the building.

Terrorist captured from Green Park Free Church, screamed the red and yellow ticker that scrolled at the bottom of the screen.

Moments later, the camera skipped to another location, a hospital whose name Asif was unable to catch. It showed the footage of an unconscious man being carried inside on a stretcher with a posse of armed cops all around him.

A second terrorist was captured from Punjabi Bagh church.

Then the camera returned to the devastation outside the Vasant Kunj church.

Asif watched carefully for several more minutes. There was nothing about the strike at the church on Sansad Marg or the capture of anyone there.

So! It's that bastard, Iqbal... he's the traitor. Asif began to shake with anger. *I'll make him pay. I'll set such an example that no one will even dream of betraying the cause again.* Realizing that his fingers had begun to crush the newspaper in his hands, Asif forced himself to relax. *I'll make him pay if it kills me... Iqbal, you treacherous bastard, you are so fucking dead.*

That was when he noticed a group of harried looking men enter the area and fan out in every direction. They had stress written large on their faces and what seemed like a photograph in their hands as they swept through the crowds. Forcing himself to stay calm, Ian Smith did what everyone else around him was doing. Turning to the elderly lady beside him, he began to discuss the latest bomb attack on Delhi. He was confident that his changed appearance would pass muster and no one other than Iqbal would be able to spot him after the changes he had made to his appearance; they were minor, but adequate for the purpose. Asif knew that the cops would not have had the time to computer-generate variants of the description Iqbal would surely have given them; variants that would have shown other appearances he could have adopted.

'Isn't that terrible,' Asif said to the lady beside him, gesturing at the television, which was showing gory footage of the carnage at Vasant Kunj. 'These days, you can't step out of the house without wondering if you will return home alive.'

From the corner of his eye Asif watched a cop walk past him as the woman nodded vigorously.

He kept his head attentively turned towards her, nodding occasionally as he engaged her in conversation.

'What was your planned escape route?' Anbu's voice came through tersely on the phone as Dhankar and Iqbal drove back towards Delhi Cantonment.

'I was to catch the Jhelum Express from New Delhi railway station at 1020 hours, sir.'

'So was the guy we caught from Punjabi Bagh, but he was going to board from the Subzi Mandi railway station.'

'And Imtiaz? The one at the Green Park church?'

'He was to take the Mumbai Rajdhani at 1630 hours, again from the New Delhi station.' Anbu paused for a moment. 'So I guess Asif had planned trains for all of you?'

'He probably had, sir,' Iqbal said hesitantly. 'That's what we normally did but then, this time he flew us all down.'

'True.' Anbu made up his mind, deciding to go with the law of averages. 'I want both of you to get back to the railway station and keep an eye out for Asif.'

'Which station, sir?'

'You go to the New Delhi one. I'll have the other stations and the airport covered by the other guys. Thanks to you, we have enough photographs of Asif.'

'You'll need lots of people, sir,' Iqbal said worriedly.

'Don't worry, son. The ATTF has plenty of men. You go ahead and see if you can spot him. Focus on the trains heading towards Pune and Mumbai.'

'What if he has managed to catch the flight back to Pune, sir?' A sudden strand of fear clutched at Iqbal's heart. 'Tanaz is alone there. What if he...'

'Good point, Iqbal,' Anbu concurred. 'I'll get someone to her right away.'

'But who, sir? The whole team is here in Delhi.'

'Don't worry, Iqbal. One of my paltan officers is posted there. In fact, he stays in Khadki, not too far from your apartment. I'll tell him to deploy a couple of men to take care of Tanaz until you get there and we can get both of you out.'

'Thank you, sir.' Iqbal heaved a sigh of relief.

Anbu got on the job right away.

'Kapur,' he said when the officer came on the line, 'something urgent has come up. I need to have an important asset protected immediately.' He quickly explained the situation and gave him the address. 'It's important that you get someone there at once. Her cover is almost certainly blown and she could be in grave danger.'

'Don't worry, sir, I'll take care of it myself.' Major Rajesh Kapur, who had once served in the battalion with Anbu, replaced the phone and ran towards the door. He knew Anbu was not the kind to cry wolf needlessly. He thought he would pick up a couple of guards from the quarter guard and go himself. Then he remembered that the quarter guard was on the other side of the unit lines, whereas the address given by Anbu was just around the corner.

Kapur turned around, rushed back to his room, grabbed his helmet and the keys to his motorbike and ran out again. A moment later he was on his way, his sense of urgency ensuring the throttle was wide open as he roared down the road. He didn't notice the deep blue Toyota Corolla hurtling down the empty road. By the time he saw the car it was too late; its front fender caught the side of his bike almost head on, catapulting him over the handlebars. His head smashed against the concrete median dividing the road. The helmet cushioned the impact considerably, protecting him from otherwise certain death, but it was unable to keep him from being knocked unconscious. His last thought as he lost consciousness was, *I didn't tell anybody about Anbu's call...*

Miles to the north, unaware that the safety net he had thrown for Tanaz had not fallen into place, Anbu was immersed in the task of getting the ATTF to scour the airport and seal the several, oh-so-porous borders of the capital.

Asif had to be found, and taken. That was the least they could do to make up for the church victims. But he was nowhere to be found. The man seemed to have simply dropped off the face of the earth. *Damn! I wish I had at least activated the jammers a few minutes earlier*, Anbu thought, clenching his fist in frustration.

'Maybe he has gone to ground.'

'Maybe he left Delhi by road.'

'Maybe...'

There were just too many maybes. Though the vigil continued, by late afternoon the hunt had begun to lose steam. It was becoming increasingly clear to the hunters that their quarry had eluded them, at least for the time being.

'Iqbal, I think you'd better get back to Pune,' Anbu finally told him as the day wore to a close, 'wind up there and both of you get back to base asap.'

'Are you sure there's nothing else I can do here, sir?'

'I'm sure. We have enough people here to keep the city locked down tight. You go,' Anbu reassured him. 'Here, I am giving the phone to Ankita; she'll tell you about the available flights to Pune.'

In the Ops Room just a few feet away, Ankita's fingers had already begun to fly over the keyboard as she took the phone from Colonel Anbu.

Launching a new browser window, she swiftly logged into MakeMyTrip.com and checked the flights available from Delhi to Pune. 'Where are you, Iqbal?'

'We're heading back from New Delhi railway station. We've just crossed Connaught Place.'

'Okay.' Ankita checked the time and then examined the flights available from Delhi to Pune. 'If you hurry up, you can make the flight at 1845 hours. Head straight to the airport. I'll book your ticket and text the e-ticket number to Dhankar's mobile phone. Get a printout from the airlines counter at the airport. Okay?'

'Fine!'

Ankita keyed in her credit card number and hit the enter key. 'There! It's done,' she said a few seconds later. 'I'm texting the PNR number to Dhankar's mobile.'

'Got it, thanks,' said Iqbal as the text message chimed in. 'We're on our way.'

Dhankar accelerated when Iqbal gave him the flight time, but traffic was heavy and the first boarding call had already been made by the time Iqbal rushed up to the airline counter. By the time he had printed his e-ticket, checked in and navigated through security, final boarding had been announced. The aircraft door closed moments after he boarded. Exhausted by the rapid turn of events and the last-minute rush, he leaned back and allowed himself to relax as the plane began to taxi down the runway.

I wish I'd had the time to call Tanaz, he thought. *She must have seen the news and will be worried sick. But I'm sure whoever Anbu sent to guard her has explained everything.*

Despite the failure to prevent Asif from exploding

the final bomb, Iqbal was smiling to himself as he leaned back and closed his eyes. It felt unbelievably good to be going home again. A few feet away, the aircrew began to serve snacks and beverages and the sound of the aircraft settled into a monotonous drone.

TWENTY-TWO

Iqbal jumped out of the prepaid cab as it drew to a halt at the gates of the Golden Heritage complex. There was a blaze of lights in the almost fully occupied Tower A, but Towers B and C were clothed in near darkness. Neither of the two elevators was on the ground floor when he reached the lobby of his building. Too impatient to wait, he turned and began to run up the stairs, two at a time. Despite the lack of sleep, the two hour flight and the exhaustion of the last few days, his body took it well. The training was paying off. He grinned to himself as he reached the third floor and walked through the corridor to his apartment on the extreme left. It was dark, the only light coming from the weak yellow bulb over the front door of Zubaida's apartment at the other end.

Iqbal wondered why Tanaz had not switched on the light outside their front door.

He was about five feet from the apartment door, his hands reaching in his jacket pocket for the house keys when he noticed that the door was slightly ajar. He halted for a second, his mind trying to process this information.

Maybe one of the guards sent by Colonel Anbu has stepped out... but why would he leave the door open?

His heartbeat escalated as Iqbal reached out and gently pushed open the door.

Mujib sat at the far end of the room, just out of reach of the solitary light that had been switched on near the living room door. He was in almost total darkness whereas anyone entering the room would be caught squarely under the light. The large, well-padded armchair had been turned to face the door and the .38 Smith and Wesson pistol in Mujib's hand was trained on Iqbal's chest when he entered, the bulky silencer fitted on the barrel adding to its menace.

Iqbal's fingers itched for the .22 pistol that Tanaz kept buried under the cushion of the red three-seater sofa about six feet to his right, but his mind reined him in. He knew that such an attempt would be nothing short of suicidal; Mujib would cut him down before he was halfway.

As he cast around for the options available to him, Iqbal realized that Tanaz was nowhere in sight. He felt a sudden nauseous churning in the pit of his stomach.

'Come in.' Mujib's voice was laconic. 'We've been waiting for you.'

'Who are you?' Iqbal brushed away the panic building inside him. He would have to retain his composure if he was to fight back and get Tanaz and himself out of this situation alive. 'What are you doing in my house?'

'Come in and close the door.' Mujib's voice was tight with anger.

Iqbal shut the door and threw the latch before he turned to face Mujib again. 'Who are you?' he repeated mechanically, trying desperately to figure out the situation. *Who else is inside? How many? Where is Tanaz?*

'You don't know who I am?'

'I've never seen you before.'

'It doesn't matter. We know who you are now.'

'What do you mean, you know who I am? You...'

'Save it, Iqbal.' Mujib waved the gun at him dismissively. 'We know! Your woman talked.' He laughed. 'She's a tough one, I'll grant you, but she talked. Everyone talks after a point.'

Iqbal felt his mind shut down as fear wrestled with rage. 'If you have so much as harmed a hair on her...' He took a step forward. Mujib brought his gun hand up menacingly, forcing him to a halt.

'Oh, we've done much more than that,' he said almost conversationally, his words chilling Iqbal to the bone. 'You have no idea of the pain she took before better sense prevailed and she decided to talk.' The words hissed out venomously. 'And you are going to suffer far worse, as will everyone who betrays the cause.'

Just then Asif and another man whom Iqbal had never seen before emerged from the bedroom to the left. Both had large splotches of blood on their hands and clothes.

'That's it, bhaijaan. I don't think she knows any more...' Asif was saying when he noticed Iqbal in the room and his tone changed. 'So! The traitor is back.'

The sight of the two men sent a tidal wave of fear through Iqbal. A red haze began to shroud his eyes, blanketing his mind to everything else. He felt only the need to kill... to kill and to save Tanaz. His body tensed for action. Then he looked at Mujib and realized that neither the man's gaze nor his gun had wavered even an inch.

I can do nothing for Tanaz if I behave stupidly and get myself killed. I need to be calm if I have to get us out of here.

'What have you done to her? Can I see her... please,' Iqbal forced himself to plead. Every fibre of his being ached to find his beloved Tanaz and save her from the pain these soulless bastards must have inflicted upon her.

'Sure!' Mujib replied as Asif sniggered. 'You must see for yourself the death that awaits all those who betray the jihad. Go!' The pistol gestured towards the bedroom door.

'She is just inches away from death,' Asif said

with a dark smile. 'After you've seen and suffered the pain she has gone through, you'll follow her straight to hell.'

Iqbal sprang to push open the bedroom door, then froze at the sight that met his eyes as he entered thc room.

They had stripped her of every shred of clothing, just as they had stripped her chest of almost every inch of skin. Her face was a bloody mess, the puffed up, bruised eyes glazed with pain. She lay on the floor, huddled against the bed, moaning in agony. There were ugly, ever increasing pools of blood all around her.

No! Allah have mercy! Tanaz... Tanaz... What have I brought upon you?

A cloth had been stuffed into her mouth to smother the screams of pain as they worked on her with a pair of knives that now lay in the blood on the floor beside her. Iqbal ran across to her and then she was in his embrace. He held her gently, propping her up in his arms, trying to will away the pain as he wiped the blood from her face and smoothed down her hair. He knew neither would make any difference to her pain, but his fingers moved of their own accord.

'Tanaz, what have they done to you? What have I allowed them to do to you?' He was crying silently, helplessly, gripped by the knowledge that this was worse, far worse than anything he could have imagined. He fought to control himself and comfort her. 'Don't worry, it will be all right soon. I'm here now.'

'Yes, it will be all right soon,' said Mujib from the doorway, where he stood flanked by Asif and the other man. 'You'll soon be in hell, where all traitors deserve to go.'

Iqbal turned to face him, still cradling Tanaz in his arms. He could feel her begin to stir as the pain of wakefulness returned.

He had to buy time, he thought fiercely. He had to think of a way out of this.

'You're right,' Iqbal said desperately. 'I have betrayed you. But this woman has nothing to do with it. She had no choice, she just did what I told her to. Spare her. Please spare her... she is due to have a baby any day now. Please allow me to take her to a doctor. I'll come back to you for whatever...'

'There's no need for a doctor where she's going,' Mujib sneered.

'No!' Iqbal shuddered with fear. 'Please let me...'

'Shut up, you bastard!' Asif said harshly. 'She is as guilty as you are and must pay the same penalty.'

While Asif was talking, Iqbal felt Tanaz's hand slowly creep up, over his back. She was reaching for the pistol that was kept inside the shoe under the bed. The movement was not visible to any of the three men standing in the doorway because Iqbal's body was in their line of sight.

'Kill me if you want, but please,' Iqbal pleaded again, 'please spare her.'

'Of course I'll kill you, but first you'll suffer seeing your woman die and then go to hell yourself.' Mujib's voice was a flat monotone.

Iqbal could feel Tanaz's body straining with the exertion of reaching out for the weapon behind him. He knew he had to give her a little more time. 'Why? At least tell me why you're doing this? Don't you realize that they're just using you, the Pakistanis and their ISI?'

'The ISI?' Mujib repeated, his voice rising. 'They think they are in control, but it's they who are being used. I owe my loyalty only to the Ameer.'

'The Ameer? The Ameer ul Momineem?'

Shock registered on Mujib's face. 'How do you know that name?' he asked in disbelief.

'I've met him.' Iqbal felt Tanaz's hand stiffen slightly as it grasped the pistol.

A moment more...

'You lie!'

'No, I swear I have.'

'You lying, treacherous bastard. And even if you have, what difference does it make; nothing on earth can stop the tidal wave the Ameer will soon unleash. In just a few months, the world will see a holocaust the likes of which it cannot even imagine.' Mujib was almost shouting now, his eyes glazed with fanatical excitement. 'Soon! Very soon, the crescent will rule the world. It's not going to be long now before India fragments and the two Pakistans are reunited. Not just that…'

Iqbal felt Tanaz's hand ease the pistol out of the shoe. He had to keep them talking. 'What are you saying? How can Pakistan and Bangladesh ever be reunited?'

'Oh yes, they can.' A smile lit up Mujib's face. 'They certainly can... once Mughalstan becomes a reality, which it will, soon.'

'Mughalstan? What is...'

Iqbal felt Tanaz use his back to steady her hand and aim the pistol.

At the same time, Mujib's gun hand came up. 'Enough talking,' he said. 'I don't have any more time to waste.' He was training the weapon on Tanaz when she fired.

If you flick your finger and point at the target, you'll almost always be aiming at the point you've selected. If either you or the target is moving, it's always better to aim for the body rather than try for the head, which is a much smaller target. The head shot will mean almost certain death whereas a body shot may still leave the wounded opponent capable of shooting back. It's a choice you have to make depending on the situation and, of course, how confident you are of your shot…

Tanaz sought certain death and she was confident. Knowing that both their lives depended on it lent her an unshakeable confidence. She knew she couldn't afford to give Mujib the chance to get a shot off. He was too close to miss either Iqbal or her, and that was a risk she couldn't afford to take. With one final superhuman effort, she freed her mind of the agonizing pain and fired, aiming straight for the hateful head that filled her vision.

The muted spit of a .22 weapon firing is confusing, especially when your opponent has no idea there is a weapon in your hand and does not believe you are in any state, mental or physical, for offensive action.

For a moment none of the three terrorists realized that a weapon had been fired. By the time realization dawned, a dark red star had blossomed on Mujib's face, where his mouth had been a moment earlier. Tanaz's aim was perfect. Mujib dropped as though he had been poleaxed. The pistol in his right hand and the mobile phone in his left fell to the ground like two discordant notes.

As the sound of the shot echoed through the room and Mujib's lifeless body crumpled slowly to the floor, the two surviving merchants of death were galvanized into action. Asif reached into his jacket pocket while the other man tried to duck out of the room. Barely alive though she was, Tanaz saw the movement and identified the threat it posed to Iqbal and her.

Her next shot thumped into Asif's chest, throwing him backwards. He slammed into the door and slumped to the floor, desperate hands clutching at the hole in his chest, trying to stem the blood that was seeping out.

By now Iqbal had snatched up the bloodstained knife lying near his feet and hurled it at the third terrorist. Arrowing across the room with a steely glint, it caught him plumb in the neck, just between the cleft in his collarbones. He fell to the floor, his hands clawing at the knife stuck in his neck, a weird gagging sound his only defence.

By now the second knife that had been lying on the floor was in Iqbal's hand. He kited across the room, landing with a soft thud next to the newcomer who was still alive. Taking hold of his shoulder, Iqbal spun him around as his knife hand sliced through the air. The man's throat yawned open with a ghastly popping sound as the sharp steel blade mowed through it. Life went out of him instantly. Without pause or wasted motion, Iqbal dropped him and moved on towards his final quarry. Asif, who was struggling to reach for the pistol that Mujib had dropped, died as the knife slammed through his ribcage and pierced his heart.

Just as suddenly as it had begun, the killing heat was over and the race for survival began. Iqbal pushed down his heaving emotions and forced his training to take over.

Grabbing the mobile phone that Mujib had dropped, Iqbal quickly dialled a number.

'Sir, we've been blown,' he said tersely. 'Tanaz is badly hurt. I need an ambulance fast. *Really* fast!'

'Where are you two? At the apartment?' Anbu reacted with all the speed and mental mobility expected of a man who perpetually operated in special conditions.

'Yes!'

'The military hospital at Khadki is just minutes away. I'll have an ambulance there immediately and will see that the hospital is ready to receive her.'

'Sir, please hurry.' Iqbal could feel his control giving way. 'Tanaz is all I have. I don't want to lose her.'

'You won't, Iqbal. Trust me.'

For once, Anbu was wrong. The doctors did their best, but it wasn't enough to compensate for the damage the terrorists had inflicted as they extracted information from her.

As the hours bled away, so did her life. She died minutes before Anbu reached the hospital; minutes after she delivered a three-kilogram baby boy, whom god in all his mercy had saved from the pain that the woman who bore him had suffered.

Tanaz died fighting, her eyes constantly seeking the man whom life had gifted her, the man who in the few months they spent together had given her a lifetime of love. And there were tears in her eyes as life left her.

The tears were not for herself. They were for the man she loved and the baby she would have loved. They were for the man who had had only hate in his heart when life had delivered them to the same crossroads; she had helped lance out the hate and filled it with love, instead. Her tears were for the man who would be bereft without her. She knew her passage from his life would once again leave behind a huge void that would allow the hate to return. She knew it would send him hurtling down the futile, violent path of death and destruction yet again.

Her tears were for the baby who would never feel the comfort of his mother's arms. She cried for the little child she had carried safely all these months and was now leaving behind in a world so full of horror.

She cried because she didn't want any of this for either of them. But even as she cried, she knew her tears were in vain, for that was the way it had been written and that was the way it would unfold.

TWENTY-THREE

Iqbal was shaking when Anbu walked into the hospital room. He sat crouched forward on the bed next to Tanaz, clutching her lifeless hand, as though by doing so he could pull her back from the afterlife she had gone to. Neither the anger nor the hate that pulsed through him was visible on his face. Nor were there any tears in his eyes. In fact, he seemed to have receded into another reality. Only the uncontrollable tremors that sporadically wracked his body betrayed his anguish.

'Iqbal!' Anbu's hand landed gently on his shoulder, his soft, compassionate voice dragging Iqbal back to the present.

Iqbal looked up at him, his eyes numb. 'I should have listened to you and never allowed her to become a part of this...'

'No one could have known it would end like this. We all take decisions that we feel are the best at the time we take them,' Anbu said quietly. 'Sometimes they go well, and sometimes...' He stopped as he realized the sheer inadequacy of his words.

Iqbal collapsed in his arms and began to cry. He cried like a baby – the tall, broad-shouldered, hardened young man who had seen so many facets of life and death so close. He cried like there was no tomorrow. And Anbu let him.

It was a long time before Iqbal broke free from Anbu's clasp. He turned and gazed silently at the broken body of the woman he loved. To Anbu it seemed as though Iqbal was branding every single scar and cut on her body onto his mind, as though he was bidding her a last farewell.

Iqbal was thinking of his mother and sister. He had not been able to see their bodies and mourn over them. This time, he would have at least this final memory to strengthen his mind for what lay ahead. From somewhere deep within, a chill began to creep through him; it spread slowly, bit by bit, driving every emotion from his heart.

'I know what has to be done next.' His tone was flat, devoid of all but cold certainty as he looked at Anbu. 'I need you to help me.'

'What do you want, son?' Anbu asked gently.

'They have to pay for this.' Iqbal gestured at Tanaz's body without looking at it. It was as though he could no longer bring himself to set eyes on her.

'That they will. The men who did this are already dead. The others we now know about and are hunting down. None of them will get away... I promise you that,' Anbu said. 'None of us will rest till we have them behind bars.'

'Iqbal.' It was Tiwathia who spoke up. He and Sami had come into the room quietly sometime earlier. 'You have done enough and given enough to this fight. You must know what a huge blow you've dealt to the terrorists. This group is totally decimated.'

'Yes, Iqbal, Vikram is right,' Sami said, 'you've done much more than could be expected from one person. You must pull back now, at least for some time.'

'No, this battle is far from over. It will not be over till we go in and hit the source where this monster came from. Tanaz would not want me to give up now, or ever. Then...' Iqbal's voice broke for a moment, before he snatched control over it again, 'her death would be futile. I cannot accept that... I *will* not accept it.' By now his voice was a hoarse whisper.

'But what do you want to do?' Anbu asked him. 'Your task is over; the Indian Mujahideen is finished.'

'I know that, sir, but before Mujib died, he mentioned a few things that...'

'Do you want to talk about all this right now?' Anbu interrupted him.

'Yes, I do.' Iqbal was adamant.

'Okay.' Anbu understood that at this moment Iqbal needed the release more than anything else. As long as he was talking, his mind could resist the pain. 'Go ahead then.'

'Do you remember that man we told you about when we returned from Pakistan – the Ameer ul Momineem?'

'Yes.'

'He's the one behind men like Mujib and Asif. They are working towards reuniting Pakistan and Bangladesh by creating what Mujib refered to as Mughalstan.'

'What the hell is that?' Tiwathia asked.

'Mughalstan is the name of an independent homeland proposed for the Muslims of India,' Anbu answered.

'Proposed by whom?' Sami was incredulous.

'Well, the comprehensive plan for a second partition of India was first developed by the Mughalstan Research Institute of Bangladesh's Jahangir Nagar University under the patronage of the ISI and the DGFI. This Mughalstan, or Greater Pakistan, is supposed to be the grand culmination of General Zia's Op TOPAC.'

'You can't be serious, sir?'

'Of course I am. The MRI even released a map of Mughalstan in which a large corridor of land runs through north and east India, linking Bangladesh and Pakistan. In fact, all the jihadi groups, especially Al Qaeda, Lashkar-e-Toiba, Hizbul Mujahideen Jaish-e-Mohammed, YPS and the Indian Mujahideen support this plan for a Greater Pakistan. They've also managed to get the support of various criminal groups in India.'

'But Pakistan itself is on the verge of disintegration, so how the hell can they be thinking of this?'

'Disintegration? Really?' Anbu asked. 'Is it disintegrating, or is it just slipping bit by bit into Taliban hands? Isn't that what the hardliners there want, and people like the Ameer are working towards?'

For a moment, no one spoke. Then Sami said, 'How the hell can they hope to convince the Indian Muslims to support crap like this?'

'They're banking on the hardliners to bulldoze the moderates and make them toe the line.'

'Do they actually believe that the Indian Muslim will ever accept being forced to live in Taliban-like conditions? Do they think we are not aware of the destruction the fundamentalists have wreaked on the parts they control in Pakistan?'

'Whether you do or don't is not the issue here,' Anbu intervened. 'The fact remains that this is what they want to achieve. Do you know that one of Jinnah's private secretaries, who stayed behind in India after partition and became a minister in the Assam ministry, wrote to him promising that in thirty years he would present Assam to Pakistan on a platter?'

'And this man was a minister in India?' Sami was the picture of disbelief. 'Why didn't they shoot him for treason?'

'Yes, he was.' Anbu nodded, ignoring the last part of Sami's question. 'And since then they have been working hard to ensure that the Muslim population attains majority in the areas they have targeted for inclusion in Mughalstan. That's why we've seen such an explosion in the number of Pak-funded madrassas in certain parts of India, Nepal and Bangladesh. That is...'

'Precisely, sir,' Iqbal interrupted. 'Mujib clearly told me before he died that the Ameer is making sure they are not far from achieving their goal.'

'He may have said so, Iqbal, but let me tell you that we have been monitoring events very closely for many years now; in fact, even more closely since you told us about the Ameer. But barring stray rumours and some unsubstantiated reports, we've come up with nothing.'

'What did these reports say?'

'That a group of people are trying to fill the gap after the death of the Sheikh in American custody and the one-eyed Mullah, the commander of the Afghan Taliban, had to go into hiding in Quetta. But you must understand, Iqbal, that there are many such people who will try to take advantage of this vacuum in leadership and assume bigger roles for themselves.'

'Absolutely,' Sami agreed. 'With the Sheikh dead and most of the Al Qaeda leadership either in hiding or on the run, there is considerable disarray in their rank and file. Most of the terrorists have either split up into smaller groups or have just gone back to wherever they came from.'

'So, that's what Mujib must have meant.' Iqbal saw the query on the faces of the Force 22 officers and added, 'Tell me, sir, what would happen if someone came forward and took charge of the situation; someone ruthless enough to seize control and restructure the shattered jihadi setup. Someone who could make all the groups function in tandem. What then?'

'If such a thing did happen...'

'It would raise the pitch of the battle and take it to a totally different level. They have already wrested control over the Swat Valley and large parts of Waziristan,' Iqbal continued, 'and if they are working with the ISI to make Mughalstan a reality, then we certainly have a lot to worry about.'

'But how on earth can the ISI hope to gain if Pakistan splits up?'

'Does anyone really know what's going on in that part of the world? Everything we see and hear is so contradictory... can we really make sense of it sitting here? Is the country really splitting up or is it just being taken over by the fundamentalists in a planned manner?' Anbu said. 'Or is there a larger plan, some devious hidden agenda that we are all missing?'

No one answered.

'We need to go after the Ameer and his group. As long as he and people like him are at large, this battle is far from over.'

'I agree with you, Iqbal, but if that's all you know

about the Ameer, it's hardly enough.' Anbu's calm voice tried to blunt the edge of Iqbal's fury. 'You won't even know where to start.'

'You may be right, sir, but I know I'll be able to find him. Don't ask me how, where, why... Here,' he tapped his heart, 'I just know I'll find him. That's enough for me.' There was a chilling, almost pathological certainty in Iqbal's tone.

'If you say so, Iqbal. In any case, you're a free agent and you know I can't stop you. I don't even want to. In fact, I'll do everything in my power to help you, but,' Anbu met his gaze squarely, 'do you think this is the time for you to go away? There is much to be done. Tanaz has to be buried...'

'No, sir,' Iqbal was dogged. 'Tanaz will be buried by me up here,' he touched his forehead with the fingers of his right hand, 'only once I have taken out the Ameer. Till then there will be no closure.' He turned to Tiwathia. 'Will you do this for me? Will you bury Tanaz for me, the way she should be, with honour and dignity... as befits any soldier, for she was no less.'

'Yes, she was a true soldier and a much braver one than most,' Tiwathia replied without hesitation. 'I would be honoured to do this for you, Iqbal. This and anything else you want me to do.'

Just then, the door swung open and a nurse entered. Cradled in her arms was the baby that Tanaz had battled death to give birth to. He was fast asleep in the warm cocoon of the woman's arms, with no inkling of the turmoil that had prefaced his arrival on earth.

'Your son.' The nurse held out the bundle to Iqbal. 'I thought you'd like to see him.'

A warmth he had never known before flooded through Iqbal as the baby slipped into his arms. He cradled the tiny bundle of life close to his heart, so close that for a moment the heartbeats of father and son merged into a single, rhythmic medley. Iqbal felt a sharp pain clamp his heart.

'What about your son, Iqbal?' Anbu murmured softly, watching the glow of attachment on the young father's face. 'He has already lost his mother. Do you think you should also take his father away from him?'

Anbu's words broke the magic of the moment, in a way he would never have imagined possible. Reality hit Iqbal like a bucket of cold water and a shadow passed over his face.

'If he stays with me, he is not going to last very long.' Like his face, his voice was flat and bereft of all feeling. 'Everyone and everything I have ever loved has been destroyed and taken away from me. I know I am cursed. Take him, sir, I beg you. Take him away from me. No one else knows about him and that's the way I'd like to keep it.' His eyes sought and held Anbu's. 'Will you keep him safe for me? Please.'

'Are you sure that's what you want, Iqbal?'

'Yes, sir. It would make me happy if you took

him and brought him up as your own. There will be no danger to him as long as no one knows he belongs to me.'

'Okay.' Anbu nodded unhesitatingly, reaching forward and taking the infant in his arms. 'If that's what you want. I promise you your son will never want for anything. He will be a son to my wife and me... and a brother to my son and daughter. He will get the best that I am able to give either of my own.'

'I have no doubt that he will, sir. But yes, there is one more thing that I will ask of you. Please bring him up as a god-fearing person, but let his god have no name, let his god have no religion.' Without meaning to, Iqbal half turned to face the love of his life, now lying dead. 'How could they have done this to her? How could any human being have...' His voice faded away as his eyes took in her battered body yet again. 'May I please be alone with Tanaz?' he whispered finally after a long pause.

Anbu nodded and gestured to the two officers who flanked him. Wordlessly, as one, the three Force 22 commandos made their way out. None of them could push away the thought that they had let them down; the young beautiful woman whose brutally tortured body now lay stiffening on the hospital bed and the tormented young man whose body was alive but whose soul seemed condemned to the uncertainty of festering hate once again.

Some time later, concerned by the prolonged silence within, the three men came back into the room and found it empty, except for the lifeless body on the bed.

Tanaz had been tended to, carefully, lovingly. Her hair had been combed back and her eyes were now closed. All that was humanly possible had been done to erase the evidence of the mutilation she had suffered. The fresh bedsheet that covered her body up to her chin hid most of the horrific wounds that had been inflicted on her. It seemed as though Tanaz was merely asleep.

And Iqbal was gone.

ACKNOWLEDGEMENTS

This book would not have been possible without the tremendous support I have received from my family over the years. They gave me the time, space and the encouragement to keep going.

I must thank my comrades-in-arms in the Indian Armed Forces who were kind enough to ensure that I did not make any major blunders while writing about tactics, weapons and weapon systems. However, I must stress that all technical data used in this book is freely and easily available on the internet and has not been provided to me by any person or persons.

A very special vote of thanks to my publisher Karthika V.K. for believing in me, keeping me on track, and for giving final shape to this book and this series. Without her watching over me I do not think I could have ever been able to achieve this incredibly difficult task of getting out each successive book within a year. And to Neelini Sarkar, Amit Sharma, Jojy and the others at HarperCollins India who helped to make this book possible.

Any errors, factual or technical, that still exist in this book are solely my fault or have been deliberately left there by me to prevent any misuse of a technology or an idea.